LUCIAN

Selections edited with Notes
and Vocabulary by

Keith Sidwell

Bristol Classical Press

Cover illustration: Dionysus afloat.
Interior of wine cup by Exekias, c. 535 BC. [Drawing by Christine Hall.]

First published in 1986 by
Bristol Classical Press
an imprint of
Gerald Duckworth & Co. Ltd
61 Frith Street
London W1D 3JL
e-mail: inquiries@duckworth-publishers.co.uk
Website: www.ducknet.co.uk

Reprinted 1990, 2001

A catalogue record for this book is available
from the British Library

ISBN 0-906515-36-X

Printed in Great Britain by
Antony Rowe Ltd., Eastbourne

For

Julius and Marc

CONTENTS

ILLUSTRATIONS

Illustrations by Christine Hall, Jean Bees and Patrick Harrison.

PREFACE

This selection has been written with the intermediate
student (at school or University) in mind. It takes as
its basis - arbitrarily, since all such decisions must be
arbitrary - the standard reached in both vocabulary and
grammar at the end of *Reading Greek* (Cambridge University
Press, 1978). The text is furnished with introductory
material, vocabulary and the parallel grammar notes designed
to give only enough help for a translation to be made and
the immediate 'who's who?' problems to be solved. The for-
mat will be familiar to users of *A World of Heroes* and *The
Intellectual Revolution* (Cambridge University Press, 1979
and 1980). The vocabulary at the end of the book contains
words which were set down for learning in *Reading Greek*,
as well as words to be learned by the student in this selec-
tion (these are indicated by an asterisk). A set of exer-
cises has been appended to help the student in the revision
of certain points of grammar and in vocabulary. The appen-
dix is an introduction to Lucian's works in their histori-
cal context. It has been excised from the main body of the
work and placed at the back since it makes detailed refer-
ence to the passages in the selection and will make little
sense if read before the text. This is followed by a biblio-
graphy with other references included.

In preparing this edition I was helped with the text by
M.D. MacLeod, who kindly allowed me to see and use his (at
the time) unpublished Oxford Classical Text of the section
from *How to Write History* included here. I have taken the
liberty, *ioci causa*, of printing the original reading of
the early Mss. in one place in that section. Otherwise the
readings are those of the O.C.T. except for the extracts from
Dialogues of the Gods and *Dialogues of the Dead*, where the
readings (and the numbering) are those of M.D. MacLeod's
Loeb vol.VII (save one change in *Dialogues of the Gods* 2).
Peter Jones read and commented with his unerring sense of
what the student requires on most of what appears here. I
am grateful to him for his suggestions, many of which I have
implemented, some of which I have not, some of which I dare
not. John Wilkins scoured the first draft of the appendix
with scholarly vim: his comments frequently rivalled Lucian
in their wit and were almost all gratefully noted. I am
very grateful to my colleague John Creed for his keen perusal
of the later version of the appendix. For the blemishes which
remain I alone am responsible. Like all writers, I say this
knowing that for any reputation this work may bring me the
blemishes will be largely to blame.

Keith Sidwell
University of Lancaster

1

I O L Y M P I A N G A M E S

The first three pieces are from a collection of short dialogues
(Lucian's favourite form), called Dialogues of the Gods (Θεῶν Διάλογοι).
They all deal with the gods of Greek mythology - a topic close to Lucian's
heart. Here we catch a glimpse of the immortals conversing together at
moments from the traditional stories. But since they are seen as only an
ironical observer can see them, it is essential first to know these
stories. The background to each piece is therefore set out at the head of
each dialogue.

The fourth and fifth pieces view the same Olympians from a slightly
different angle. In 'God's in his heaven...', drawn from the Ἰκαρομένιππος
ἤ Ὑπερνέφελος - 'Menippos as Ikaros' (the son of Daidalos, inventor of
flight) or 'Man above the clouds' - Menippos, frustrated by the philosophers
he has consulted in his search for the truth about the universe and the gods,
flies up to heaven to get the answers from the one place they can be found.
'A sceptical interviewer' is taken from the Ζεὺς ἐλεγχόμενος - 'Zeus proved
wrong'; here at the start, Kyniskos calls up Zeus on 'the prayer hot-line'
and asks some embarrassing questions about the various forms of fate menti-
oned by the epic poet Homer, in the Iliad and Odyssey. These embroil the
king of the gods in some difficult philosophical arguments.

1. ZEUS' POST-NATAL DEPRESSION

(Θεῶν Διάλογοι - Dialogi Deorum 12)

Semele, a daughter of Kadmos, king of Thebes, was loved by Zeus.
Hera, Zeus' wife, jealous of the liaison, persuaded Semele to test her
lover's claim to be king of the gods by asking him to appear to her in
his true shape. Zeus, tricked into granting this request, complied and
thus killed Semele with the fire of his thunderbolts. Semele was pregnant
with Dionysos. Zeus took the embryo from her womb and sewed it into his
thigh, until it was ready to be born. Poseidon is god of the sea and
Zeus' brother. Hermes (son of Zeus and Maia) is the messenger of Zeus.

(a) Poseidon wants an interview with Zeus. Hermes (on guard outside)
puts him off. Poseidon tries to guess what Zeus is up to.

1. ΠΟΣΕΙΔΩΝ: ἔστιν, ὦ Ἑρμῆ, νῦν ἐντυχεῖν τῷ Διί;

   ΕΡΜΗΣ : οὐδαμῶς, ὦ Πόσειδον.

   ΠΟΣ : ὅμως προσάγγειλον αὐτῷ.

2

1. ZEUS' POST-NATAL DEPRESSION

ἐστιν: it is possible
'Ερμῆς, ὁ (ld): Hermes
ἐντυγχάνω (ἐντυχ-) (+ dat.):
  I talk to
* οὐδαμῶς: by no means
προσαγγέλλω (προσαγγειλ-): I
  announce (sc. 'my presence')

Birth of Dionysus from
Zeus. From a volute
crater by the Semele Paint-
er, c.410 B.C., Museo
Nazionale, Taranto.

EPM: μὴ ἐνόχλει, φημί· ἄκαιρον γάρ ἐστιν, ὥστε οὐκ ἄν

ἴδοις αὐτὸν ἐν τῷ παρόντι.   5

ΠΟΣ: μῶν τῇ ῞Ηρᾳ σύνεστιν;

EPM: οὔκ, ἀλλ᾽ ἑτεροῖόν τί ἐστιν.

ΠΟΣ: συνίημι· ὁ Γανυμήδης ἔνδον.

EPM: οὐδὲ τοῦτο· ἀλλὰ μαλακῶς ἔχει αὐτός.

ΠΟΣ: πόθεν, ὦ ῾Ερμῆ; δεινὸν γὰρ τοῦτο φής.   10

EPM: αἰσχύνομαι εἰπεῖν, τοιοῦτόν ἐστιν.

ΠΟΣ: ἀλλὰ οὐ χρὴ πρὸς ἐμὲ θεῖόν γε ὄντα.

(b) *Hermes admits the truth. Zeus has just become a mother. The strange manner of the pregnancy is revealed to Poseidon, together with the name of the real mother.*

EPM: τέτοκεν ἀρτίως, ὦ Πόσειδον.

ΠΟΣ: ἄπαγε, τέτοκεν ἐκεῖνος; ἐκ τίνος; οὐκοῦν ἐλελήθει

ἡμᾶς ἀνδρόγυνος ὤν; ἀλλὰ οὐδὲ ἐπεσήμανεν ἡ γαστὴρ αὐτῷ   15

ὄγκον τινά.

EPM: εὖ λέγεις· οὐ γὰρ ἐκείνη εἶχε τὸ ἔμβρυον.

ΠΟΣ: οἶδα· ἐκ τῆς κεφαλῆς ἔτεκεν αὖθις ὥσπερ τὴν ᾿Αθηνᾶν.

τοκάδα γὰρ τὴν κεφαλὴν ἔχει.   19

EPM: οὔκ, ἀλλὰ ἐν τῷ μηρῷ ἐκύει τὸ τῆς Σεμέλης βρέφος.

ἐνοχλέω: I trouble (sc.
'him'), am a nuisance
4 ἄκαιρος -ον: ill-timed
Ἥρα, ἡ: (1b) Hera
*σύνειμι (+ dat.): I am with,
have intercourse with
ἑτεροῖος, -α, ον: of
another kind
τί: something (the accent
is thrown back from
ἐστιν)
*συνίημι (συνε-): I under-
stand, am aware of
Γανυμήδης, ὁ (3d): Ganymede
(Phrygian boy abducted by
Zeus to be his lover)
μαλακῶς: poorly
10 πόθεν: tr. 'how?'
*θεῖος, ὁ (2a): uncle
τέτοκα = perf. of τίκτω
ἀρτίως: just now
ἄπαγε: come off it!
ἐκ τίνος: tr. 'who's the
father?'
ἐλελήθει = 3rd s. pluperf. of
λανθάνω
15 ἀνδρόγυνος, ὁ (2a): herma-
phrodite, man-woman
ἐπισημαίνω (ἐπισημαν-): I
show x (acc.) as a
symptom
*γαστήρ (γαστερ-), ἡ (3a):
stomach
ὄγκος, ὁ (2a): swelling
*ἔμβρυον, τό (2b): embryo,
baby
*ἔτεκον = aor. of τίκτω
ὥσπερ: sc. 'he did'
Ἀθηνᾶ, ἡ (1b): Athena
(daughter of Zeus, born
fully-armed from his head,
after he had swallowed
his pregnant girlfriend
Metis 'Thought')
τοκάς (τοκαδ-), ἡ (3a):
prolific, for breeding
20 μηρός, ὁ (2a): thigh
κύω: I conceive
*βρέφος, το (3c, uncontr.):
foetus, new-born baby

6

ΠΟΣ: εὖ γε ὁ γενναῖος, ὡς ὅλος ἡμῖν κυοφορεῖ καὶ παντα-
χόθι τοῦ σώματος. ἀλλὰ τίς ἡ Σεμέλη ἐστί;

2. ΕΡΜ: Θηβαία, τῶν Κάδμου θυγατέρων μία. ταύτῃ συνελθὼν
ἐγκύμονα ἐποίησεν.

ΠΟΣ: εἶτα ἔτεκεν, ὦ 'Ερμῆ, ἀντ' ἐκείνης;   25

(c) Hermes tells the rest of Semele's story, then hastens to his
midwifely duties.

ΕΡΜ: καὶ μάλα, εἰ καὶ παράδοξον εἶναί σοι δοκεῖ· τὴν μὲν
γὰρ Σεμέλην ὑπελθοῦσα ἡ Ἥρα - οἶσθα ὡς ζηλότυπός ἐστι -
πείθει αἰτῆσαι παρὰ τοῦ Διὸς μετὰ βροντῶν καὶ ἀστραπῶν ἥκ-
ειν παρ' αὐτήν· ὡς δὲ ἐπείσθη καὶ ἧκεν ἔχων καὶ τὸν κεραυ-
νόν, ἀνεφλέγη ὁ ὄροφος, καὶ ἡ Σεμέλη μὲν διαφθείρεται ὑπὸ   30
τοῦ πυρός, ἐμὲ δὲ κελεύει ἀνατεμόντα τὴν γαστέρα τῆς γυν-
αικὸς ἀνακομίσαι ἀτελὲς ἔτι αὐτῷ τὸ ἔμβρυον ἑπτάμηνον·
καὶ ἐπειδὴ ἐποίησα, διελὼν τὸν ἑαυτοῦ μηρὸν ἐντίθησιν, ὡς
ἀποτελεσθείη ἐνταῦθα, καὶ νῦν τρίτῳ ἤδη μηνὶ ἐξέτεκεν αὐτὸ
καὶ μαλακῶς ἀπὸ τῶν ὠδίνων ἔχει.   35

ΠΟΣ: νῦν οὖν ποῦ τὸ βρέφος ἐστίν;

ΕΡΜ: ἐς τὴν Νῦσαν ἀποκομίσας παρέδωκα ταῖς Νύμφαις ἀνα-
τρέφειν Διόνυσον αὐτὸν ἐπονομασθέντα.

ΠΟΣ: οὐκοῦν ἀμφότερα τοῦ Διονύσου τούτου καὶ μήτηρ καὶ
πατὴρ ὁ ἀδελφός ἐστιν;   40

ΕΡΜ: ἔοικεν. ἄπειμι δ' οὖν ὕδωρ αὐτῷ πρὸς τὸ τραῦμα οἴ-
σων καὶ τὰ ἄλλα ποιήσων ἃ νομίζεται ὥσπερ λεχοῖ.

Σεμέλη, ἡ (1a): Semele
εὖ γε: well done!
ἡμῖν: tr. 'as we can see'
(lit. 'for us')
κυοφορέω: I become
pregnant
πανταχόθι: in every
part
Θηβαῖος, -α, ον: Theban
Κάδμος, ὁ (2a): Kadmos
(founder of Thebes)
συνελθ- = aor. stem of
συνέρχομαι (+ dat.): I
have sexual intercourse
with
24 ἐγκύμων (ἐγκυμον-):
pregnant
*καὶ μάλα: yes, indeed
*παράδοξος, -ον: incred-
ible, paradoxical, un-
expected
ὑπελθ- = aor. stem of
ὑπέρχομαι: I trick
ζηλότυπος, -ον: jealous
βροντή, ἡ (1a): thunder
ἀστραπή, ἡ (1a): lightning
κεραυνός, ὁ (2a): thunder-
bolt
30 ἀναφλέγω (aor. pass.
ἀνεφλέγην): I set on
fire
ὄροφος, ὁ (2a): roof
*ἀνατεμ- = aor. stem of
ἀνατέμνω: I cut open
ἀνακομίζω: I bring back
(safely)
ἀτελής, -ές: imperfect,
not fully developed
ἑπτάμηνος, ον: seven
months old
διαιρέω (διελ-): I cut
open
ἀποτελέω: I complete
τρίτος, -η, -ον: third
*μεις (μην-), ὁ (3a): month
ἐξέτεκον = aor. of
ἐκτίκτω: I produce, give
birth to
35 ὠδίς (ὠδιν-), ἡ (3a): pain
of childbirth
Νῦσα, ἡ (1c): Nysa (a city
on Mt. Meros in India)
ἀποκομίζω: I take away

παρέδωκα = aor. of
παραδίδωμι
Νύμφη, ἡ (1a): Nymph
ἀνατρέφω: I bring up
Διόνυσος, ὁ (2a):
Dionysos (god of wine)
ἐπονομαζω: I name
39 ἀμφότερα: both together
ἔοικεν: tr. 'it looks
like it'
ἄπειμι = fut. of ἀπέρχομαι
*δ᾽ οὖν: however that may be,
all the same
πρός (+ acc.): for
τραῦμα, τό (3b): wound
οἴσω fut. of φέρω. οἴσων ...
ποιήσων (fut. parts. expres-
sing purpose) tr. 'to'
λεχώ, ἡ (dat. λεχοῖ): woman
who has just given birth

2. A WORD OF WARNING FOR EROS

(Θεῶν Διάλογοι - Dialogi Deorum 6)

Eros was, for Lucian, the son of Aphrodite, and had the form of a young winged child, carrying bow and arrows, and sometimes a torch. His arrows had the power to make his victims fall passionately in love. Zeus was often a victim, but always required some subterfuge to gain his satisfaction. He courted Antiope as a satyr (a man with goat's legs, horse's tail and ears), Europa as a bull, Danaë as a shower of gold, Leda as a swan and Ganymede as an eagle. Dionysos (son of Zeus and Semele) was god of living things and of wine. His worship was conducted amid high emotion and ecstasy by Maenads, women dressed in fawnskins and waving thyrsoi (wands wreathed in ivy and vine leaves, topped with a pine-cone) and torches, to the sound of the double pipes and the tambourine. Dionysos was frequently represented as effeminate in appearance.

(a) Zeus has collared Eros and complains about the metamorphoses he has had to undergo in pursuit of his passions.

1. ΕΡΩΣ: ἀλλ᾽ εἰ καί τι ἥμαρτον, ὦ Ζεῦ, σύγγνωθί μοι· παιδίον γάρ εἰμι καὶ ἔτι ἄφρων.

ΖΕΥΣ: σὺ παιδίον ὁ Ἔρως, ὃς ἀρχαιότερος εἶ πολὺ Ἰαπετοῦ; ἢ διότι μὴ πώγωνα μηδὲ πολιὰς ἔφυσας, διὰ ταῦτα καὶ βρέφος ἀξιοῖς νομίζεσθαι γέρων καὶ πανοῦργος ὤν;   5

ΕΡΩΣ: τί δαί σε μέγα ἠδίκησα ὁ γέρων ὡς φῂς ἐγώ, διότι με καὶ πεδῆσαι διανοῇ;

ΖΕΥΣ: σκόπει, ὦ κατάρατε, εἰ μικρά, ὃς ἐμοὶ μὲν οὕτως ἐν-τρυφᾷς, ὥστε οὐδέν ἐστιν ὃ μὴ πεποίηκάς με, σάτυρον, ταῦ-ρον, χρυσόν, κύκνον, ἀετόν· ἐμοῦ δὲ ὅλως οὐδεμίαν ἥντινα   10 ἐρασθῆναι πεποίηκας, οὐδὲ συνῆκα ἡδὺς γυναικὶ διὰ σὲ γε-γενημένος, ἀλλά με δεῖ μαγγανεύειν ἐπ᾽ αὐτὰς καὶ κρύπτειν ἐμαυτόν· αἱ δὲ τὸν μὲν ταῦρον ἢ κύκνον φιλοῦσιν, ἐμὲ δὲ ἢν ἴδωσι, τεθνᾶσιν ὑπὸ τοῦ δέους.

9

2. A WORD OF WARNING FOR EROS

*εἰ καί: even if
τι: tr. 'in some way'
(accusative of respect)
ἥμαρτον = aor. of ἁμαρτάνω
συγγιγνώσκω (συγγνο-)(+ dat.):
I forgive
ἄφρων, -ον: without sense
Ἔρως ('Ερωτ-), ὁ (3a):
Passion, Cupid
ἀρχαῖος, -α, -ον: old,
ancient
Ἰαπετός, ὁ (2a): Iapetos
(Son of Earth and Heaven,
father of Prometheus; the
expression ἀρχαιότερος ...
Ἰαπετοῦ is proverbial)
*πώγων (πωγων-), ὁ (3a):
beard
πολιαί, αἱ (1b): grey
hairs
*φύω (trans.): I grow
καί tr. actually (καί is
often used this way,
esp. before verbs, to
emphasis what follows:
see line 7 below)
5 ἀξιόω: I expect
πανοῦργος, ὁ (2a): villain
τί δαί ...: what ever ...?
πεδάω: I put in chains
κατάρατος, ον: cursed,
abominable (sc. 'wretch')
*εἰ: whether (indir. ques-
tion)
μικρά: sc. ἠδίκησας tr.
'they are small wrongs you
have done me'
ἐντρυφάω: I treat x(dat.)
with contempt
σάτυρος, ὁ (2a): satyr (when
pursuing Antiope, who bore
him the twins Amphion and
Zethus)
ταῦρος, ὁ (2a): bull (when
seducing Europa, who
bore him Minos, Rhadamanthys
and, in some accounts,
Sarpedon
10 χρυσός, ὁ (2a): gold (when
seducing Danae, whose
father Akrisios had shut
her in a bronze tower,

and who bore Zeus
Perseus)
κύκνος, ὁ (2a): swan (when
seducing Leda, who bore
Helen and the Dioscuri)
ἀετός, ὁ (2a): eagle (when
carrying off Ganymede,
son of Tros, whom he
repaid with a marvellous
breed of horses)
*ὅλως: completely,
altogether
ἐρασθῆναι = aor. inf. of
ἔραμαι: I desire x(gen.)
*ποιέω: I make x(acc.) do
y(inf.)
συνῆκα = aor. of συνίημι
(constr. is nom. + part.,
tr. 'that I ...')
ἡδύς: tr. pleasing
μαγγανεύω: I use magic
on (ἐπί + acc.)
κρύπτω: I hide
*ἤν (+ subj.): if
τεθνᾶσιν = 3rd pl. perf. of
θνῄσκω, tr. 'they are dead'
*ὑπό (+ gen.): through,
because of
14 δέος, τό (3c): fear

2. ΕΡΩΣ: εἰκότως· οὐ γὰρ φέρουσιν, ὦ Ζεῦ, θνηταὶ οὖσαι τὴν
σὴν πρόσοψιν.   16

(b) *Zeus demands to know why he alone suffers this ignominy, and
Eros explains what he must do to become desirable to women.*

ΖΕΥΣ: πῶς οὖν τὸν Ἀπόλλω ὁ Βράγχος καὶ ὁ Ὑάκινθος φιλοῦσιν;

ΕΡΩΣ: ἀλλὰ ἡ Δάφνη κἀκεῖνον ἔφευγε καίτοι κομήτην καὶ
ἀγένειον ὄντα. εἰ δ᾽ ἐθέλεις ἐπέραστος εἶναι, μὴ ἐπίσειε τὴν
αἰγίδα μηδὲ τὸν κεραυνὸν φέρε, ἀλλ᾽ ὡς ἥδιστον ποίει σεαυτόν,   20
ἀπαλὸν ὀφθῆναι, καθειμένος βοστρύχους, τῇ μίτρᾳ τούτους
ἀνειλημμένος, πορφυρίδα ἔχε, ὑποδέου χρυσίδας, ὑπ᾽ αὐλῷ καὶ
τυμπάνοις εὔρυθμα βαῖνε, καὶ ὄψει ὅτι πλείους ἀκολουθήσουσι
σοι τῶν Διονύσου Μαινάδων.

ΖΕΤΣ: ἄπαγε· οὐκ ἂν δεξαίμην ἐπέραστος εἶναι τοιοῦτος   25
γενόμενος.

ΕΡΩΣ: οὐκοῦν, ὦ Ζεῦ, μηδὲ ἐρᾶν θέλε· ῥᾴδιον γὰρ τοῦτό γε.

ΖΕΥΣ: οὔκ, ἀλλὰ ἐρᾶν μέν, ἀπραγμονέστερον δὲ αὐτῶν ἐπι-
τυγχάνειν· ἐπὶ τούτοις αὐτοῖς ἀφίημί σε.

3. 'HIS FATHER'S SON'?

(Θεῶν Διάλογοι - Dialogi Deorum 2)

   Pan, an Arcadian god often associated with Dionysos, half goat, half
man, was the son of Hermes (who also originated in Arcadia) by Penelope,
daughter of Ikarios. His form derived from the disguise of a goat which
Hermes wore in visiting Penelope. He was supposed to make the flocks
fertile, a trait reflected by his amorous nature in mythology. He was
given a cult at Athens after the battle of Marathon (490 B.C.) for allegedly
helping the Athenians during the battle. Hermes is usually depicted in
art as a handsome young man with no beard.

πρόσοψις, ἡ (*3e*): appear-
ance
Ἀπόλλων, ὁ (*3a, but acc.
Ἀπόλλω*): Apollo (*god
of prophecy and music*)
Βράγχος, ὁ (*2a*): Brankhos
(*a son of Apollo or of
Smikros of Delphi, in-
spired by Apollo with
prophecy; gave oracles at
Didyme*)
Ὑάκινθος, ὁ (*2a*): Hyakin-
thos (*a beautiful boy,
loved by Apollo, who was
killed by the god's own
discus*)
Δάφνη, ἡ (*1a*): Daphne
(*daughter of a river-god;
loved by Apollo, but, un-
willing to accept his
caresses, turned into the
laurel-tree*)
καίτοι (+ *part.*): although
*κομήτης, ὁ (*1d*): wearing
long hair; person wearing
long hair
ἀγένειος, -ον: beardless
ἐπέραστος, -ον: lovable,
desirable
ἐπισείω: I shake
20 κεραυνός, ὁ (*2a*): thunder-
bolt
ἁπαλός, -ή, -όν: tender,
gentle
ὀφθῆναι = *aor. pass. inf.
of* ὁράω
καθειμένος = *perf. mid. part.
of* καθίημι: I let fall, let
down, put down
βόστρυχος, ὁ (*2a*): curl
καθειμένος βοστρύχους *lit.
'letting down curls' tr.
'letting your hair grow
long and curly'*
μίτρα, ἡ (*1b*): ribbon
ἀνειλημμένος = *perf. part.
of* ἀναλαμβάνομαι: I take
up, tie up
πορφυρίς (πορφυριδ-), ἡ (*3a*):
purple robe
*ἔχω: I wear
ὑποδέομαι: I bind on, put
on

χρυσίδες, αἱ (*3a*): gold
embroidered shoes
ὑπό (+ *dat.*): to the
accompaniment of
δύλός, ὁ (*2a*): reed-pipe
τύμπανον, τό (*2b*): tam-
bourine
εὔρυθμα: in time
ὄψομαι = *fut. of* ὁράω
πλείους = *nom. pl. of*
πλείων, -ον: more
Μαινάς (Μαιναδ-), ἡ (*3a*):
Maenad, Bacchante (*female
follower of Dionysos*)
25 ἄπαγε: come off it!
δέχομαι: I choose
μηδέ (+ *imper.*): don't ...
either
ἐράω: I am a lover
θέλω: I wish
τοῦτό γε *tr. 'this (way
I've mentioned)'*
ἀπράγμων, -ον: without
trouble (*comp. adv.
ἀπραγμονέστερον*)
ἐπιτυγχάνω: I succeed
with *x*(*gen.*)
ἐπί (+ *dat.*): on the
condition of

12

(a) *Pan greets Hermes as 'father'. Hermes is surprised and comments on their dissimilarity of appearance.*

1. ΠΑΝ: χαῖρε, ὦ πάτερ ᾿Ερμῆ.

ΕΡΜΗΣ: νὴ·καὶ σύ γε. ἀλλὰ πῶς ἐγὼ σὸς πατήρ;

ΠΑΝ: οὐχ ὁ Κυλλήνιος ᾿Ερμῆς ὢν τυγχάνεις;

ΕΡΜ: καὶ μάλα. πῶς οὖν υἱὸς ἐμὸς εἶ;

ΠΑΝ: μοιχίδιός εἰμι, ἐξ ἔρωτός σοι γενόμενος. 5

ΕΡΜ: νὴ Δία, τράγου ἴσως τινὸς μοιχεύσαντος αἶγα· ἐμοὶ
γὰρ πῶς, κέρατα ἔχων καὶ ῥῖνα τοιαύτην καὶ πώγωνα λάσιον
καὶ σκέλη διχαλὰ καὶ τραγικὰ καὶ οὐρὰν ὑπὲρ τὰς πυγάς;

ΠΑΝ: ὅσα ἂν ἀποσκώψῃς με, τὸν σεαυτοῦ υἱόν, ὦ πάτερ,
ἐπονείδιστον ἀποφαίνεις, μᾶλλον δὲ σεαυτόν, ὃς τοιαῦτα γεννᾷς
καὶ παιδοποιεῖς, ἐγὼ δὲ ἀναίτιος. 11

(b) *Hermes asks who Pan's mother was and Pan tells the story. Hermes remembers and is worried.*

ΕΡΜ: τίνα καὶ φὴς σου μητέρα; ἦ που ἔλαθον αἶγα μοιχεύσας
ἔγωγε;

ΠΑΝ: οὐκ αἶγα ἐμοίχευσας, ἀλλ᾿ ἀνάμνησον σεαυτόν, εἴ
ποτε ἐν ᾿Αρκαδίᾳ παῖδα ἐλευθέραν ἐβιάσω. τί δακὼν τὸν δάκτυλον
ζητεῖς καὶ ἐπὶ πολὺ ἀπορεῖς; τὴν ᾿Ικαρίου λέγω Πηνελόπην. 16

ΕΡΜ: εἶτα τί παθοῦσα ἐκείνη ἀντ᾿ ἐμοῦ τράγῳ σε ὅμοιον
ἔτεκεν;

3. 'HIS FATHER'S SON'?

νὴ καὶ σύ γε: the same to
you too
κυλλήνιος: from Kyllene
(the mountain in
Arkadia where Hermes
was born)
μοιχίδιος, -α, -ον: begotten
in adultery, a love-child
5 ἔρως (ἐρωτ-), ὁ (3a): love-
affair
*τραγός, ὁ (2a): billy-
goat
*μοιχεύω: I commit adult-
ery with
*αἴξ (αἰγ-), ἡ: nanny-
goat
ἐμοί tr. '(can you be) mine'
κέρας (κερατ-), τό (3b):
horn
*ἔχων: with (lit. 'having')
ῥίς (ῥιν-), -ἡ (3a): nose
λάσιος, -α, -ον: shaggy
*σκέλος, τό (3c): leg
διχαλός, -ον: cloven-
hoofed
πραγικός, -ή, -όν: like a
goat, goat's
*οὐρά, ἡ (1b): tail
*ὑπέρ (+ acc.): over
πυγή, ἡ (1a): buttock
ἀποσκώπτω: I fling insults
at
ὅσα ἂν ἀποσκώψῃς: tr. 'what-
ever insults ...'
10 ἐπονείδιστος, -ον: (sc. 'as')
disgraceful
γεννάω: I beget
παιδοποιέω: I father
που: perhaps
ἀναμιμνήσκω (ἀναμνησ-): I
remind
15 Ἀρκαδία, ἡ (1b): Arkadia
(mountainous district in
the Peloponnese)
παῖς, ἡ (3a): girl
ἐλευθέραν: sc. born
βιάζομαι: I rape, force
my attentions on
*δάκτυλος, ὁ: finger
ζητεῖς: sc. 'in your
memory'
ἐπὶ πολύ: for a long time
τὴν Ἰκαρίου: tr. 'the
daughter of ...'

Ἰκάριος, ὁ (2a): Ikarios
(father of Penelope,
brother of Tyndareus
king of Sparta)
Πηνελόπη, ἡ (1a): Penelope
(daughter of Ikarios -
later or in a different
tradition, wife of
Odysseus)
τί παθοῦσα ...: tr. 'what
made her...' (lit. 'suf-
fering what did she...',
a very common idiom, also
found with βούλομαι)

2. ΠΑΝ: αὐτῆς ἐκείνης λόγον σοι ἐρῶ· ὅτε γάρ με ἐξέπεμπεν
ἐπι τὴν Ἀρκαδίαν, Ὦ παῖ, μήτηρ μέν σοι, ἔφη, ἐγώ εἰμι,   20
Πηνελόπη ἡ Σπαρτιᾶτις, τὸν πατέρα δὲ γίνωσκε θεὸν ἔχων
Ἑρμῆν Μαίας καὶ Διός. εἰ δὲ κερασφόρος καὶ τραγοσκελὴς
εἶ, μὴ λυπείτω σε· ὁπότε γάρ μοι συνῄει ὁ πατὴρ ὁ σός,
τράγῳ ἑαυτὸν ἀπείκασεν, ὡς λάθοι, καὶ διὰ τοῦτο ὅμοιος
ἀπέβης τῷ τράγῳ.   25

ΕΡΜ: νὴ Δία, μέμνημαι ποιήσας τοιοῦτόν τι. ἐγὼ οὖν ὁ
ἐπι κάλλει μέγα φρονῶν, ἔτι ἀγένειος αὐτὸς ὢν σὸς πατὴρ
κεκλήσομαι καὶ γέλωτα ὀφλήσω παρὰ πᾶσιν ἐπὶ τῇ εὐπαιδίᾳ;

(c) Pan lists his accomplishments - musician, shepherd, dancer,
fighter - and reveals his erotic proclivites. Hermes asks a favour.

3. ΠΑΝ: καὶ μὴν οὐ καταισχυνῶ σε, ὦ πάτερ. μουσικός τε γάρ
εἰμι καὶ συρίζω πάνυ καπυρόν, καὶ ὁ Διόνυσος οὐδὲν ἐμοῦ   30
ἄνευ ποιεῖν δύναται, ἀλλὰ ἑταῖρον καὶ θιασώτην πεποίηταί
με, καὶ ἡγοῦμαι αὐτῷ τοῦ χοροῦ· καὶ τὰ ποίμνια δὲ εἰ θεά-
σαιό μου, ὁπόσα περὶ Τεγέαν καὶ ἀνὰ τὸ Παρθένιον ἔχω,
πάνυ ἡσθήσῃ· ἄρχω δὲ καὶ τῆς Ἀρκαδίας ἁπάσης· πρῴην δὲ
καὶ Ἀθηναίοις συμμαχήσας οὕτως ἠρίστευσα Μαραθῶνι, ὥστε   35
καὶ ἀριστεῖον ᾑρέθη μοι τὸ ὑπὸ τῇ ἀκροπόλει σπήλαιον. ἢν
γοῦν εἰς Ἀθήνας ἔλθῃς, εἴσῃ ὅσον ἐκεῖ τοῦ Πανὸς ὄνομα.

ΕΡΜ: εἰπὲ δέ μοι, γεγάμηκας, ὦ Πάν, ἤδη; τοῦτο γάρ,
οἶμαι, καλοῦσίν σε.

ΠΑΝ: οὐδαμῶς, ὦ πάτερ· ἐρωτικὸς γάρ εἰμι καὶ οὐκ ἂν   40
ἀγάπησαιμι συνὼν μιᾷ.

ΕΡΜ: ταῖς οὖν αἰεὶ δηλαδὴ ἐπιχειρεῖς.

αὐτῆς ἐκείνης: tr. 'her'
σοι: tr. 'your' (lit. 'to you')
Σπαρτιᾶτις, ἡ (3a): Spartan
  woman
*γινώσκω = γιγνώσκω
Μαῖα, ἡ (1b): Maia (mother
  of Hermes)
Μαίας καὶ Διός: sc. 'the
  son of ...'
κερασφόρος, -ον: horned,
  having horns
τραγοσκελής, -ές: with
  goat's legs
λυπέω: I vex, upset
συνῄει = imperf. of
  συνέρχομαι: I have
  intercourse with (+
  dat.)
ἀπεικάζω: I make x (acc.)
  like y (dat.)
25 ἀποβαίνω (ἀποβα-): I turn
  out
*μέμνημαι: I remember
  (perf. of μιμνήσκομαι)
*ἐπί (+ dat.): for,
  because of
κάλλος, τό (3c): beauty
μέγα φρονέω: I am proud,
  think a lot of myself
ἀγένειος, -ον: beardless
κεκλήσομαι = fut. perf.
  pass. of καλέω
γέλωτα ὀφλισκάνω (fut.
  ὀφλήσω): I incur laugh-
  ter from, I am laughed
  at by (παρά + dat.)
εὐπαιδία, ἡ (1b): being
  blest in one's children,
  having beautiful child-
  ren
καταισχύνω: I disgrace
  (fut. κατασχυνέω)
μουσικός, -ή, -όν: skil-
  led in music, musical
30 συρίζω: I play the reed-
  pipe
καπυρός, -ά, -όν: clear
ἄνευ: take with ἐμοῦ
θιασώτης, ὁ (1d): fellow-
  reveller
ἡγέομαι: I am x's (dat.)
  leader in y (gen.)
καί ... δέ: yes, and
ποίμνιον, τό (2b): flock

μου: tr. 'my' (take with
  ποίμνια: μου, σου are
  often used instead of the
  possessive adjs. ἐμός, σός)
Τεγέα, ἡ (1b): Tegea
  (a city of Arkadia)
ἀνά (+ acc.): up
Παρθένιον, τό (2b):
  Parthenion (a mountain
  in Arkadia)
ἡσθήσῃ = fut. of ἥδομαι
εἰ θεάσαιο ... ἡσθήσῃ: 'if
  you were to ... you will'
  (a mixed condition)
πρῴην: just now, the
  other day
35 συμμαχέω (+ dat.): I
  fight as an ally with
ἀριστεύω: I gain the
  highest distinction
Μαραθῶνι: at Marathon
  (the Athenian victory
  over the invading
  Persians in 490 B.C.)
ἀριστεῖον, τό (2b): (sc.
  'as a ...') prize for
  valour
*ἡρέθην = aor. pass. of
  αἱρέομαι
σπήλαιον, τό (2b): cave
Πάν (Παν-), ὁ (3a): Pan
40 ἐρωτικός, -ή, -όν:
  passionate
ἀγαπάω: I am content
δηλαδή: clearly, doubtless
ἐπιχειρέω (+ dat.): I
  try my hand with

16

ΠΑΝ: σὺ μὲν σκώπτεις, ἐγὼ δὲ τῇ τε ᾽Ηχοῖ καὶ τῇ Πίτυϊ
σύνειμι καὶ ἁπάσαις ταῖς τοῦ Διονύσου Μαινάσι καὶ πάνυ
σπουδάζομαι πρὸς αὐτῶν.   45

ΕΡΜ: οἶσθα οὖν, ὦ τέκνον, ὅ τι χαρίσῃ τὸ πρῶτον
αἰτοῦντί μοι;

ΠΑΝ: πρόσταττε, ὦ πάτερ· ἡμεῖς μὲν ἴδωμεν ταῦτα.

ΕΡΜ: καὶ πρόσιθί μοι καὶ φιλοφρονοῦ· πατέρα δὲ ὅρα
μὴ καλέσῃς με ἄλλου ἀκούοντος.   50

4. 'GOD'S IN HIS HEAVEN ...'

(᾽Ικαριμένιππος ἥ ῾Υπερνέφελος - Icaromenippus 24-28)

A friend comes across Menippos muttering astronomical calculations.
Asking for an explanation, the friend is told that Menippos has just
visited Zeus. Menippos tells the story. He was puzzled about the nature
of the physical universe and the identity of its creator. Since the
philosophers whom he consulted only confused him with their contradictory
hypotheses, he decided to go straight to 'the horse's mouth' and fly to
heaven to ask. He equipped himself with a pair of wings (one an eagle's,
the other a vulture's) and after preliminary flight tests over some
Greek mountains, he set off. He had a brief stop on the moon. Here the
natural philosopher Empedokles, whose soul, after his suicide in the crater
of Mt. Etna, wafted up - half-burnt - to the moon, helped him to see the
amusing picture of life on earth in a new perspective. Menippos set off
again, bearing a message for Zeus from the moon, complaining about the
philosophers. They were meddling in the moon's affairs, asking what
her measurements were and why she changed shape. She demanded their
punishment. When Menippos finally arrived at the door of heaven, he
knocked and was let in by Hermes. After telling his story and delivering
his message he was taken by Zeus to the prayer room. On the way Zeus
asked him a lot of questions about the state of things in Greece.

(a)   Zeus asked what men thought of him. Menippos replied piously.
But Zeus knew better and detailed their neglect of his worship.

σκώπτω: I joke
Ἠχώ, ἡ: Echo (dat.
  Ἠχοῖ) (a nymph loved in
  vain by Pan, who caused
  her to be ripped to
  pieces by shepherds he
  had driven mad: Earth
  hid the pieces which
  still sing and imitate
  other sounds)
Πίτυς, ἡ (3h): Pitys
  (nymph of the fir-tree,
  who ran away from Pan's
  advances and changed
  into her tree shape)
Μαινάς (Μαιναδ-), ἡ (3a):
  Maenad, Bacchante (fe-

male follower of
  Dionysos)
45 σπουδάζομαι: I am
  courted
πρός (+ gen.) by
ὅ' τι: tr. 'in what way'
*τὸ πρῶτον: for the first
  time
*ὁράω (ἰδ-): I see to.
  ἴδωμεν tr. 'let us (i.e.
  me) ...'
πρόσιθι = imper. of
  προσέρχομαι/πρόσειμι
φιλοφρονέομαι: I embrace
*ὅρα μὴ (+ subj.): tr.
  'see to it that ...
  not'

Pan pursuing a goatherd.
From a bell crater by the
Pan Painter, mid-5th cen-
tury B.C.; Museum of Fine
Arts, Boston.

24. ἐπεὶ δὲ περὶ τούτων ἀπεκρινάμην, Εἰπέ μοι, Μένιππε,
ἔφη, περὶ δὲ ἐμοῦ οἱ ἄνθρωποι τίνα γνώμην ἔχουσιν; Τίνα,
ἔφην, δέσποτα, ἢ τὴν εὐσεβεστάτην, βασιλέα σε πάντων εἶναι
θεῶν;
παίζεις ἔχων, ἔφη· τὸ δὲ φιλόκαινον αὐτῶν ἀκριβῶς οἶδα,   5
κἂν μὴ λέγῃς: ἦν γάρ ποτε χρόνος, ὅτε καὶ μάντις ἐδόκουν
αὐτοῖς καὶ ἰατρὸς καὶ πάντα ὅλως ἦν ἐγώ,

　　　　　μεσταὶ δὲ Διὸς πᾶσαι μὲν ἀγυιαί,
　　　　πᾶσαι δ᾽ ἀνθρώπων ἀγοραί·

καὶ ἡ Δωδώνη τότε καὶ ἡ Πῖσα λαμπραὶ καὶ περίβλεπτοι πᾶσιν   10
ἦσαν, ὑπὸ δὲ τοῦ καπνοῦ τῶν θυσιῶν οὐδὲ ἀναβλέπειν μοι
δυνατόν· ἐξ οὗ δὲ ἐν Δελφοῖς μὲν 'Απόλλων τὸ μαντεῖον κατε-
στήσατο, ἐν Περγάμῳ δὲ τὸ ἰατρεῖον ὁ 'Ασκληπιὸς καὶ τὸ Βεν-
δίδειον ἐγένετο ἐν Θρᾴκῃ καὶ τὸ 'Ανουβίδειον ἐν Αἰγύπτῳ
καὶ τὸ 'Αρτεμίσιον ἐν 'Εφέσῳ, ἐπὶ ταῦτα μὲν ἅπαντες θέουσιν   15
καὶ πανηγύρεις ἀνάγουσι καὶ ἑκατόμβας παριστᾶσιν καὶ χρυσᾶς
πλίνθους ἀνατιθέασιν, ἐμὲ δὲ παρηβηκότα ἱκανῶς τετιμηκέναι
νομίζουσιν, ἂν διὰ πέντε ὅλων ἐτῶν θύσωσιν ἐν 'Ολυμπίᾳ. τοι-
γαροῦν ψυχροτέρους ἂν μου τοὺς βωμοὺς ἴδοις τῶν Πλάτωνος
νόμων ἢ τῶν Χρυσίππου συλλογισμῶν.   20

4. 'GOD'S IN HIS HEAVEN...'

Μένιππος, ὁ (2a): Menippos
εὐσεβής, -ές: reverent (sup.
εὐσεβέστατος). τὴν
εὐσεβεστάτην (sc. 'γνώμην,
namely that ...'
5 παίζεις ἔχων: tr. 'you keep
on joking' (a common idiom:
the imperf. (pres.) part.
emphasises the duration of
action)
φιλόκαινον, τό (2b): love
of novelty
κἂν = καὶ ἐάν: even if
μάντις, ὁ (3e): prophet
μεσταί ... ἀγοραί: one of
Lucian's favourite quot-
ations: lines 2-3 of the
Phainomena, a work on
astronomy by Aratos, a
3rd cent. B.C. Alexandrian
poet
*μεστός, -ή, -όν (+ gen.):
full (of)
ἀγυιά, ἡ (1b): street
10 Δωδώνη, ἡ (1a): Dodona
(site of an ancient
oracle of Zeus in the
mountains of Epirus;
already mentioned in
Homer)
Πῖσα, ἡ (1c): Pisa
(district in the
Peloponnese where the
Olympian games were
held)
*λαμπρός, -ά, -όν: famous,
illustrious; splendid
περίβλεπτος, -ον (+ dat.):
generally admired (by)
*καπνός, ὁ (2a): smoke
ἀναβλέπω: I open my eyes
ἐξ οὗ: since
Δελφοί, οἱ (2a): Delphi
(site of Apollo's chief
oracular shrine - extrem-
ely popular already in
5th. cent. B.C.)
μαντεῖον, τό (2b): oracle
καθίσταμαι: I set up my
own (aor. κατεστησάμην)

Πέργαμον, τό (2b): Pergamum
(this shrine was perhaps
established in 4th cent.
B.C.)
ἰατρεῖον, τό (2b): surgery
'Ασκληπιός, ὁ (2a): Asklepios
(son of Apollo and Coronis;
god of medicine)
Βενδιδεῖον, τό (2b): shrine
of Bendis (a Thracian god-
dess worshipped with
orgiastic rites in Thrace;
introduced into Athens in
the 5th cent. B.C. with
rites including a torch-
race on horseback)
Θράκη, ἡ (1d): Thrace
'Ανουβίδειον, τό (2b):
shrine of Anubis (an
Egyptian god, with the
head of a dog)
Αἴγυπτος, ἡ (2a): Egypt
15 'Αρτεμίσιον, τό (2b): shrine
of Artemis (one of the
Seven Wonders of the World;
first established in 6th.
cent. B.C., burned down in
356)
Ἔφεσος, ἡ (2a): Ephesos
(town on the west coast
of Asia Minor)
πανήγυρις, ἡ (3e): festival
ἀνάγω: I celebrate
ἑκατόμβη, ἡ (1a): hecatomb
(a sacrifice of 100 oxen)
παρίστημι: I offer
πλίνθος, ἡ (2a): brick
ἀνατίθημι: I dedicate, set
up as a votive gift
παρηβάω: I am elderly, past
my prime
*ἱκανῶς: sufficiently
*ἂν (+ subj.) = ἐάν: if
διά (+ gen.): after
*πέντε: five
'Ολυμπία, ἡ (1b): Olympia
(site of the Olympian games,
held every four years -
Lucian uses the Roman method
of inclusive reckoning)
τοιγαροῦν: for this reason
ψυχρός, -ά, -όν: frigid
Πλάτων (Πλάτων-), ὁ (3a):

20

(b) *They arrived at 'prayer H.Q.'. The communication system was
described. Zeus dealt with the prayers, which were often contradictory,
and gave him pause in his decisions about them.*

25. τοιαῦθ᾽ ἅμα διεξιόντες ἀφικνούμεθα ἐς τὸ χωρίον ἔνθα
ἔδει αὐτὸν καθεζόμενον διακοῦσαι τῶν εὐχῶν. θυρίδες δὲ
ἦσαν ἑξῆς τοῖς στομίοις τῶν φρεάτων ἐοικυῖαι πώματα ἔχου-
σαι, καὶ παρ᾽ ἑκάστῃ θρόνος ἔκειτο χρυσοῦς. καθίσας οὖν
ἑαυτὸν ἐπὶ τῆς πρώτης ὁ Ζεὺς καὶ ἀφελὼν τὸ πῶμα παρεῖχε   25
τοῖς εὐχομένοις ἑαυτόν· εὔχοντο δὲ πανταχόθεν τῆς γῆς διά-
φορα καὶ ποικίλα. συμπαρακύψας γὰρ καὶ αὐτὸς ἐπήκουον ἅμα
τῶν εὐχῶν. ἦσαν δὲ τοιαίδε, ῏Ω Ζεῦ, βασιλεῦσαί μοι γένοιτο·
῏Ω Ζεῦ, τὰ κρόμμυά μοι φῦναι καὶ τὰ σκόραδα· ῏Ω θεοί, τὸν
πατέρα μοι ταχέως ἀποθανεῖν· ὁ δέ τις ἂν ἔφη, Εἴθε κληρο-   30
νομήσαιμι τῆς γυναικός, Εἴθε λάθοιμι ἐπιβουλεύσας τῷ
ἀδελφῷ, Γένοιτό μοι νικῆσαι τὴν δίκην, Δὸς στεφθῆναι τὰ
Ὀλύμπια. τῶν πλεόντων δὲ ὁ μὲν βορέαν εὔχετο ἐπιπνεῦσαι,
ὁ δὲ νότον, ὁ δὲ γεωργὸς ᾔτει ὑετόν, ὁ δὲ γναφεὺς ἥλιον.
    ἐπακούων δὲ ὁ Ζεὺς καὶ τὴν εὐχὴν ἑκάστην ἀκριβῶς ἐξ-   35
ετάζων οὐ πάντα ὑπισχνεῖτο,

    ἀλλ᾽ ἕτερον μὲν ἔδωκε πατήρ, ἕτερον δ᾽ ἀνένευσεν.

Plato (c.429-347 B.C.,
founder of the Academy.
The Laws, his last work,
outlines a constitution
and legal system for a
new colony. This tract
was considered to have a
forbidding style)

20 Χρύσιππος, ὁ (2a): Khrysippos
(c.280-204 B.C., Stoic
philosopher. His 'Syllo-
gisms' would include such
favourites as the 'Man
in the Hood': Khrysippos
questions a dealer who is
considering buying him:
'Answer me now: do you
know your own father?'
Dealer: 'Yes'. K.: 'Well
now, if I present to you
a man in a hood, will you
know him?' D.: 'Of course
not'. K.: 'Ah, but the
man in the hood is your
father. You don't know
the man in the hood.
Therefore you don't know
your own father'. (Lucian,
Sale of Creeds 22-3).
Philosophers were a
favourite target with
Lucian: see pieces 18 and
19 below)

συλλογισμός, ὁ (2a): syl-
logism
ἅμα (+ part.): at the same
time as
διεξίοντες = pres. part. of
διεξέρχομαι
καθέζομαι: I sit down
διακούω: I hear x (gen.)
to the end
*θυρίς (θυριδ-), ἡ (3a):
opening
ἑξῆς: in a row
στόμιον, τό (2b): mouth
φρέαρ (φρεατ-), τό (3b):
well
ἑοικυῖα = f. part. of
ἔοικα
πῶμα, τό (3b): lid
*θρόνος, ὁ (2a): throne,
seat

καθίζω: I seat
25 ἐπί (+ gen.): near
τῆς πρώτης: sc. θυρίδος
*ἀφαιρέω (ἀφελ-): I re-
move
πανταχόθεν: from every
part
διάφορος, -ον: different
ποικίλος, -η, -ον: diver-
sified
συμπαρακύπτω: I bend down
as well
ἐπακούω (+ gen.): I
listen in to
μοι γένοιτο (+ inf.): may
it happen to me to ...
i.e. may I ...
κρόμμυον, τό (2b): onion
μοι: sc. γένοιτο as in
line 28
φῦναι = aor. inf. of
φύομαι: I grow
σκόροδον, τό (2b): garlic
30 ὁ δέ τις: and someone
else
κληρονομέω (+ gen.): I
am heir to
ἐπιβουλεύω (+ dat.): I
plot against
δός sc. μοι: grant that
I ...
στεφθῆναι = aor. inf. of
στέφομαι: I win a
wreath at (+ acc.)
Ὀλύμπια, τά (2b): Olym-
pian games
βορέας, ὁ (1d): north
wind
ἐπιπνέω (ἐπιπνευσ-): I
blow behind
νότος, ὁ (2a): south wind
ὑετός, ὁ (2a): rain
34 γναφεύς, ὁ (3g): fuller
(ancient equivalent of
a launderer)
ἀλλ' ... ἀνένευσεν: a
slightly altered version
of Homer, Iliad 16.250,
where Zeus has just heard
Akhilleus' prayer for
Patroklos to beat back
the Trojans and return
safely to the Greek camp.

22

τὰς μὲν γὰρ δικαίας τῶν εὐχῶν προσίετο ἄνω διὰ τοῦ στομίου
καὶ ἐπὶ τὰ δεξιὰ κατετίθει φέρων, τὰς δὲ ἀνοσίους ἀπράκ-
τους αὖθις ἀπέπεμπεν ἀποφυσῶν κάτω, ἵνα μηδὲ πλησίον γέ-   40
νοιντο τοῦ οὐρανοῦ. ἐπὶ μιᾶς δέ τινος εὐχῆς καὶ ἀποροῦντα
αὐτὸν ἐθεασάμην· δύο γὰρ ἀνδρῶν τἀναντία εὐχομένων καὶ
τὰς ἴσας θυσίας ὑπισχνουμένων οὐκ εἶχεν ὁποτέρῳ μᾶλλον
ἐπινεύσειεν αὐτῶν, ὥστε δὴ τὸ 'Ακαδημαϊκὸν ἐκεῖνο ἐπεπόνθει
καὶ οὐδέν τι ἀποφήνασθαι δυνατὸς ἦν, ἀλλ' ὥσπερ ὁ Πύρρων   45
ἐπεῖχεν ἔτι καὶ διεσκέπτετο.

(c) Zeus next moved round to deal with the oaths and omens in turn.
Then he smelt the sacrifice smoke. Finally he gave orders to the
weather.

26.   ἐπεὶ δὲ ἱκανῶς ἐχρημάτισεν ταῖς εὐχαῖς, ἐπὶ τὸν ἑξῆς
μεταβὰς θρόνον καὶ τὴν δευτέραν θυρίδα κατακύψας τοῖς
ὅρκοις ἐσχόλαζεν καὶ τοῖς ὀμνύουσιν. χρηματίσας δὲ καὶ
τούτοις καὶ τὸν 'Επικούρειον 'Ερμόδωρον ἐπιτρίψας μετε-   50
καθέζετο ἐπὶ τὸν ἑξῆς θρόνον κληδόσι καὶ φήμαις καὶ οἰ-
ωνοῖς προσέξων. εἶτ' ἐκεῖθεν ἐπὶ τὴν τῶν θυσιῶν θυρίδα
μετήει, δι' ἧς ὁ καπνὸς ἀνιὼν ἀπήγγελλεν τῷ Διὶ τοῦ
θύοντος ἑκάστου τοὔνομα. ἀποστὰς δὲ τούτων προσέταττεν
τοῖς ἀνέμοις καὶ ταῖς ὥραις ἃ δεῖ ποιεῖν· Τήμερον παρὰ   55
Σκύθαις ὑέτω, παρὰ Λίβυσιν ἀστραπτέτω, παρ' "Ελλησι
νιφέτω, σὺ δὲ ὁ Βορέας πνεῦσον ἐν Λυδίᾳ, σὺ δὲ ὁ Νότος
ἡσυχίαν ἄγε, ὁ δὲ Ζέφυρος τὸν 'Αδρίαν διακυμαινέτω, καὶ
τῆς χαλάζης ὅσον μέδιμνοι χίλιοι διασκεδασθήτωσαν ὑπὲρ
Καππαδοκίας.   60

23

The latter is not:
granted in Homer.
ἀνανεύω: I refuse
προσίεμαι: I admit,
·let in
ἀνόσιος, -ον: impious
ἄπρακτος, -ον: unfulfilled
40 ἀποφυσάω: I blow away
*μηδέ: not even
ἐπί (+ gen.): in the case
of
δύο: with ἀνδρῶν
*ἐναντίος, -α, -ον: op-
posite
*ἴσος, -η, -ον: equal
ὁπότερος, -α, -ον: which
(of two). οὐκ εἶχεν
ὁποτέρῳ: tr. 'he didn't
know to which ...'
ἐπινεύω (+ dat.) I give my
assent to
τὸ ᾽Ακαδημαϊκὸν ἐκεῖνο:
tr. 'the sort of exper-
ience the Academics
have'
ἐπεπόνθει = pluperf. of
πάσχω
45 οὐδέν τι: tr. 'no opin-
ion at all'
ἀποφαίνομαι (ἀποφην-):
I declare (an opinion)
Πύρρων, ὁ: Pyrrhon (c.365-
275 B.C., founder of the
school of philosophy known
as Scepticism; based on
the Academy, its adherents
were known as Academics.
Pyrrho's view was that
sense and intellect gave
such contrary evidence
that true knowledge was
impossible. One could
only 'hold back from
judgement' (ἐπέχω) and
'keep examining all sides
of a question' (δια-
σκέπτομαι), hence the
comment in line 44)
ἑξῆς: next, following
μεταβαίνω (μεταβα-): I
change position, move
*δεύτερος, -α, -ον:
second
κατακύπτω: I bend down

σχολάζω (+ dat.): I
devote my time to
50 ὀμνύω: I swear (an oath)
᾽Επικούρειος, -ον: Epicurean
(a follower of the philo-
sopher Epicurus (341-270
B.C.) according to whom the
gods existed, but did not
interfere in human life)
᾽Ερμόδωρος, ο (2a):
Hermodoros
ἐπιτρίβω: I destroy, kill
μετακαθέζομαι: I change
my seat
κληδών (κληδον-), ὁ (3a):
chance utterance
φήμη, ἡ (1a): prophecy
οἰωνός, ὁ (2a): omen (drawn
from the flight of birds)
προσέξων = fut. part. of
προσέχω (sc. τὸν νοῦν and
remember that fut. part. can
express purpose)
*ἐκεῖθεν: from there
μετῄει = imperf. of μετέρ-
χομαι: I move
ἀνιών = pres. part. of
ἀνέρχομαι: I go up
ἀποστάς = aor. part. intrans.
of ἀφίσταμαι: I leave (+
gen.)
55 ὥρα, ἡ (1b): weather
ἃ sc. 'as to...'
δεῖ sc. 'they...'
*παρά (+ dat.): among
Σκύθης, ὁ (1d): Scythian
ὕει: it rains
ὑέτω ... διασκεδασθήτωσαν:
-ετω, -τωσαν are 3rd. s. pl.
imper. forms, tr. 'let'
*Λίβυς, ὁ (3h): Libyan
ἀστράπτει: there is lightning
νίφει: it snows
πνέω (πνευσ-): I blow
Λυδία, ἡ (1b): Lydia
Νότος, ὁ (2a): South Wind
Ζέφυρος, ὁ (2a): West Wind
᾽Αδρίας, ὁ (1d): the Adriatic
διακυμαίνω: I raise into waves
χαλάζα, ἡ (1c): hail
*ὅσον: about, as far as
μέδιμνος, ὁ (2a): gallon
(a corn measure)
διασκεδάννυμι: I scatter

24

(d) *Menippos and Zeus next joined the other gods at the divine
dinner-party. Menippos tasted the food of the immortals. He con-
firms an Homeric observation.*

27. ἀπάντων δὲ ἤδη σχεδὸν αὐτῷ διῳκημένων ἀπήειμεν ἐς τὸ
     συμπόσιον· δείπνου γὰρ ἤδη καιρὸς ἦν· καί με ὁ Ἑρμῆς
     παραλαβὼν κατέκλινε παρὰ τὸν Πᾶνα καὶ τοὺς Κορύβαντας καὶ
     τὸν Ἄττην καὶ τὸν Σαβάζιον, τοὺς μετοίκους τούτους καὶ
     ἀμφιβόλους θεούς. καὶ ἄρτον δὲ ἡ Δημήτηρ παρεῖχε καὶ ὁ   65
     Διόνυσος οἶνον καὶ ὁ Ἡρακλῆς κρέα καὶ μύρτα ἡ Ἀφροδίτη
     καὶ ὁ Ποσειδῶν μαινίδας. ἅμα δὲ καὶ τῆς ἀμβροσίας ἠρέμα
     καὶ τοῦ νέκταρος παρεγευόμην· ὁ γὰρ βέλτιστος Γανυμήδης
     ὑπὸ φιλανθρωπίας εἰ θεάσαιτο ἀποβλέποντά που τὸν Δία,
     κοτύλην ἂν ἢ καὶ δύο τοῦ νέκταρος ἐνέχει μοι φέρων. οἱ   70
     δὲ θεοί, ὡς Ὅμηρός που λέγει (καὶ αὐτός, οἶμαι, καθάπερ
     ἐγὼ τἀκεῖ τεθεαμένος), οὔτε "σῖτον ἔδουσιν, οὐ πίνουσ'
     αἴθοπα οἶνον", ἀλλὰ τὴν ἀμβροσίαν παρατίθενται καὶ τοῦ
     νέκταρος μεθύσκονται, μάλιστα δὲ ἤδονται σιτούμενοι τὸν
     ἐκ τῶν θυσιῶν καπνὸν αὐτῇ κνίσῃ ἀνενηνεγμένον καὶ τὸ αἷμα   75
     δὲ τῶν ἱερείων, ὃ τοῖς βωμοῖς οἱ θύοντες περιχέουσιν.

about (the form in
the text is aor. pass.)
*ὑπέρ (+ gen.): over
60 Καππαδοκία, ἡ (1b):
Cappadocia
αὐτῷ: tr. 'by' (dat. of
agent after perf. pass.
verb)
ἀπῇειμεν = imperf. of
ἀπέρχομαι
*συμπόσιον, τό (2b):
dinner-party,
symposium.
*δεῖπνον, τό (2b): dinner
καιρός, ὁ (2a): time
κατακλίνω: I make x (acc.)
recline
παρά (+acc.): alongside
Κορυβάς (Κορυβαντ-), ὁ (3a):
Korybant (companions of
the Asiatic goddess Kybele,
the Great Mother)
Ἄττης, ὁ (1d): Attis (a
Phrygian god, son of
Kybele - she forced him
to castrate himself be-
cause she was jealous of
his intended marriage)
Σαβάζιος, ὁ (2a): Sabazios
(a Phrygian and Thracian
god; worshipped in Italy
during the early empire)
μέτοικος, ὁ (2a): metic
(someone living in a city
other than his own, there-
fore without citizen
rights)
65 ἀμφίβολος, -ον: doubtful,
ambiguous.
καί ... δέ: well,
furthermore
ἄρτος, ὁ (2a): bread
Δημήτηρ, ἡ (3a): Demeter
(goddess of crops)
*οἶνος, ὁ (2a): wine
Ἡρακλῆς: Herakles (one
of his twelve labours was
to steal the cattle of
Geryon - whence this
meat?)
κρέας, τό (pl. κρέα):
meat
μύρτον, τό (2a): myrtle-
berry

Ἀφροδίτη, ἡ (1a): Aphrodite
(goddess of love)
μαινίς (μαινιδ-), ἡ (3a):
sprat, sardine
ἀμβροσία, ἡ (1b): ambrosia
(food of the gods)
ἠρέμα: a bit
νέκταρ (νεκταρ-), τό (3b):
nectar (drink of the gods)
παραγεύομαι (+ gen.): I
have a slight taste of
βέλτιστος: tr. 'splendid'
φιλανθρωπία, ἡ (1b):
humanity, kindliness
ἀποβλέπω: I look away
70 κοτύλη, ἡ (1a): ladle
ἐγχέω: I pour in
Ὅμηρος, ὁ (2a): Homer
(composer of the Iliad and
the Odyssey)
*καθάπερ: like, as
τεθεαμένος = perf. part. of
θεάομαι
σῖτον ... οἶνον: the quot-
ation is from Homer Iliad 5,
341 - where the gods' diet
is given as a reason for
their having 'ichor' not
blood in their veins
σῖτος, ὁ (2a): bread
ἔδω: I eat
αἴθοψ (αἰθοπ-): gleaming
παρατίθεμαι: I have set
before me
μεθύσκομαι (+ gen.): I
get drunk on
σιτέομαι: I feed on, eat
75 αὐτῇ κνίσῃ: tr. 'smell
and all'
ἀνενηνεγμένον = perf. pass.
part. of ἀναφέρω: I
carry up
καί ... δέ: and, moreover
αἷμα, τό (3b): blood
ἱερεῖον, τό (2b): sacrificial
victim
περιχέω: I pour x (acc.)
over y (dat.)
κιθαρίζω: I play the kithara
Σιληνός, ὁ (2a): Silenos
(an elderly, simian, drunken
fellow-reveller with
Dionysos)
κόρδαξ (κορδακ-), ὁ (3a):

26

(e) *Menippos describes the singing and dancing at the dinner-party.*
He slept badly, trying to resolve some problems about Apollo and the
sun.

ἐν δὲ τῷ δείπνῳ ὅ τε ᾿Απόλλων ἐκιθάρισεν καὶ ὁ Σιληνὸς
κόρδακα ὠρχήσατο καὶ αἱ Μοῦσαι ἀναστᾶσαι τῆς τε ᾿Ησιόδου
Θεογονίας ᾖσαν ἡμῖν καὶ τὴν πρώτην ᾠδὴν τῶν ὕμνων τῶν
Πινδάρου. κἀπειδὴ κόρος ἦν, ἀνεπαυόμεθα ὡς εἶχεν ἕκαστος   80
ἱκανῶς ὑποβεβρεγμένοι.

28.   ἄλλοι μέν ῥα θεοί τε καὶ ἀνέρες ἱπποκορυσταὶ
           εὗδον παννύχιοι, ἐμὲ δ᾿ οὐκ ἔχε νήδυμος ὕπνος·

ἀνελογιζόμην γὰρ πολλὰ μὲν καὶ ἄλλα, μάλιστα δὲ ἐκεῖνα, πῶς
ἐν τοσούτῳ χρόνῳ ὁ ᾿Απόλλων οὐ φύει πώγωνα ἢ πῶς ἐγένετο   85
νὺξ ἐν οὐρανῷ τοῦ ἡλίου παρόντος ἀεὶ καὶ συνευωχουμένου.

Next day Zeus called a meeting to discuss the moon's complaint.
Angry voices were raised against the impiety of the philosophers in
seeking to know about the moon more than was proper.
   It was agreed that they would be exterminated. 'But of course',
Zeus explained. 'we can't do it right this minute, since there's an
amnesty. But soon ... ' Menippos had his wings removed and was
dropped back to earth. He informs his friend that he now intends to
break the news to the philosophers.

5. A SCEPTICAL INTERVIEWER

(Ζεὺς ἐλεγχόμενος - *Iuppiter Confutatus 1-4*)

   In the poems of Homer (Iliad and Odyssey) and Hesiod (Theogony -
'The Genealogy of the Gods'), the ideas of destiny and fate are impor-
tant in describing the lot of man. In Homer especially there are
many different words for fate. Three are important here: (i) Εἱμαρ-
μένη *- alloted portion; (ii)* Μοῖρα *- goddess of fate (literally a*
portion or lot). Hesiod said there were three. They were envisaged
as spinning a thread for each man's life. Lakhesis assigned the lot
or length of the thread, Klotho spun it and Atropos cut it at the
required length; (iii) Τύχη *- fortune (not a goddess in Homer).*

kordax, can-can (an
obscene dance)
ὀρχέομαι: I dance
Μοῦσα, ἡ (1c): Muse
(one of the nine god-
desses of the arts)
ἀναστᾶσαι = aor. part.
intrans. of ἀνίσταμαι
Ἡσίοδος, ὁ (2a): Hesiod
(Boiotian poet, 7th cent.
B.C. (?): a farmer whose
poems include the did-
actic Works and Days and
Theogony - a genealogy
of the gods)
θεογονία, ἡ (1b). τῆς θ...:
sc. 'a part of ...'
ᾖσαν = 3rd pl. aor. of
ᾄδω
ᾠδή, ἡ (1a): ode, song
ὕμνος, ὁ (2a): hymn
80 Πίνδαρος, ὁ (2a): Pindar
(518-438 B.C., lyric poet
from Kynoskephalai in
Boiotia, many of whose
poems are works commis-
sioned to celebrate vic-
tories at the Olympian,
Nemean and Pythian games.
The 1st Olympian ode was
in celebration of Hieron
of Syracuse's victory
at Olympia in the horse-
race. It begins 'Water
is best, but gold like
gleaming fire in the
night outshines wealth
which makes men great.'
Lucian often quotes
this opening.)
κόρος, ὁ (2a): satisfaction,
fullness
ἀναπαύομαι: I take a rest,
sleep
ὡς εἶχεν ἕκαστος: tr. 'just
as we each were'
ὑποβεβρεγμένος, -η, -ον:
tight, sozzled
ἄλλοι ... ὕπνος: the quot-
ation is from Iliad 2.1-2,
but Lucian has altered the
line to ἐμὲ: in Homer the
word is Δία - there it is
Zeus who cannot sleep!

ῥα: then
ἀνέρες = ἄνδρες
ἱπποκορυστής, ὁ (1d): mar-
shaller of chariots
εὕδω (imperf. εὖδον): I
sleep
παννύχιος, -ον: all night
long
ἔχε (imperf. with no augment)
= εἶχε
νήδυμος, -ον: sweet
ἀναλογίζομαι: I consider
85 ἐκεῖνα: tr. 'the following'
πώγωνα: Apollo is always
represented as a young man,
therefore without a beard
συνευωχέομαι: I feast to-
gether (sc. 'with the
others')

The kordax. From a
relief from the Athenian
Agora.

Zeus is sitting down in heaven in the room where he deals with
oaths, prayers and other communications between men and the gods.
He has taken the lid off the prayer-hole and hears the modest but
self-confident voice of Kyniskos.

(a) Kyniskos rejects the idea of praying to Zeus for wealth etc.,
but merely wishes to ask a question. Zeus agrees to this.

1. ΚΥΝΙΣΚΟΣ: ἐγὼ δέ ὦ Ζεῦ, τὰ μὲν τοιαῦτα οὐκ ἐνοχλήσω σε

πλοῦτον ἢ χρυσὸν ἢ βασιλείαν αἰτῶν, ἅπερ εὐκταιότατα τοῖς

πολλοῖς, σοὶ δ' οὐ πάνυ ῥᾴδια παρασχεῖν· ὁρῶ γοῦν σε τὰ

πολλὰ παρακούοντα εὐχομένων αὐτῶν. ἓν δέ, καὶ τοῦτο ῥᾷσ-

τον, ἐβουλόμην παρὰ σοῦ μοι γενέσθαι.   5

ΖΕΥΣ: τί τοῦτό ἐστιν, ὦ Κυνίσκε; οὐ γὰρ ἀτυχήσεις, καὶ

μάλιστα μετρίων, ὡς ἔφης, δεόμενος.

ΚΥΝ: ἀπόκριναί μοι πρός τινα οὐ χαλεπὴν ἐρώτησιν.

ΖΕΥΣ: μικρά γε ὡς ἀληθῶς ἡ εὐχὴ καὶ πρόχειρος· ὥστε

ἐρώτα ὁπόσα ἂν ἐθέλῃς.   10

(b) Kyniskos asks if fate's decree is unavoidable. Zeus replies
that it is. Homer, as poets will when inspiration leaves them, made
a mistake.

ΚΥΝ: ἰδοὺ ταῦτα, ὦ Ζεῦ· ἀνέγνως γὰρ δῆλον ὅτι καὶ σὺ τὰ

Ὁμήρου καὶ Ἡσιόδου ποιήματα· εἰπὲ οὖν μοι εἰ ἀληθῆ ἐστιν

ἃ περὶ τῆς Εἱμαρμένης καὶ τῶν Μοιρῶν ἐκεῖνοι ἐρραψῳδήκασιν,

ἄφυκτα εἶναι ὁπόσα ἂν αὗται ἐπινήσωσιν γεινομένῳ ἑκάστῳ;

ΖΕΥΣ: καὶ πάνυ ἀληθῆ ταῦτα· οὐδὲν γάρ ἐστιν ὅ τι μὴ αἱ 15

Μοῖραι διατάττουσιν, ἀλλὰ πάντα ὁπόσα γίνεται, ὑπὸ τῷ

τούτων ἀτράκτῳ στρεφόμενα εὐθὺς ἐξ ἀρχῆς ἕκαστον ἐπικε-

κλωσμένην ἔχει τὴν ἀπόβασιν, καὶ οὐ θέμις ἄλλως γενέσθαι.

5. A SCEPTICAL INTERVIEWER

τὰ ... τοιαῦτα: i.e. πλοῦτον
etc.; take as object of
αἰτῶν
ἐνοχλέω: I bother
πλοῦτος, ὁ (2a): wealth
χρυσός, ὁ (2a): gold
βασιλεία, ἡ (1b): kingship
εὔκταῖος, -α, -ον: prayed
for
τοῖς πολλοῖς: 'by' (dat. of
agent after passive idea)
τὰ. πολλά: tr. 'in most cases' 14
παρακούω: I disregard,
ignore
5 μοι γενέσθαι: tr. 'to have'
(lit. 'to be to me')
Κυνισκος, ὁ (2a): Kyniskos
(his name has associations
with the words 'dog' and
'Cynic philosopher')
ἀτυχέω: I meet with refusal
μετρίων: sc. 'things'
ἐρώτησις, ἡ (3e): question
*ἀληθής, -ές: true
9 πρόχειρος, -ον: easy to grant

ἀνέγνως = aor. of ἀναγιγνώσκω
(ἀναγνο-): I read
ποίημα, τό (3b): poem
Εἱμαρμένη, ἡ (1a): see intro-
ductory note to this
piece.
Μοῖραι, αἱ (1b): see
introductory note to
this piece
ῥαψῳδέω: I recite
ἄφυκτος, -ον: inescapable
(sc. 'that ...')
ἐπινέω: I spin
γείνομαι: I am born
διατάττω: I ordain
ὑπό (+ dat.): on, by
*ἄτρακτος, ὁ (2a): spindle
(of the Fates)
στρέφω: I spin
ἕκαστον: is in apposition
to πάντα (tr. 'of all ...
each ...')
ἐπικεκλωσμένην = perf.
pass. part. of ἐπικλώθω:
I assign
ἀπόβασις, ἡ (3e): outcome
οὐ θέμις: it isn't lawful
(sc. 'for things to ...')

2. ΚΥΝ: οὐκοῦν ὁπόταν ὁ αὐτὸς Ὅμηρος ἐν ἑτέρῳ μέρει
τῆς ποιήσεως λέγῃ,   20

μὴ καὶ ὑπὲρ μοῖραν δόμον Ἄϊδος

καὶ τὰ τοιαῦτα, ληρεῖν δηλαδὴ φήσομεν τότε αὐτόν;

ΖΕΥΣ: καὶ μάλα· οὐδὲν γὰρ οὕτω γένοιτ' ἂν ἔξω τοῦ νόμου
τῶν Μοιρῶν, οὐδὲ ὑπὲρ τὸ λίνον. οἱ ποιηταὶ δὲ ὁπόσα μὲν
ἂν ἐκ τῶν Μουσῶν κατεχόμενοι ᾄδωσιν, ἀληθῆ ταῦτά ἐστιν·   25
ὁπόταν δὲ ἀφῶσιν αὐτοὺς αἱ θεαὶ καὶ καθ' αὑτοὺς ποιῶσι,
τότε δὴ καὶ σφάλλονται καὶ ὑπεναντία τοῖς πρότερον δι-
εξίασι· καὶ συγγνώμη, εἰ ἄνθρωποι ὄντες ἀγνοοῦσι τάληθές,
ἀπελθόντος ἐκείνου ὃ τέως παρὸν ἐρραψῴδει δι' αὐτῶν.

(c) *Kyniskos asks about the Fates. Is Zeus subject to them? The
answer is 'yes'.*

ΚΥΝ: ἀλλὰ τοῦτο μὲν οὕτω φήσομεν. ἔτι δὲ κάκεῖνό μοι   30
ἀπόκριναι· οὐ τρεῖς αἱ Μοῖραί εἰσι, Κλωθὼ καὶ Λάχεσις, οἶμαι,
καὶ Ἄτροπος;

ΖΕΥΣ: πάνυ μὲν οὖν.

3. ΚΥΝ: ἡ Εἱμαρμένη τοίνυν καὶ ἡ Τύχη - πολυθρύλητοι
γὰρ πάνυ καὶ αὗται - τίνες ποτ' εἰσιν ἢ τί δύναται αὐτῶν   35
ἑκατέρα; πότερον τὰ ἴσα ταῖς Μοίραις ἢ τι καὶ ὑπὲρ ἐκεί-
νας; ἀκούω γοῦν ἁπάντων λεγόντων μηδὲν εἶναι Τύχης καὶ
Εἱμαρμένης δυνατώτερον.

ΖΕΥΣ: οὐ θέμις ἅπαντά σε εἰδέναι, ὦ Κυνίσκε· τίνος δ'
οὖν ἕνεκα ἠρώτησας τὸ περὶ τῶν Μοιρῶν;   40

4. ΚΥΝ: ἢν πρότερόν μοι, ὦ Ζεῦ, κάκεῖνο εἴπῃς, εἰ καὶ
ὑμῶν αὗται ἄρχουσιν καὶ ἀνάγκη ὑμῖν ἠρτῆσθαι ἀπὸ τοῦ λίνου
αὐτῶν.

20 ποίησις, ἡ (3e): poem
μή (+ subj.): lest, in
case (Lucian has missed
out εἰσαφίκηαι 'you arrive
at' at the end of the line,
Il. 20.336: Poseidon warns
Aineias what may happen to
him if he persists in fac-
ing Akhilleus, from whom
P. has just rescued him.)
ὑπὲρ μοῖραν: 'beyond your
fate'
δόμον ῎Αϊδος: 'the house
of Hades'
ληρέω: I speak nonsense
δηλαδή: obviously
οὐδέ: nor
λίνον, τό (2b): thread
(of destiny)
ὁπόσα: take this as first
word in the sentence
25 κατέχομαι (ἐκ + gen.): I
am possessed by
ἀφῶσιν = aor. subj. of
ἀφίημι
καθ' αὑτούς: off their
own bat, unaided
ποιέω: I compose, write
poetry
σφάλλομαι: I make a
mistake
ὑπεναντίος, -ον (+ dat.):

contrary to
τοῖς πρότερον: tr. 'to their
previous efforts'
διέξειμι = fut. of διεξέρχομαι
συγγνώμη: sc. 'one must
accord them ...'
*ἀγνοέω: I do not understand/
perceive/know
ἐκείνου ὅ: tr. 'the thing
which ...'
τέως: until then
30 κἀκεῖνο: tr. 'the following
question too'
Κλωθώ ... Λάχεσις ...῎Ατροπος
see introductory note to
this piece
πολυθρύλητος, -ον: well known
35 δύναμαι: I have power
τὰ ἴσα ... τι: sc. δύναται
αὐτῶν ἑκατέρα
δύνατος, -η, -ον: strong,
powerful. δυνατώτερον here
takes gen. of comparison
θέμις: right, allowed (by the
law of the gods) (followed
by acc. + inf.)
40 τὸ περὶ τῶν Μοιρῶν: sc.
'question'
*πρότερον: first (of two)
ἠρτῆσθαι = perf. inf. of
ἀρτάομαι: I depend on,
I am hung from (ἀπό + gen.)

ΖΕΥΣ: ἀνάγκη, ὦ Κυνίσκε. τί δ' οὖν ἐμειδίασας;

(d) *Kyniskos reminds Zeus of the passage in the Iliad where he claims to be stronger than all the rest of the gods together. Fate, it seems, is stronger than he.*

ΚΥΝ: ἀνεμνήσθην ἐκείνων τῶν Ὁμήρου ἐπῶν, ἐν οἷς   45
πεποίησαι αὐτῷ ἐν τῇ ἐκκλησίᾳ τῶν θεῶν δημηγορῶν, ὁπότε ἠπεί-
λεις αὐτοῖς ὡς ἀπὸ σειρᾶς τινος χρυσῆς ἀναρτησόμενος τὰ πάντα·
ἔφησθα γὰρ αὐτὸς μὲν τὴν σειρὰν καθήσειν ἐξ οὐρανοῦ, τοὺς
θεοὺς δὲ ἅμα πάντας, εἰ βούλοιντο, ἐκκρεμαμένους κατασπᾶν
βιάσεσθαι, οὐ μὴν κατασπάσειν γε, σὲ δέ, ὁπόταν ἐθελήσῃς,   50
ῥᾳδίως ἅπαντας

          αὐτῇ κεν γαίῃ ἐρύσαι αὐτῇ τε θαλάσσῃ.

τότε μὲν οὖν θαυμάσιος ἐδόκεις μοι τὴν βίαν καὶ ὑπέφριττον
μεταξὺ ἀκούων τῶν ἐπῶν· νῦν δὲ καὶ αὐτόν σε ἤδη ὁρῶ μετὰ
τῆς σειρᾶς καὶ τῶν ἀπειλῶν ἀπὸ λεπτοῦ νήματος, ὡς φής,   55
κρεμάμενον. δοκεῖ γοῦν μοι δικαιότερον ἂν ἡ Κλωθὼ μεγαλ-
αυχήσασθαι, ὡς καὶ αὐτόν σε ἀνάσπαστον αἰωροῦσα ἐκ τοῦ
ἀτράκτου καθάπερ οἱ ἁλιεῖς ἐκ τοῦ καλάμου τὰ ἰχθύδια.

The interview goes from bad to worse for Zeus. Kyniskos' next point is that sacrifices and prayers can have no effect, since nothing the Fates decree can be altered; the gods are only the tools of the Fates; oracles are superfluous, since one cannot do anything about them, punishments in Hades should not be inflicted on men, since, from these arguments, they do not have any free will. At this point Zeus shuts the prayer lid in disgust and leaves Kyniskos to muse on the evil fate of being a Fate, and all the hard work it entails.

μειδιάω: I smile
45 ἀνεμνήσθην = aor. of ἀναμιμνή-
σκομαι (+ gen.): I recall
αὐτῷ: 'by' (dat. of agent
after passive verb)
δημηγορέω: I speak in the
assembly, I make popular
speeches, I use clap-trap
ἀπειλέω (+ dat.): I threaten
σειρά, ἡ (1b): cord
ἀναρτάομαι: I attach
καθήσειν = fut. inf. of καθίημι
ἐκκρέμαμαι: I am suspended,
I hang on
κατασπάω: I pull down (sc.
'you')
50 βάσεσθαι: tr. 'would use
force ...'
οὐ μὴν ... γε: but all the
same
κεν (+ inf.) = ἄν: (in indir.
st. after ἔφησθα) tr.
'would'
αὐτῇ ... γαίῃ: land
and all
ἐρύω: I pull (up)
αὐτῇ ... θαλάσσῃ: sea and
all (Lucian has adapted
Il. 8.24 to his own sen-
tence, altering ἐρύσαιμ'
to ἐρύσαι - which thus

does not scan. In Homer
the context is as L. des-
cribes it)
*θαυμάσιος, -α, -ον: wonder-
ful, amazing (sc. 'in ...')
βία, ἡ (1b): strength.
ὑποφρίττω: I shudder
μεταξύ (+ part.): in the
middle of, while
55 ἀπειλαί, αἱ (1a): threats
*λεπτός, -ή, -όν, thin,
weak
νῆμα, τό (3b): thread
κρέμαμαι (ἀπό + gen.): I
hang (from)
δικαιότερον (comp. adv.):
more justly
ἄν (+ inf.): tr. 'able
to ...' (lit. 'Kl. seems
... to be able to ...')
μεγαλαυχέομαι: I boast
ἀνάσπαστος, -ον: drawn
up
αἰωρέω: I hang x (acc.)
from υ (ἐκ + gen.)
ἁλιεύς, ὁ (3g): fisherman
κάλαμος, ὁ (2a): fishing-
rod
ἰχθύδιον, τό (2b): little
fish

Zeus. From exterior of
wine cup by Oltos, c.515
B.C.; Museo Nazionale,
Tarquinia.

I I B E Y O N D T H E G R A V E

The extract which makes up this section is from a collection
of short pieces entitled Dialogues of the Dead (Νεκρικοὶ Διάλογοι).
In these Lucian portrays the world as it looks from Hades. Some
of the dialogues deal with stock characters from satire (e.g. the
young legacy-hunter or the rich and childless old man) and show
how futile their behaviour in life has been in the light of their
death. Others involve famous figures from history or mythology (e.g.
Tantalus, Herakles and Alexander the Great), whose presence in the
Underworld gives an opportunity to cast light - or doubt - on their
stories. In this dialogue Menippos (see also 4 above) meets Sokrates.

6. SOKRATES OWNS UP

(Νεκρικοὶ Διάλογοι - Dialogi Mortuorum 6.4-6)

Menippos has died and requested from Aiakos (the gatekeeper of
Hades and one of the judges of the dead) a guided tour of the famous
deceased. He is shown the Greek heroes of the Trojan war, some famous
oriental despots and the well-known philosophers. In each of these
cases he makes apt remarks about the vanity of their existence on
earth. Then he asks to meet Sokrates.

(a) *Menippos enquires the whereabouts of Sokrates. Aiakos' descrip-*
tion does not help.

4. ΜΕΝΙΠΠΟΣ: ὁ Σωκράτης δέ, ὦ Αἰακέ, ποῦ ποτε ἆρα ἐστίν;

ΑΙΑΚΟΣ: μετὰ Νέστορος καὶ Παλαμήδους ἐκεῖνος ληρεῖ τὰ
πολλά.

ΜΕΝ: ὅμως ἐβουλόμην ἰδεῖν αὐτόν, εἴ που ἐνθάδε ἐστίν.

ΑΙΑ: ὁρᾷς τὸν φαλακρόν;   5

ΜΕΝ: ἅπαντες φαλακροί εἰσιν· ὥστε πάντων ἂν εἴη τοῦτο
τὸ γνώρισμα.

6. SOKRATES OWNS UP

Αἰακός, ὁ (2a): Aiakos
Νέστωρ (Νεστορ-), ὁ (3a):
  Nestor (King of Pylos;
  an old counsellor and in-
  veterate talker in Homer's
  Iliad)
Παλαμήδης, ὁ (3c): Palamedes 5
  (inventor of the alphabet,
  a cunning helper of Agamem-

non during the Trojan war -
he tricked Odysseus into
coming and was paid back by
Odysseus 'framing' him and
getting him killed)
ληρέω: I speak rubbish
τὰ πολλά: tr. 'most of
  the time'
*φαλακρός, -ά, -όν: bald
γνώρισμα, τό (3b): mark,
  way of recognising

Sokrates. From a Roman
copy, probably based on a
lost bronze seated statue
by Lysippos, c.324 B.C.

36

AIA: τὸν σιμὸν λέγω.

MEN: καὶ τοῦτο ὅμοιον· σιμοὶ γὰρ ἅπαντες.

(b) Sokrates makes himself known and enquires about the situation
in Athens. Menippos' views of philosophers are sceptical.

5. ΣΩΚΡΑΤΗΣ: ἐμὲ ζητεῖς, ὦ Μένιππε;   10

MEN: καὶ μάλα, ὦ Σώκρατες.

ΣΩΚ: τί τὰ ἐν ᾿Αθήναις;

MEN: πολλοὶ τῶν νέων φιλοσοφεῖν λέγουσι, καὶ τά γε
σχήματα αὐτὰ καὶ τὰ βαδίσματα εἰ θεάσαιτό τις, ἄκροι φιλόσοφοι.

ΣΩΚ: μάλα πολλοὺς ἑώρακα.   15

MEN: ἀλλὰ ἑώρακας, οἶμαι, οἷος ἧκε παρὰ σοὶ ᾿Αρίστιππος
ἢ Πλάτων αὐτός, ὁ μὲν ἀποπνέων μύρον, ὁ δὲ τοὺς ἐν Σικελίᾳ
τυράννους θεραπεύειν ἐκμαθών.

(c) Sokrates asks about his own reputation and affirms the truth
of his famous claim to ignorance.

ΣΝΚ: περὶ ἐμοῦ δὲ τί φρονοῦσιν;

MEN: εὐδαίμων, ὦ Σώκρατες, ἄνθρωπος εἶ τά γε τοιαῦτα. 20
πάντες γοῦν σε θαυμάσιον οἴονται ἄνδρα γεγενῆσθαι καὶ πάντα
ἐγνωκέναι καὶ ταῦτα - οἶμαι γὰρ τἀληθῆ λέγειν - οὐδὲν
εἰδότα.

σιμός, -ή, όν: snub-nosed
9 ὅμοιον: tr. 'the same'
τί: sc. ἐστι
τὰ ἐν 'Αθήναις: sc.
  'news ...'
φιλοσοφέω: I practise
  philosophy, I am a
  philosopher
σχῆμα, τό (3b): dress,
  appearance; form, figure
τὰ ... σχήματα: the object
  of θεάσαιτο
βάδισμα, τό (3b): walk,
  gait
ἄκρος, -α, -ον: top (sc.
  εἰσι)
15 ἑώρακα = perf. of ὁράω
οἷος: tr. 'in what
  condition'
'Αρίστιππος, ὁ (2a):
  Aristippos (founder of the
  Cyrenaic school of philo-
  sophy; he taught that
  immediate pleasure was the
  only end of action. Lucian
  may be confusing him with
  his grandfather, a friend
  of Socrates)
Πλάτων: Plato (in 367 B.C.
  he made an abortive visit to

Syracuse to try to realise
  the idea of the philosopher-
  king from his Republic in
  the person of Dionysius II.
  Dion, who had invited him,
  later ousted Dionysius and
  became tyrant, despite his
  Platonic ideaology, in his
  stead.)
ἀποπνέω: I smell of, breathe
  out
*μύρον, τό (2b): myrrh,
  Chanel No.5 (?)
Σικελία, ἡ (1b): Sicily
τύραννος, ὁ (2a): tyrant
θεραπεύω: I flatter
*ἐκμαθ- = aor. stem of
  ἐκμανθάνω (+ inf.): I
  learn well/thoroughly (how
  to)
τὰ ... τοιαῦτα: tr. 'in
  these respects' (acc.
  of respect)
οἴονται = 3rd. pl. of
  οἶμαι
ἐγνωκέναι = perf. inf.
  of γιγνώσκω
καὶ ταῦτα: and at that,
  although

38

ΣΩΚ: καὶ αὐτὸς ἔφασκον ταῦτα πρὸς αὐτούς, οἱ δὲ
εἰρωνείαν τὸ πρᾶγμα ᾤοντο εἶναι.   25

(d) Menippos comments on Sokrates' choice of companions and chooses a place to spend his death.

6. ΜΕΝ: τίνες δέ εἰσιν οὗτοι οἱ περὶ σέ;

ΣΩΚ: Χαρμίδης, ὦ Μένιππε, καὶ Φαῖδρος καὶ ὁ τοῦ
Κλεινίου.

ΜΕΝ: εὖ γε, ὦ Σώκρατες, ὅτι κἀνταῦθα μέτει τὴν
σεαυτοῦ τέχνην καὶ οὐκ ὀλιγωρεῖς τῶν καλῶν.   30

ΣΩΚ: τί γὰρ ἂν ἥδιον ἄλλο πράττοιμι; ἀλλὰ πλησίον
ἡμῶν κατάκεισο, εἰ δοκεῖ.

ΜΕΝ: μὰ Δί', ἐπεὶ παρὰ τὸν Κροῖσον καὶ τὸν Σαρδα-
νάπαλλον ἄπειμι πλησίον οἰκήσων αὐτῶν· ἔοικα γοῦν οὐκ ὀλίγα
γελάσεσθαι οἰμωζόντων ἀκούων.   35

25 εἰρωνεία, ἡ (1b): irony
(in ancient rhetoric
'saying the opposite
of what you mean')
ᾤοντο = 3rd. pl. imperf.
of οἶμαι
Χαρμίδης, ὁ (1d):
Kharmides (d.403 B.C.,
Plato's uncle; a central
character in Plato's
Kharmides and a compan-
ion of Sokrates)
Φαῖδρος, ὁ (2a): Phaidros
(c.450-408 B.C., a char-
acter in several of Plato's
dialogues - a Sokratic
philosopher)
Κλεινίας, ὁ (1d): Kleinias
ὁ τοῦ K: the son of ...
(i.e. Alkibiades, c.450-
404 B.C., companion of
Sokrates and leading
politician during the
second half of the Pelopon-
nesian War)
εὖ γε: nice one, well done
μέτειμι: I pursue

30 ὀλιγωρέω (+ gen.): I spurn,
take no account of
γάρ: yes, for; well
κατάκεισο = imper. of
κατάκειμαι: I lie down
Κροῖσος, ὁ (2a): Kroisos
(King of Lydia c.560-546
B.C., who once deemed him-
self the happiest man in
the world because of his
vast wealth)
Σαρδανάπαλλος, ὁ (2a):
Sardanapallos (King of
Assyria, who eventually
burned himself together
with his treasures; he
was noted for transvestism
and effeminacy)
ἄπειμι = fut. of ἀπέρχομαι
πλησίον: take with αὐτῶν
οἰκήσων = fut. part. expres-
sing purpose, tr. 'to ...'
ἔοικα: tr. 'I reckon'
οὐκ ὀλίγα: tr. 'a great
deal'
35 οἰμώζω: I cry alas (οἴμοι),
lament

III THE TRUTH, THE HALF TRUTH AND NOTHING LIKE THE TRUTH

A True Story ('Αληθῶν Διηγημάτων A and B), *perhaps Lucian's best work is self-confessedly in conception an extended literary satire. Lucian says at the beginning that he wrote it because he saw authors like Ktesias and Iamboulos getting away with writing histories which contained very few grains of truth. He blames Homer's Odysseus for starting the trend, with his tales to Alkinoos of bags of wind, Kyklopes and cannibals. But, Lucian claims, his reaction is not one of moral indignation, merely surprise that people can tell such lies and expect to get away with them. So if you can't beat them ... and Lucian himself embarked on a history of amazing sights. But he gives fair warning: 'the only true thing I'll say, is that I'm lying ... The things I'm writing about I never saw, experienced or heard from anyone else. They don't exist and couldn't. My readers should beware of giving my words any credence.'*

7. 'IN VINO VERITAS'?

('Αληθῶν Διηγημάτων A - *Verae Historiae* 1.6-9)

Lucian set sail from the Pillars of Herakles (Straits of Gibraltar) and headed westward with a crew of fifty. They ran into a storm, which lasted seventy-nine days, but eventually the sun reappeared and they saw an island.

(a) *Lucian and his crew landed and investigated the place. They found inscriptional evidence of a visit by Herakles and Dionysos, which was confirmed by some startling phenomena - footprints and a river of wine.*

6. προσσχόντες οὖν καὶ ἀποβάντες ὡς ἂν ἐκ μακρᾶς ταλαι-
πωρίας πολὺν μὲν χρόνον ἐπὶ γῆς ἐκείμεθα, διαναστάντες
δὲ ὅμως ἀπεκρίναμεν ἡμῶν αὐτῶν τριάκοντα μὲν φύλακας τῆς
νεὼς παραμένειν, εἴκοσι δὲ σὺν ἐμοὶ ἀνελθεῖν ἐπὶ κατα-
7. σκοπῇ τῶν ἐν τῇ νήσῳ. προελθόντες δὲ ὅσον σταδίους τρεῖς   5
ἀπὸ τῆς θαλάττης δι' ὕλης ὁρῶμέν τινα στήλην χαλκοῦ πε-
ποιημένην, Ἑλληνικοῖς γράμμασιν καταγεγραμμένην, ἀμυδροῖς

7. 'IN VINO VERITAS'?

προσσχ- = aor. stem of
προσέχω: I put in (to
harbour)
*ἀποβα- = aor. stem of
ἀποβαίνω: I disembark
ὡς ἄν: tr. 'as (you) would
(expect). ...'
ἐκ (+ gen.): after
ταλαιπωρία, ἡ (1b): suffering
διαναστάντες = aor. part. in-
trans. of διανίσταμαι: I
stand up
ἀποκρίνω (ἀποκριν-): I de-
tail, choose
τριάκοντα: thirty
*παραμένω: I stay near/behind/
put
ἀνελθ- = aor. stem of
ἀνέρχομαι: I go up
κατασκοπή, ἡ (1a): spying out

5 προελθ = aor. stem of
προέρχομαι: I go forward
στάδιοι, οἱ (2a): stades
(a stade was a distance of
c.200 yds.)
*ὐλή, ἡ (1a): forest, wood.
στήλη, ἡ (1a): inscribed
plaque, monument
χαλκός, ὁ (2a): bronze
χαλκοῦ is gen. of material
out of which it is made (as
in English)
'Ελληνικός, -ή, -όν: Greek
γράμμα, τό (3b): letter
καταγεγραμμένην = perf. pass.
part. of καταγράφω: I
inscribe, engrave
ἀμυδρός, -ά, -όν: dim, faint.
ἐκτετριμμένος = perf. pass.
part. of ἐκτρίβω: I rub
out

Dionysus afloat. Inside
of a wine cup by Exekias,
c. 535 B.C.

δὲ καὶ ἐκτετριμμένοις, λέγουσαν "Αχρι τούτων 'Ηρακλῆς καὶ
Διόνυσος ἀφίκοντο. ἦν δὲ καὶ ἴχνη δύο πλησίον ἐπὶ πέτρας,
τὸ μὲν πλεθριαῖον, τὸ δὲ ἔλαττον - ἐμοὶ δοκεῖν, τὸ μὲν   10
τοῦ Διονύσου, τὸ μικρότερον, θάτερον δὲ 'Ηρακλέους. προσ-
κυνήσαντες δ' οὖν προῆμεν· οὔπω δὲ πολὺ παρῆμεν καὶ ἐφ-
ιστάμεθα ποταμῷ οἶνον ῥέοντι ὁμοιότατον μάλιστα οἶόσπερ
ὁ Χῖός ἐστιν. ἄφθονον δὲ ἦν τὸ ῥεῦμα καὶ πολύ, ὥστε
ἐνιαχοῦ καὶ ναυσίπορον εἶναι δύνασθαι. ἐπῄει οὖν ἡμῖν   15
πολὺ μᾶλλον πιστεύειν τῷ ἐπὶ τῆς στήλης ἐπιγράμματι,
ὁρῶσι τὰ σημεῖα τῆς Διονύσου ἐπιδημίας.

(b) Lucian found the source of the river and caught some fish, which
manifested many of the qualities of the wine in which they lived.

7.   δόξαν δέ μοι καὶ ὅθεν ἄρχεται ὁ ποταμὸς καταμαθεῖν,
cont. ἀνῄειν παρὰ τὸ ῥεῦμα, καὶ πηγὴν μὲν οὐδεμίαν εὖρον αὐτοῦ,
πολλὰς δὲ καὶ μεγάλας ἀμπέλους, πλήρεις βοτρύων, παρὰ δὲ   20
τὴν ῥίζαν ἑκάστην ἀπέρρει σταγὼν οἴνου δαυγοῦς, ἀφ' ὧν
ἐγίνετο ὁ ποταμός. ἦν δὲ καὶ ἰχθῦς ἐν αὐτῷ πολλοὺς ἰδεῖν,
οἴνῳ μάλιστα καὶ τὴν χρόαν καὶ τὴν γεῦσιν προσεοικότας·
ἡμεῖς γοῦν ἀγρεύσαντες αὐτῶν τινας καὶ ἐμφαγόντες ἐμεθύσ-
θημεν· ἀμέλει καὶ ἀνατεμόντες αὐτοὺς εὑρίσκομεν τρυγὸς   25
μεστούς. ὕστερον μέντοι ἐπινοήσαντες τοὺς ἄλλους ἰχθῦς,
τοὺς ἀπὸ τοῦ ὕδατος παραμιγνύντες ἐκεράννυμεν τὸ σφοδρὸν
τῆς οἰνοφαγίας.

(c) Lucian and his comrades discovered some vine-women. He narrates
the tragic consequences of two men's erotic indulgences.

8.   τότε δὲ τὸν ποταμὸν διαπεράσαντες ᾗ διαβατὸς ἦν, εὕ-
ρομεν ἀμπέλων χρῆμα τεράστιον· τὸ μὲν γὰρ ἀπὸ τῆς γῆς,   30
ὁ στέλεχος αὐτὸς εὐερνὴς καὶ παχύς, τὸ δὲ ἄνω γυναῖκες
ἦσαν, ὅσον ἐκ τῶν λαγόνων ἅπαντα ἔχουσαι τέλεια - τοιαύ-
την παρ' ἡμῖν τὴν Δάφνην γράφουσιν ἄρτι τοῦ 'Απόλλωνος

ἄχρι (+ gen.): as far as,
up to.
τούτων: sc. 'point'.
ἴχνος, τό (3c): footprint
πέτρα, ἡ (1b): rock
10 πλεθριαῖος, -α, -ον: 100
feet long.
*ἐμοὶ δοκεῖν: in my opinion,
as it seems to me (a
number of such idioms
occur with inf. where you
might expect indic. e.g.
μικροῦ δεῖν: almost).
θάτερος, -α, -ον: other
(of two).
προσκυνέω: I make obei-
sance, fall down and
worship.
προῆμεν = 1st. pl. imperf.
of προέρχομαι: I go for-
ward/on.
ἐφίσταμαι (+ dat.): I come
upon suddenly.
ῥέω (+ acc.): I flow with.
οἷοσπερ: as.
Χῖος, ὁ (2a): Khian wine.
ἄφθονος, -ον: plentiful.
ῥεῦμα, τό (3b): stream.
15 ἐνιαχοῦ: in some places.
ναυσίπορος, -ον: navigable.
ἐπήει = 3rd. s. imperf. of
ἐπέρχομαι (+ dat.): I
occur to, I come into x's
head.
ἐπίγραμμα, το (3b): in-
scription.
ὁρῶσι = dat. pl. pres. part.
with ἡμῖν.
ἐπιδημία, ἡ (1b): stay.
δόξαν ... μοι: tr. 'since
I had decided' (acc. abs.,
lit. 'it seeming good to
me...')
ἀνῄειν = ἀνῇα, 1st s. imperf.
of ἀνέρχομαι: I go up.
ῥεῦμα, τό (3b): stream.
*πηγή, ἡ (1a): spring,
source.
αὐτοῦ: on the spot (or
'of it' i.e. the stream).
20 *ἄμπελος, ἡ (2a): grape-
vine.
πλήρης, -ές (+ gen.): full
of.

*βότρυς, ὁ (3h): bunch of
grapes.
ῥίζα, ἡ (1c): root.
ἀπορρέω: I flow out.
σταγών, ὁ (3a): drop.
διαυγής, -ές: translucent.
ἦν: 'it was possible'.
ἰχθῦς, ὁ (3h): fish.
προσέοικα (+ dat.): I
resemble.
χρόα, ἡ (1b): colour.
γεῦσις, ἡ (3e): taste.
τὴν χρόαν καὶ τὴν γεῦσιν
(acc. of respect): tr.
'in ... and ...'
ἀγρεύω: I catch.
ἐμφαγεῖν: to eat hastily.
μεθύσκομαι (aor. ἐμεθύσθην):
I get drunk.
25 ἀμέλει: of course.
εὑρίσκομεν: imperf. (εὑ-
vbs. augment either εὑ-
or ηὑ-).
τρύξ (τρυγ-), ἡ (3a): dregs,
wine-lees.
ἐπινοέω: I have an idea.
παραμίγνυμι: I add by mixing.
κεράννυμι: I temper,
moderate.
σφοδρόν, τό (2b): vehemence,
excess.
οἰνοφαγία, ἡ (1b): solid
alcohol intake (lit. 'wine-
eating').
διαπεράω: I cross.
ᾗ: where.
διαβατός, -ον: fordable.
εὕρομεν = aor. (cf. εὑρίσκομεν
in line 25 above)
30 ἀμπέλων χρῆμα τεράστιον: tr.
'a prodigious sort of vine'
(a common idiom with χρῆμα).
περάστιος, -ον: prodigious,
monstrous.
τὸ μὲν ... τὸ δὲ (acc. of
respect): id the part ...
in the part ...
στέλεχος, ὁ (2a): crown of
the root, trunk.
εὐερνής, -ές: flourishing
παχύς, -εῖα, -ύ: thick.
λαγών (λαγον-), ὁ (3a):
thigh.
τέλειος, -α, -ον: perfect,
complete.

καταλαμβάνοντος ἀποδενδρουμένην. ἀπὸ δὲ τῶν δακτύλων ,
ἄκρων ἐξεφύοντο αὐταῖς οἱ κλάδοι καὶ μεστοὶ ἦσαν βοτρύων.   35
καὶ μὴν καὶ τὰς κεφαλὰς ἐκόμων ἕλιξί τε καὶ φύλλοις καὶ
βότρυσι. προσελθόντας δὲ ἡμᾶς ἡσπάζοντο καὶ ἐδεξιοῦντο,
αἱ μὲν Λύδιον, αἱ δ' 'Ινδικήν, αἱ πλεῖσται δὲ τὴν 'Ελλάδα
φωνὴν προϊέμεναι. καὶ ἐφίλουν δὲ ἡμᾶς τοῖς στόμασιν· ὁ
δὲ φιληθεὶς αὐτίκα ἐμέθυεν καὶ παράφορος ἦν. δρέπεσθαι   40
μέντοι οὐ παρεῖχον τοῦ καρποῦ, ἀλλ' ἤλγουν καὶ ἐβόων
ἀποσπωμένου. αἱ δὲ καὶ μίγνυσθαι ἡμῖν ἐπεθύμουν· καὶ δύο
τινὲς τῶν ἑταίρων πλησιάσαντες αὐταῖς οὐκέτι ἀπελύοντο,
ἀλλ' ἐκ τῶν αἰδοίων ἐδέδεντο· συνεφύοντο γὰρ καὶ συνερ-
ριζοῦντο. καὶ ἤδη αὐτοῖς κλάδοι ἐπεφύκεσαν οἱ δάκτυλοι,   45
καὶ ταῖς ἕλιξι περιπλεκόμενοι ὅσον οὐδέπω καὶ αὐτοὶ καρπο-
9. φορήσειν ἔμελλον. καταλιπόντες δὲ αὐτοὺς ἐπὶ ναῦν
ἐφεύγομεν καὶ τοῖς ἀπολειφθεῖσιν διηγούμεθα ἐλθόντες τά
τε ἄλλα καὶ τῶν ἑταίρων τὴν ἀμπελομιξίαν. καὶ δὴ λαβόντες
ἀμφορέας τινὰς καὶ ὑδρευσάμενοί τε ἅμα καὶ ἐκ τοῦ ποταμοῦ   50
οἰνισάμενοι καὶ αὐτοῦ πλησίον ἐπὶ τῆς ἠόνος αὐλισάμενοι
ἕωθεν ἀνήχθημεν οὐ σφόδρα βιαίῳ πνεύματι.

8. 'DE LA TERRE A LA LUNE'

(' Αληθῶν Διηγημάτων Α - Verae Historiae 1.9-11)

(a) The breeze soon turned into a typhoon. Lucian's ship was whirled
into the air, where it sailed on until docking at the moon. Lucian
describes the night sky.

9.   περὶ μεσημβρίαν δὲ οὐκέτι τῆς νήσου φαινομένης ἄφνω
cont. τυφὼν ἐπιγενόμενος καὶ περιδινήσας τὴν ναῦν καὶ μετεωρίσας
ὅσον ἐπὶ σταδίους τριακοσίους οὐκέτι καθῆκεν εἰς τὸ πέλαγος,
ἀλλ' ἄνω μετέωρον ἐξηρτημένην ἄνεμος ἐμπεσὼν τοῖς ἱστίοις

γράφω: I paint.
ἀποδενδρόομαι: I am
turned into a tree.
35 ἄκρος, -α, -ον: tip.
ἐκφύομαι: I grow.
αὐταῖς: tr. 'their' (lit.
to them', dat. of pos-
session).
*κλάδος, ὁ (2a): branch.
τὰς κεφαλάς (acc. of re-
spect): sc. 'on ...'
κομάω (+ dat.): I have
long hair made of.
ἕλιξ (ἑλικ-), ἡ (3a): vine
tendril.
*φύλλον, τό (2b): leaf.
δεξιόομαι: I welcome (with
the right hand), I shake
hands with.
Λύδιος, -ον: Lydian.
'Ινδικός, -ή, -όν: Indian.
"Ελλας ('Ελλαδ-), ἡ (adj.):
Greek.
προΐεμαι: I utter, speak.
40 μεθύω: I am intoxicated,
I am tipsy/tight.
παράφορος, -ον: staggering,
legless.
δρέπομαι: I pick.
παρέχω: I allow,
*καρπός, ὁ (2a): fruit.
τοῦ καρποῦ: sc. 'any
of ...'
ἀλγέω: I feel pain,
ἀποσπάω: I pull off.
ἀποσπωμένου (gen. abs.):
if it (i.e. the fruit)
were ...
μίγνυμαι (+ dat.): I have
intercourse with.
πλησιάζω (+ dat.): I get
to grips with, have sex
with.
*αἰδοῖα, τά (2b): genitals.
ἐδέδεντο = 3rd pl. pluperf.
pass. of δέω: I hold
fast.
συμφύομαι: I grow together,
am assimilated.
συρριζόομαι: I am joined
by the root.
45 αὐτοῖς (dat. of possession):
tr. 'their'

ἐπεφύκεσαν pluperf. of
φύομαι: I become.
περιπλέκομαι: I an en-
twined.
ὅσον οὐδέπω: tr. 'any minute
now'
καρποφορέω: I bear fruit.
*ἀπολείπω (ἀπολιπ-): I leave
behind, desert (aor. pass.
stem ἀπολειφθ-)
διηγούμεθα: imperf. (η-
verbs stay the same when
augmented).
ἀμπελομιξία, ἡ (1b): vintage-
sex, sexual vintnercourse.
50 *ἀμφορεύς, ὁ (3g): amphora,
storage jar.
ὑδρεύομαι: I draw water.
οἰνίζομαι: I draw wine.
αὐτοῦ: here, on the spot.
ἠών (ἠον-), ἡ (3a): shore,
beach.
αὐλίζομαι: I encamp.
ἕωθεν: at dawn.
ἀνήχθην = aor. of ἀνάγομαι:
I set sail.
βίαιος, -α, -ον: violent.
πνεῦμα, τό (3b): wind,
breeze.

8. 'DE LA TERRE A LA LUNE'

μεσημβρία, ἡ (1b): midday.
ἄφνω: all of a sudden.
τυφῶν, ὁ (3a): typhoon.
ἐπιγεν- = aor. stem of
ἐπιγίγνομαι: I arise, come
on.
περιδινέω: I whirl round.
μετεωρίζω: I raise aloft
(normally = I put (a ship)
to sea).
ἐπί (+ acc.): as far as, up
to.
τριακόσιοι, -αι, -α: three
hundred.
καθῆκεν = aor. of καθίημι.
πέλαγος, τό (3c): sea.
μετέωρος, -ον: in mid-air
(usually = in mid-ocean
(of a ship)).
ἐξαρτάομαι: I hang.

ἔφερεν κολπώσας τὴν ὀθόνην. ἑπτὰ δὲ ἡμέρας καὶ τὰς ἴσας   5
νύκτας ἀεροδρομήσαντες, ὀγδόῃ καθορῶμεν γῆν τινα μεγάλην
ἐν τῷ ἀέρι καθάπερ νῆσον, λαμπρὰν καὶ σφαιροειδῆ καὶ φωτὶ
μεγάλῳ καταλαμπομένην· προσενεχθέντες δὲ αὐτῇ καὶ ὁρμισά-
μενοι ἀπέβημεν, ἐπισκοποῦντες δὲ τὴν χώραν εὑρίσκομεν
οἰκουμένην τε καὶ γεωργουμένην. ἡμέρας μὲν οὖν οὐδὲν αὐτό-   10
θεν ἑωρῶμεν, νυκτὸς δὲ ἐπιγενομένης ἐφαίνοντο ἡμῖν καὶ
ἄλλαι πολλαὶ νῆσοι πλησίον, αἱ μὲν μείζους, αἱ δὲ μικρό-
τεραι, πυρὶ τὴν χρόαν προσεοικυῖαι, καὶ ἄλλη δέ τις γῆ
κάτω, καὶ πόλεις ἐν αὐτῇ καὶ ποταμοὺς ἔχουσα καὶ πελάγη
καὶ ὕλας καὶ ὄρη. ταύτην οὖν τὴν καθ' ἡμᾶς οἰκουμένην   15
εἰκάζομεν.

(b) Lucian and his friends were captured by the Vulture Cavalry who
took them to the king of the moon, Endymion. He offered them hospitality.

11.   δόξαν δὲ ἡμῖν καὶ ἔτι πορρωτέρω προελθεῖν, συνελήφ-
θημεν τοῖς 'Ιππογύποις παρ' αὐτοῖς καλουμένοις ἀπαντήσα-
αντες. οἱ δὲ 'Ιππόγυποι οὗτοί εἰσιν ἄνδρες ἐπὶ γυπῶν
μεγάλων ὀχούμενοι καὶ καθάπερ ἵπποις τοῖς ὀρνέοις χρώ-   20
μενοι· μεγάλοι γὰρ οἱ γῦπες καὶ ὡς ἐπίπαν τρικέφαλοι.
μάθοι δ' ἄν τις τὸ μέγεθος αὐτῶν ἐντεῦθεν· νεὼς γὰρ
μεγάλης φορτίδος ἱστοῦ ἕκαστον τῶν πτερῶν μακρότερον
καὶ παχύτερον φέρουσι. τούτοις οὖν τοῖς 'Ιππογύποις
προστέτακται περιπετομένοις τὴν γῆν, εἴ τις εὑρεθείη   25
ξένος, ἀνάγειν ὡς τὸν βασιλέα· καὶ δὴ καὶ ἡμᾶς συλλαβ-
όντες ἀνάγουσιν ὡς αὐτόν. ὁ δὲ θεασάμενος καὶ ἀπὸ τῆς
στολῆς εἰκάσας, Ἕλληνες ἄρα, ἔφη, ὑμεῖς, ὦ ξένοι;
συμφησάντων δέ, Πῶς οὖν ἀφίκεσθε, ἔφη, τοσοῦτον ἀέρα δι-
ελθόντες; καὶ ἡμεῖς τὸ πᾶν αὐτῷ διηγούμεθα· καὶ ὃς ἀρξά-   30
μενος τὸ καθ' αὐτὸν ἡμῖν διεξῄει, ὡς καὶ αὐτὸς ἄνθρωπος
ὢν τοὔνομα 'Ενδυμίων ἀπὸ τῆς ἡμετέρας γῆς καθεύδων ἀναρ-
πασθείη ποτὲ καὶ ἀφικόμενος βασιλεύσειε τῆς χώρας· εἶναι
δὲ τὴν γῆν ἐκείνην ἔλεγε τὴν ἡμῖν κάτω φαινομένην σελήνην.
ἀλλὰ θαρρεῖν τε παρεκελεύετο καὶ μηδένα κίνδυνον ὑφορᾶσθαι.   35
πάντα γὰρ ἡμῖν παρέσεσθαι ὧν δεόμεθα.

ἱστία, τά (2b): sails.
5 κολπόω: I make x (acc.)
belly/swell.
ὀθόνη, ἡ (1a): sail.
*ἑπτά: seven.
ἴσας: sc. 'number of
...'
ἀεροδρομέω: I traverse
the air.
ὄγδοος, -η, -ον: eighth.
*ἀήρ (ἀερ-), ὁ (3a): air.
*λαμπρός, -ά, -όν: bright,
shining.
σφαιροειδής, -ές: spher-
ical.
καταλάμπομαι: I am shone
upon, lit up.
προσενεχθέντες = aor. part.
of προσφέρομαι (+ dat.):
I approach.
ὁρμίζομαι: I anchor.
ἐπισκοπέω: I inspect,
observe.
εὑρίσκομεν: imperf. (see
7.25 above)
10 γεωργέω: I farm.
ἡμέρας (gen. of time during
which): tr. 'during'.
αὐτόθεν: from this spot,
from where we stood.
μείζους = μείζονες (n. pl.
f.).
χρόα, ἡ (1b): colour.
τὴν χρόαν: tr. 'in ...'
(acc. of respect)
προσέοικα (+ dat.): I
resemble.
καί ... δέ: and moreover.
15 οἰκουμένη, ἡ (1a): the in-
habited region.
*εἰκάζω: I guess x (acc.)
to be y (acc.), infer.
δόξαν: tr. 'when we had
decided ...' (acc. abs.,
lit. 'it seeming good to
us ...')
πορρωτέρω: further.
προελθ- = aor. stem of
προέρχομαι: I advance.
συνελήφθημεν = aor. pass.
of συλλαμβάνω: I arrest.
Ἱππόγυποι, οἱ (2a):
Vulture Cavalry.
ἀπαντάω (+ dat.): I meet.
γύψ (γυπ-), ὁ (3a): vulture

20 ὀχέομαι: I ride.
ὄρνεον, τό (2b): bird.
ὡς ἐπίπαν: for the most part.
τρικέφαλος, -ον: three-
headed.
ἐντεῦθεν i.e. what follows.
φορτίς (φορτιδ-), ἡ (3a adj.):
merchant.
ἱστόν, τό (2b): mast. ἱστοῦ
is gen. of comparison after
μακρότερον.
πτερόν, τό (2b): wing.
παχύς, -εῖα, -ύ: thick.
25 προστέτακται = perf. pass.
of προστάττω used imperson-
ally, i.e. orders have been
given.
περιπέτομαι: I fly round.
εὑρεθ- = aor. pass. stem of
εὑρίσκω.
ἀνάγω: I bring back.
στολή, ἡ (1a): dress,
clothing.
σύμφημι (συμφησ-): I agree,
concur. συμφησάντων sc.
ἡμῶν.
διελθ- = aor. stem of
διέρχομαι: I cross.
30 διηγούμεθα: imperf., see 7.48
above.
*ὅς: he.
τὸ καθ' αὐτόν: tr. 'his story'
(lit. 'the thing in relation
to himself').
διεξήει = imperf. of
διεξέρχομαι.
τοὔνομα: tr. 'in name' (acc.
of respect).
Ἐνδυμίων, ὁ (3a): Endymion
(a remarkably beautiful young
man, said to have been loved
by the moon).
ἀναρπάζω: I snatch, steal.
ἀναρπασθείη = aor. (pass.) opt.
because it is secondary se-
quence in ind. speech: so too
for βασιλεύσειε (act.).
εἶναι: ind. statement depen-
dent on ἔλεγε.
35 θαρρέω: I cheer up, am of good
heart.
παρακελεύομαι: I encourage.
ὑποράομαι: I suspect.
παρέσεσθαι = fut. inf. of
πάρειμι.

9. THE LUNATIC FRINGE

(᾿Αληϑῶν Διηγημάτων Α - *Verae Historiae* 1.22-25)

Endymion was for the moment engaged upon a war with Phaethon
(king of the sun) over a colony on Lucifer. Lucian and his comrades
assisted in a battle crowded with extraordinary participants wielding
curious weapons. After an initial victory by the moon-men, Lucian
and his two companions were captured and taken off to the sun. En-
dymion was brought to terms by the erection of a wall between sun
and moon which cut off his light supply. A treaty was signed, Lucian
and his friends were returned to the moon and they spent the seven
days before their departure at the dinner table.

Lucian now breaks off, and in a passage designed to be remin-
iscent of Herodotos, the fifth century B.C. historian of the Persian
Wars, he gives an account of the strange things he noticed while
living on the moon.

(a) Lucian relates the strange marriage customs of the moon-people
and their bizarre method of giving birth from the calf.

22.   ἃ δὲ ἐν τῷ μεταξὺ διατρίβων ἐν τῇ σελήνῃ κατενόησα
καινὰ καὶ παράδοξα, ταῦτα βούλομαι εἰπεῖν. πρῶτα μὲν τὸ
μὴ ἐκ γυναικῶν γεννᾶσθαι αὐτούς, ἀλλ᾿ ἀπὸ τῶν ἀρρένων·
γάμοις γὰρ τοῖς ἄρρεσι χρῶνται καὶ οὐδὲ ὄνομα γυναικὸς
ὅλως ἴσασι. μέχρι μὲν οὖν πέντε καὶ εἴκοσι ἐτῶν γαμεῖται   5
ἕκαστος, ἀπὸ δὲ τούτων γαμεῖ αὐτός· κύουσι δὲ οὐκ ἐν τῇ
νηδύϊ, ἀλλ᾿ ἐν ταῖς γαστροκνημίαις· ἐπειδὰν γὰρ συλλάβῃ
τὸ ἔμβρυον, παχύνεται ἡ κνήμη, καὶ χρόνῳ ὕστερον ἀνα-
τεμόντες ἐξάγουσι νεκρά, ἐκθέντες δὲ αὐτὰ πρὸς τὸν ἄνεμον
κεχηνότα ζῳοποιοῦσιν. δοκεῖ δέ μοι καὶ ἐς τοὺς ῞Ελληνας   10
ἐκεῖθεν ἥκειν τῆς γαστροκνημίας τοὔνομα, ὅτι παρ᾿ ἐκείνοις
ἀντὶ γαστρὸς κυοφορεῖ.

(b) The Dendritai (tree-men) are born in an alternative way. Lucian
describes the reproductive organs of the moon-people and the manner
of their death.

9. THE LUNATIC FRINGE

ἅ: tr. 'the things which ...'
  (it is picked up by ταῦτα
  in the next line).
τὸ μεταξύ: the meantime.
κατανοέω: I notice.
καινός, -ή, -όν: new,
  unusual.
*πρῶτα: first.
τὸ μή ... γεννᾶσθαι: tr.
  'their not ...' (τὸ + inf.
  = a noun).
γεννάομαι: I am born.
ἄρρην (ἀρρεν-), ὁ (3a):
  male, man.
γάμοις: tr. 'for ...'
5 μέχρι (+ gen.): up to.
γαμέομαι: I marry, give my-
  self as a wife, am a wife.

τούτων: sc. 'age'.
κύω: I conceive.
νηδύς, ἡ (3h): womb,
  stomach.
γαστροκνημία, ἡ (1b): calf
  (of the leg).
συλλαβ- = aor. stem of
  συλλαμβάνω: I conceive.
παχύνομαι: I grow fat.
κνήμη, ἡ (1a): thigh.
χρόνῳ ὕστερον: tr. 'a
  bit later'.
ἐκθε- = aor. stem of
  ἐκτίθημι: I expose.
10 κέχηνα: I gape, have my
  mouth open.
ζῳοποιέω: I bring to life.
δοκεῖ: it seems to x (dat.),
  x thinks.
παρά (+ acc.): among.
κυοφορέω: I am pregnant.

22.   μεῖζον δὲ τούτου ἄλλο διηγήσομαι. γένος ἐστί παρ'
cont. αὐτοῖς ἀνθρώπων οἱ καλούμενοι Δενδρῖται, γίνεται δὲ τὸν
τρόπον τοῦτον. ὄρχιν ἀνθρώπου τὸν δεξιὸν ἀποτεμόντες ἐν   15
γῇ φυτεύουσιν, ἐκ δὲ αὐτοῦ δένδρον ἀναφύεται μέγιστον,
σάρκινον, οἶον φαλλός· ἔχει δὲ καὶ κλάδους καὶ φύλλα·
ὁ δὲ καρπός ἐστι βάλανοι πηχυαῖοι τὸ μέγεθος. ἐπειδὰν
οὖν πεπανθῶσιν, τρυγήσαντες αὐτὰς ἐκκολάπτουσι τοὺς ἀν-
θρώπους. αἰδοῖα μέντοι πρόσθετα ἔχουσιν, οἱ μὲν ἐλεφάν-   20
τινα, οἱ δὲ πένητες αὐτῶν ξύλινα, καὶ διὰ τούτων ὀχεύουσι
23. καὶ πλησιάζουσι τοῖς γαμέταις τοῖς ἑαυτῶν. ἐπειδὰν δὲ
γηράσῃ ὁ ἄνθρωπος, οὐκ ἀποθνήσκει, ἀλλ' ὥσπερ καπνὸς δια-
λυόμενος ἀὴρ γίνεται.

(c) *Lucian describes food and drink on the moon and how a moon-man
relieves himself.*

τροφὴ δὲ πᾶσιν ἡ αὐτή· ἐπειδὰν γὰρ πῦρ ἀνακαύσωσιν,   25
βατράχους ὀπτῶσιν ἐπὶ τῶν ἀνθράκων· πολλοὶ δὲ παρ' αὐτοῖς
εἰσιν ἐν τῷ ἀέρι πετόμενοι· ὀπτωμένων δὲ περικαθεσθέντες
ὥσπερ δὴ περὶ τράπεζαν κάπτουσιν τὸν ἀναθυμιώμενον καπνὸν
καὶ εὐωχοῦνται. σίτῳ μὲν δὴ τρέφονται τοιούτῳ· ποτὸν δὲ
αὐτοῖς ἐστιν ἀὴρ ἀποθλιβόμενος εἰς κύλικα καὶ ὑγρὸν ἀνι-   30
εἰς ὥσπερ δρόσον. οὐ μὴν ἀπουροῦσίν γε καὶ ἀφοδεύουσιν,
ἀλλ' οὐδὲ τέτρηνται ἧπερ ἡμεῖς, οὐδὲ τὴν συνουσίαν οἱ
παῖδες ἐν ταῖς ἕδραις παρέχουσιν, ἀλλ' ἐν ταῖς ἰγνύσιν
ὑπὲρ τὴν γαστροκνημίαν· ἐκεῖ γάρ εἰσι τετρημένοι.

(d) *After considering the diverse standards of beauty on the moon
and elsewhere, Lucian describes further peculiarities of the moon-
people's physique and environment.*

τούτου: gen. of comparison
after μεῖζον.
Δενδρίτης, ὁ (1d): Tree-
man.
τὸν τρόπον τοῦτον (acc. of
respect): tr. 'in the
following...'
15 ὄρχις, ὁ (3e): testicle.
ἀποτεμ- = aor. stem of
ἀποτέμνω: I cut off.
φυτεύω: I plant.
ἀναφύομαι: I grow up.
σάρκινος, -η, -ον: made
of flesh.
οἷον: like.
φαλλός, ὁ (2a): phallos.
βάλανος, ἡ (2a): acorn.
πηχυαῖος, -α, -ον: a cubit
long (the distance from the
elbow to the end of the
middle finger).
τὸ μέγεθος (acc. of respect):
tr. 'in ...'.
πεπανθῶσιν = aor. subj. of
πεπαίνομαι: I ripen.
τρυγάω: I gather.
ἐκκολάπτω: I hatch.
20 πρόσθετος, -ον: detachable,
false.
ἐλεφάντινος, -η, -ον: of
ivory.
ξύλινος, -η, -ον: of wood.
ὀχεύω: I mount, copulate
(usually of animals).
πλησιάζω (+ dat.): I have
intercourse with.
γαμέτης, ὁ (1d): wife.
γηράσκω: I grow old.
διαλύομαι: I dissolve.
25 ἀνακαύω: I light.
βάτραχος, ὁ (2a): frog.
ὀπτάω: I roast, bake.
ἄνθραξ (ἀνθρακ-), ὁ (3a):
charcoal.

πέτομαι: I fly.
ὀπτωμένων: sc. των βατράχων.
περικαθεσθέντες: sitting
down around (aor. of
περικαθίζομαι)
τράπεζα, ἡ (1c): table.
κάπτω: I gulp down, guzzle.
ἀναθυμιάομαι: I rise in vapour.
εὐωχέομαι: I feast upon.
ποτόν, τό (2b): drink.
30 ἀποθλίβω: I squeeze out.
κύλιξ (κυλικ-), ὁ (3a): wine-
bowl.
ὑγρόν, τό (2b): moisture,
liquid.
ἀνίημι: I send out, let out.
*δρόσος, ὁ (2a): dew.
οὐ μήν ... γε: but ...
not; one should note
carefully that they
don't ...
ἀπουρέω: I urinate,
ἀφοδεύω: I excrete, dis-
charge excrement.
οὐδέ ... οὐδέ: neither
... nor...
τέτρηνται = 3rd pl. perf.
pass. of τιτραίνω: I
pierce (line 34 εἰσι
τετρημένοι is an equiv-
alent)
ᾗπερ: (sc. in the same
place) where.
συνουσία, ἡ (1b): sexual
intercourse.
οἱ παῖδες: tr. 'their
lovers'.
ἕδρα, ἡ (1b): sit-upon,
behind.
ἰγνύς, ἡ (3a): ham (part
behind the knee and
thigh).
γαστροκνημία, ἡ (1b): calf.

52

23.   καλὸς δὲ νομίζεται παρ' αὐτοῖς ἤν πού τις φαλακρὸς   35
cont.·καὶ ἄκομος ᾖ, τοὺς δὲ κομήτας καὶ μυσάττονται. ἐπὶ δὲ
τῶν κομητῶν ἀστέρων τοὐναντίον τοὺς κομήτας καλοὺς νομ-
ίζουσιν· ἐπεδήμουν γάρ τινες, οἵ καὶ περὶ ἐκείνων δι-
ηγοῦντο. καὶ μὴν καὶ γένεια φύουσιν μικρὸν ὑπὲρ τὰ γόνατα.
καὶ ὄνυχας ἐν τοῖς ποσὶν οὐκ ἔχουσιν, ἀλλὰ πάντες εἰσὶν   40
μονοδάκτυλοι. ὑπὲρ δὲ τὰς πυγὰς ἑκάστῳ αὐτῶν κράμβη ἐκ-
πέφυκε μακρὰ ὥσπερ οὐρά, θάλλουσα ἐς ἀεὶ καὶ ὑπτίου ἀνα-
24.πίπτοντος οὐ κατακλωμένη. ἀπομύττονται δὲ μέλι δριμύτατον·
κἀπειδὰν ἤ πονῶσιν ἤ γυμνάζωνται, γάλακτι πᾶν τὸ σῶμα
ἱδροῦσιν, ὥστε καὶ τυροὺς ἀπ' αὐτοῦ πήγνυνται, ὀλίγον   45
τοῦ μέλιτος ἐπιστάξαντες· ἔλαιον δὲ ποιοῦνται ἀπὸ τῶν
κρομμύων πάνυ λιπαρόν τε καὶ εὐῶδες ὥσπερ μύρον. ἀμπέλους
δὲ πολλὰς ἔχουσιν ὑδροφόρους· αἱ γὰρ ῥᾶγες τῶν βοτρύων
εἰσὶν ὥσπερ χάλαζα, καὶ, ἐμοὶ δοκεῖν, ἐπειδὰν ἐμπεσὼν
ἄνεμος διασείσῃ τὰς ἀμπέλους ἐκείνας, τότε πρὸς ἡμᾶς   50
καταπίπτει ἡ χάλαζα διαρραγέντων τῶν βοτρύων. τῇ μέντοι
γαστρὶ ὅσα πήρᾳ χρῶνται τιθέντες ἐν αὐτῇ ὅσων δέονται·
ἀνοικτὴ γὰρ αὐτοῖς αὕτη καὶ πάλιν κλειστή ἐστιν· ἐντέρων
δὲ οὐδὲν ὑπάρχειν αὐτῇ φαίνεται, ἤ τοῦτο μόνον, ὅτι δασεῖα
πᾶσα ἔντοσθε καὶ λάσιός ἐστιν, ὥστε καὶ τὰ νεογνά, ἐπει-   55
δὰν ῥιγώσῃ, ἐς ταύτην ὑποδύεται.

(e)   Lucian describes the moon-people's clothing and some remarkable
features of their physique.

25.   ἐσθὴς δὲ τοῖς μὲν πλουσίοις ὑαλίνη μαλθακή, τοῖς πέν-
ησι δὲ χαλκῆ ὑφαντή· πολύχαλκα γὰρ τὰ ἐκεῖ χωρία, καὶ
ἐργάζονται τὸν χαλκὸν ὕδατι ὑποβρέξαντες ὥσπερ τὰ ἔρια.
περὶ μέντοι τῶν ὀφθαλμῶν, οἵους ἔχουσιν, ὀκνῶ μὲν εἰπεῖν,   60
μή τίς με νομίσῃ ψεύδεσθαι διὰ τὸ ἄπιστον τοῦ λόγου. ὅμως

35 ἦν πού τις: tr. 'anyone at
all who ...'
ἄκομος, -ον: without hair.
μυσάττομαι: I loathe, feel
disgust at, abominate.
ἀστήρ (ἀστερ-), ὁ (3a):
star. τῶν κομητῶν ἀστερῶν
the comets.
τοὔναντίον: on the contrary
γένειον, τό (2a): beard.
μικρόν (adv.): a little.
γόνυ (γονατ-), τό (3b):
knee.
40 ὄνυξ (ὀνυχ-), ὁ (3a): nail.
μονοδάκτυλος, -ον: single-
toed.
πυγή, ἡ (1a): buttock.
κράμβη, ἡ (1a): cabbage.
ἐκπέφυκα = perf. of
ἐκφύομαι (+ dat.): I grow
on.
θάλλω: I flourish, grow,
sprout.
ἐς ἀεί: always.
ὕπτιος, -α, -ον: on one's
back.
ἀναπίπτω: I lie back.
κατακλάω: I break off,
crush.
ἀπομύττομαι: I wipe from
my nose.
μέλι (μελιτ-), τό (3b):
honey.
δριμύς, -εῖα, -ύ: bitter.
*ἤ ... ἤ: either ... or.
πονέω: I work.
γυμνάζομαι: I exercise.
γάλα (γαλακτ-), τό (3b):
milk.
πᾶν τὸ σῶμα (acc. of respect)
tr. 'on ...'
45 ἱδρόω: I sweat.
τυρός, ὁ (2a): cheese.
αὐτοῦ: i.e. the milk.
πήγνυμαι: I set for myself.
ὀλίγον: a little.
ἐπιστάζω: I let fall in
drops.
ἔλαιον, τό (2b): oil.
κρόμμυον, τό (2b): onion.

λιπαρός, -ά, -όν: rich.
εὐώδης, -ες: fragrant.
ὑδροφόρος, -ον: water-bearing.
ῥάξ (ῥαγ-), ὁ (3a): grape.
χάλαζα, ἡ (1c): hail.
50 διασείω: I shake violently.
καταπίπτω: I fall down.
διαρραγέντων = aor. part. of
διαρρήγνυμαι: I burst.
ὅσα: as like.
πήρα, ἡ (1b): pouch, wallet.
ἀνοικτός, -ή, -όν: openable,
can be opened.
αὐτοῖς: tr. 'by them' (dat.
of agent after pass. idea).
κλειστός, -ή, -όν: can be
closed.
ἔντερα, τά (2b): guts.
ὑπάρχω (+ dat.): I belong
to.
ἐντέρων ... φαίνεται: tr.
'there is no sign of intest-
ines in the stomach' (lit.
'nothing of guts appears to
belong to it (the stomach)')
δασύς, -εῖα, -ύ: hairy,
shaggy.
55 πᾶσα: sc. 'the stomach'.
ἔντοσθε: inside.
λάσιος, -α, -ον: woolly, hairy.
νεογνά, τά (2b): new born
babies, young.
ῥιγόω: I am cold.
ταύτην: i.e. the stomach.
ὑποδύομαι: I go down into,
creep into.
*ὑάλινος, -η, -ον: of crystal,
of glass.
μαλθακός, -ή, -όν: soft.
ὑφαντος, -ή, -όν: woven.
πολύχαλκος, -ον: full of
bronze.
χαλκός, ὁ (2a): bronze.
ὑποβρέχω: I moisten.
ἔριον, τό (2b): wool.
60 ὀκνέω: I hesitate.
ἄπιστος, -ον: incredible.
τὸ ἄπιστον: tr. 'the un-
believable nature ...'

δὲ καὶ τοῦτο ἐρῶ· τοὺς ὀφθαλμοὺς περιαιρετοὺς ἔχουσι, καὶ
ὁ βουλόμενος ἐξελὼν τοὺς αὐτοῦ φυλάττει ἔστ' ἂν δεηθῇ
ἰδεῖν· οὕτω δὲ ἐνθέμενος ὁρᾷ· καὶ πολλοὶ τοὺς σφετέρους
ἀπολέσαντες παρ' ἄλλων χρησάμενοι ὁρῶσιν. εἰσὶ δ' οἳ καὶ   65
πολλοὺς ἀποθέτους ἔχουσιν, οἱ πλούσιοι. τὰ ὦτα δὲ πλατάνων
φύλλα ἐστὶν αὐτοῖς πλήν γε τοῖς ἀπὸ τῶν βαλάνων· ἐκεῖνοι
γὰρ μόνοι ξύλινα ἔχουσιν.

10. 'SHANGRI-LA'

(Ἀληθῶν Διηγημάτων Β -Verae Historiae 2.11-14)

Lucian and his men left the moon and returned to earth, stopping
en route in Lamp City, where there dwelt only lamps - their death
penalty was to be snuffed - and passing Cloudcuckooland - how wrong
it was to doubt the evidence of Aristophanes' Birds! Once on the
sea they were promptly swallowed, ship and all, by a whale. Inside
the whale they came across an old man, Skintharos, and his son Kin-
yras, who dwelt on an island in the monster's belly, growing veget-
ables. They were being troubled by some fishy neighbours, but these
were soon finished off by concerted action under Lucian's leadership.
For a year and nine months or so life continued very comfortably -
the only event of note being a spectacle, seen through the open
jaws of the whale, of giants fighting with each other from floating
islands. This ends the first book of the True Story.

Lucian and his friends got bored with their prison and managed,
by dint of setting fire to the forest on their island, to kill the
whale. They levered the ship out of its mouth and set sail again.
They experienced the freezing of the sea - they lived on fish hacked
out of the ice! - passed through a sea of milk, witnessed the cork-
foot people, whose anatomy enabled them to run over the sea, and
finally approached the Island of the Blest. Here they docked, but
were arrested and led, hands bound with rose-garlands, to Rhadaman-
thys' court, where they listened to various 'legal' cases including
a suit between Menelaos and Theseus over who should have Helen. They
were eventually allowed to stay for a while.

(a) Lucian describes the city of the Island of the Blest and gives
details of the physical appearance of the shades (or spirits) who
live there.

11.   αὐτὴ μὲν οὖν ἡ πόλις πᾶσα χρυσῆ, τὸ δὲ τεῖχος περί-
κειται σμαράγδινον· πύλαι δὲ εἰσιν ἑπτά, πᾶσαι μονόξυλοι
κινναμώμιναι· τὸ μέντοι ἔδαφος τῆς πόλεως καὶ ἡ ἐντὸς

περιαιρετός, -ή, -όν: re-
  movable.
ἐξελ- = aor. stem of
  ἐξαιρέω: I take out.
*αὐτοῦ = ἑαυτοῦ
ἔστ' ἄν (+ subj.): until.
δεηθῇ = aor. subj. of
  δέομαι.
ἐνθε- = aor. stem of
  ἐντίθημι.
σφέτερος, -α, -ον: their
  (own).
65 ἀπόλλυμι (ἀπολεσ-): I lose.
χράομαι (χρησ-): I borrow.
εἰσί ... οἵ: tr. 'some'
  (lit. 'there are who ...')
ἀπόθετος, -ον: stored up,
  in reserve.
ὠτ- = stem of οὖς, τό (3b):
  ear.
πλάτανος, ἡ (2a): plane-
  tree.

τὰ ὦτα ... αὐτοῖς: tr.
  'their ears are ...'
βάλανος, ἡ (2a): acorn.
ξύλινος, -η, -ον: wooden,
  of wood.

10. 'SHANGRI-LA'

περίκειμαι: I am (lit.
  'I lie around'),
σμαράγδινος, -η, ον: of
  emerald.
μονόξυλος, -ον: in one
  block, made from one tree.
κινναμώμινος, -ον: of
  cinnamon.
ἔδαφος, τό (3c): floor.
ἐντός (+ gen.): inside.

Symposium scene. From a
cup by the Foundry Painter,
c.475 B.C.; Corpus Christi,
Cambridge.

τοῦ τείχους γῆ ἐλεφαντίνη· ναοὶ δὲ πάντων θεῶν βηρύλλου
λίθου ᾠκοδομημένοι, καὶ βωμοὶ ἐν αὐτοῖς μέγιστοι μονό-   5
λιθοι ἀμεθύστινοι, ἐφ' ὧν ποιοῦσι τὰς ἐκατόμβας. περὶ δὲ
τὴν πόλιν ῥεῖ ποταμὸς μύρου τοῦ καλλίστου, τὸ πλάτος
πηχέων ἑκατὸν βασιλικῶν, βάθος δὲ πέντε ὥστε νεῖν εὐ-
μαρῶς. λουτρὰ δέ ἐστιν αὐτοῖς οἶκοι μεγάλοι ὑάλινοι, τῷ
κινναμώμῳ ἐγκαιόμενοι· ἀντὶ μέντοι τοῦ ὕδατος ἐν ταῖς   10
12.πυέλοις δρόσος θερμὴ ἔστιν. ἐσθῆτι δὲ χρῶνται ἀραχνίοις
λεπτοῖς, πορφυροῖς. αὐτοὶ δὲ σώματα μὲν οὐκ ἔχουσιν,
ἀλλ' ἀναφεῖς καὶ ἄσαρκοί εἰσιν, μορφὴν δὲ καὶ ἰδέαν μόνην
ἐμφαίνουσιν, καὶ ἀσώματοι ὄντες ὅμως συνεστᾶσιν καὶ κιν-
οῦνται καὶ φρονοῦσι καὶ φωνὴν ἀφιᾶσιν, καὶ ὅλως ἔοικε   15
γυμνή τις ἡ ψυχὴ αὐτῶν περιπολεῖν τὴν τοῦ σώματος ὁμοιό-
τητα περικειμένη· εἰ γοῦν μὴ ἅψαιτό τις, οὐκ ἂν ἐξελέγ-
ξειε μὴ εἶναι σῶμα τὸ ὁρώμενον· εἰσὶ γὰρ ὥσπερ σκιαὶ
ὀρθαί, οὐ μέλαιναι. γηράσκει δὲ οὐδείς, ἀλλ' ἐφ' ἧς ἂν
ἡλικίας ἔλθῃ παραμένει.   20

(b)   There is only one time of day and one season on the island.
Flowers blossom and trees bear fruit all year round. There are
springs of all kinds.

οὐ μὴν οὐδὲ νὺξ παρ' αὐτοῖς γίνεται, οὐδὲ ἡμέρα πάνυ
λαμπρά· καθάπερ δὲ τὸ λυκαυγὲς ἤδη πρὸς ἕω, μηδέπω ἀνα-
τείλαντος ἡλίου, τοιοῦτο φῶς ἐπέχει τὴν γῆν. καὶ μέντοι
καὶ ὥραν μίαν ἴσασιν τοῦ ἔτους· αἰεὶ γὰρ παρ' αὐτοῖς ἔαρ
13.ἐστὶ καὶ εἷς ἄνεμος πνεῖ παρ' αὐτοῖς ὁ Ζέφυρος. ἡ δὲ χώρα   25
πᾶσι μὲν ἄνθεσιν, πᾶσι δὲ φυτοῖς ἡμέροις τε καὶ σκιεροῖς
τέθηλεν· αἱ μὲν γὰρ ἄμπελοι δωδεκάφοροί εἰσιν καὶ κατὰ
μῆνα ἕκαστον καρποφοροῦσιν· τὰς δὲ ῥοιὰς καὶ τὰς μηλέας
καὶ τὴν ἄλλην ὀπώραν ἔλεγον εἶναι τρισκαιδεκάφορον· ἑνὸς
γὰρ μηνὸς τοῦ παρ' αὐτοῖς Μινῴου δὶς καρποφορεῖν· ἀντὶ   30
δὲ πυροῦ οἱ στάχυες ἄρτον ἕτοιμον ἐπ' ἄκρων φύουσιν ὥσπερ
μύκητας. πηγαὶ δὲ περὶ τὴν πόλιν ὕδατος μὲν πέντε καὶ ἑξ-
ήκοντα καὶ τριακόσιαι, μέλιτος δὲ ἄλλαι τοσαῦται, μύρου

ἐλεφάντινος, -η, -ον: of
ivory.
ναός, ὁ (2a): shrine,
temple.
βήρυλλος, ἡ (2a): beryl.
5 ᾠκοδομημένοι = perf. pass.
part. of οἰκοδομέω: I
build.
μονόλιθος, -ον: made out
of one stone.
ἀμεθύστινος, -η, -ον: of
amethyst.
ἑκατόμβη, ἡ (1a): hecatomb
(sacrifice of 100 animals)
ῥέω: I flow.
πλάτος, τό (3c): breadth.
πῆχυς, ὁ (3e): cubit (nor-
mally 24 fingers (18 inches)
the 'royal' cubit was 3
fingers longer).
ἑκατόν: one hundred.
βασιλικός, -ή, -όν: royal.
βάθος, τό (3c): depth.
ὥστε: sc. 'it is possible'.
νέω: I swim.
εὐμαρῶς: comfortably.
λουτρόν, τό (2b): bath.
οἶκος, ὁ (2a): room.
10 κιννάμωμον, τό (2b): cinnamon
wood.
ἐγκαίομαι: I am heated.
πυέλος, ἡ (2a): bath-tub.
θερμός, -ή, -όν: warm.
ἀράχνιον, τό (2b): spider's
web.
πορφυροῦς, -ᾶ, -οῦν: purple.
ἀναφής, -ές: impalpable, in-
substantial.
ἄσαρκος, -ον: without flesh.
μορφή, ἡ (1a): shape.
ἰδέα, ἡ (1b): appearance.
ἐμφαίνω: I display.
ἀσώματος, -ον: without body,
incorporeal.
συνεστᾶσιν = 3rd pl. perf. of
συνίσταμαι: I band together
κινέομαι: I move.
15 φωνὴν ἀφίημι: I speak.
γυμνός, -ή, -όν: naked.
περιπολέω: I wander about.
ὁμοιότης (ὁμοιοτητ-), -ἡ (3a):
likeness.
περίκειμαι: I wear, I am
clad in
μὴ εἶναι: tr. 'that it was'.
ὁρώμενον = pres. pass. part.

of ὁράω.
σκία, ἡ (1b): shadow.
ὀρθαί: tr. 'upright'.
γηράσκω: I grow old.
ἐπί (+ gen.): at.
20 ἡλικία, ἡ (1b): age.
μήν: furthermore, nay.
οὐδέ ... οὐδέ...: not x
... nor y either...
τὸ λυκαυγές: early dawn.
πρός (+ acc.): near.
μηδέπω: not yet.
ἀνατέλλω (ἀνατειλ-): I
rise.
ἐπέχω: I extend over.
καὶ μέντοι: tr. 'and
what's more'.
ὥρα, ἡ (1b): season.
ἔαρ (ἐαρ-), τό (3b):
spring.
25 πνέω: I blow.
Ζέφυρος, ὁ (2a): West
Wind (warm wind of
spring).
ἄνθος, τό (3c): flower.
φυτόν, τό (2b): plant.
ἥμερος, -α, -ον: cultivated.
σκιερός, -ά, -όν: shady.
τέθηλεν = 3rd s. perf. of
θάλλω: I bloom.
δωδεκάφορος, -ον: bearing
12 times per year.
καρποφορέω: I bear fruit.
ῥοιά, ἡ (1b): pomegranate-
tree.
μηλέα, ἡ (1b): apple-
tree.
ὀπώρα, ἡ (1b): fruit.
τρισκαιδεκάφορος, -ον: bear-
ing 13 times per year.
30 Μινῷον, τό: the month
Minoon (lit. 'of Minos' -
one of the 3 judges of
the dead).
δίς: twice.
καρποφορεῖν: sc. 'they said
that they ...'.
πυρός, ὁ (2a): wheat.
στάχυς, ὁ (3h/3a): ear of
wheat/corn.
ἄρτος, ὁ (2a): loaf of
bread.
ἄκρα, ἡ (1b): end.
μύκης (μυκητ-), ὁ (3a):
mushroom.

δὲ πεντακόσιαι, μικρότεραι μέντοι αὖται, καὶ ποταμοὶ γάλ-
ακτος ἑπτὰ καὶ οἴνου ὀκτώ.   35

(c) The inhabitants hold their dinner-party in the Elysian fields,
where they benefit among other things from automatic wine-glasses
and perfume-bearing clouds.

14. τὸ δὲ συμπόσιον ἔξω τῆς πόλεως πεποίηνται ἐν τῷ Ἠλυ-
σίῳ καλουμένῳ πεδίῳ· λειμὼν δέ ἐστιν κάλλιστος καὶ περὶ
αὐτὸν ὕλη παντοία πυκνή, ἐπισκιάζουσα τοὺς κατακειμένους.
καὶ στρωμνὴν μὲν ἐκ τῶν ἀνθῶν ὑποβέβληνται, διακονοῦνται
δὲ καὶ παραφέρουσιν ἕκαστα οἱ ἄνεμοι πλήν γε τοῦ οἰνοχο-   40
εῖν· τούτου γὰρ οὐδὲν δέονται, ἀλλ᾽ ἐστι δένδρα περὶ τὸ
συμπόσιον ὑάλινα μεγάλα τῆς διαυγεστάτης ὑάλου, καὶ καρ-
πός ἐστι τῶν δένδρων τούτων ποτήρια παντοῖα καὶ τὰς κατα-
σκευὰς καὶ τὰ μεγέθη. ἐπειδὰν οὖν παρίῃ τις ἐς τὸ συμ-
πόσιον, τρυγήσας ἓν ἢ καὶ δύο τῶν ἐκπωμάτων παρατίθεται,   45
τὰ δὲ αὐτίκα οἴνου πλήρη γίνεται. οὕτω μὲν πίνουσιν, ἀντὶ
δὲ τῶν στεφάνων αἱ ἀηδόνες καὶ τὰ ἄλλα τὰ μουσικὰ ὄρνεα
ἐκ τῶν πλησίον λειμώνων τοῖς στόμασιν ἀνθολογοῦντα κατα-
νίφει αὐτοὺς μετ᾽ ᾠδῆς ὑπερπετόμενα. καὶ μὴν καὶ μυρίζον-
ται ὧδε. νεφέλαι πυκναὶ ἀνασπάσασαι μύρον ἐκ τῶν πηγῶν   50
καὶ τοῦ ποταμοῦ καὶ ἐπιστᾶσαι ὑπὲρ τὸ συμπόσιον ἠρέμα
τῶν ἀνέμων ὑποθλιβόντων ὕουσι λεπτὸν ὥσπερ δρόσον.

11. THE HOMERIC QUESTION

(Ἀληθῶν Διηγημάτων Β - Verae Historiae 2.20)

    Lucian goes on to describe the poetic and musical taste of the
islanders and the famous people there. There were the demi-gods,
the heroes of the Trojan War, and among many others Sokrates (Plato
was off living in his own Republic, submitting to his own Laws; the
Stoics were still clambering up the steep hill of virtue; the Scep-
tics couldn't agree whether the island existed or not!). In affairs
of love there were no barriers - a Platonic 'communism' reigned un-
checked. After a few days Lucian, being a literary sort of fellow,
approached Homer for a chat.

ἑξήκοντα: sixty.
τριακόσιοι, -αι, -α: three-
  hundred.
μέλι (μελιτ-), τό (3b):
  honey.
πεντακόσιοι, -αι, -α: five-
  hundred.
γάλα (γαλακτ-), τό (3b):
  milk.
35 ὀκτώ: eight.
πεποίηνται = 3rd pl. perf.
  of ποιέομαι.
Ἠλύσιον πεδίον, τό (2b):
  the Elysian fields.
λειμών (λειμων-), ὁ (3a):
  meadow.
παντοῖος, -α, -ον: of all
  sorts, of assorted (sc.
  'trees').
πυκνός, ή, όν: thick.
ἐπισκιάζω: I shade.
κατάκειμαι: I lie beneath.
ἄνθος, τό (3c): flower.
ὑποβέβληνται = 3rd pl. (mid.)
  of ὑποβάλλομαι: I place
  under myself.
*διακονέομαι (+ dat.): I act
  as a servant to.
40 παραφέρω: I serve, set on
  the table.
οἰνοχοέω: I pour wine.
τούτου: i.e. τὸ οἰνοχοεῖν.
οὐδέν: in no way.
διαυγής, -ές: translucent.
ὕαλος, ἡ (2a): glass.
ποτήριον, τό (2b): drinking-

cup.
κατασκευή, ἡ (1a): con-
  struction.
παρίῃ = subj. of παρέρχομαι.
45 τρυγάω: I pick.
ἔκπωμα, τό (3b): cup.
παρατίθεμαι: I place beside
  me.
τὰ δέ: i.e. the cups.
πλήρης, -ες (+ gen.): full of.
στέφανος, ὁ (2a): garland.
ἀηδών (ἀηδον-), ἡ (3a):
  nightingale.
μουσικός, -ή, -όν: musical.
ὄρνεον, τό (2b): bird.
ἀνθολογέω: I pick flowers.
κατανίφω: I sprinkle
  down like snow.
αὐτούς: i.e. the flowers.
ᾠδή, ἡ (1a): singing, song.
ὑπερπέτομαι: I fly over.
μυρίζομαι: I put on
  perfume.
50 νεφέλη, ἡ (1a): cloud.
πυκνός, -ή, -όν: thick.
ἀνασπάω: I draw up.
ἐπιστᾶσαι = aor. part. of
  ἐφίσταμαι (+ dat.): I
  stand over/near.
ἠρέμα: gently.
ὑποθλίβω: I press under-
  neath.
ὕω: I rain.
λεπτόν: tr. 'a fine rain'
  (cognate acc. with
  ὕουσι).

(a) *Lucian asked about Homer's birthplace and received an unexpected answer.*

20. οὔπω δὲ δύο ἢ τρεῖς ἡμέραι διεληλύθεσαν, καὶ προσελθὼν
ἐγὼ Ὁμήρῳ τῷ ποιητῇ, σχολῆς οὔσης ἀμφοῖν, τά τε ἄλλα
ἐπυνθανόμην καὶ ὅθεν εἴη, λέγων τοῦτο μάλιστα παρ' ἡμῖν
εἰσέτι νῦν ζητεῖσθαι. ὁ δὲ οὐδ' αὐτὸς μὲν ἀγνοεῖν ἔφασκεν
ὡς οἱ μὲν Χῖον, οἱ δὲ Σμυρναῖον, πολλοὶ δὲ Κολοφώνιον   5
αὐτὸν νομίζουσιν· εἶναι μέντοι γε ἔλεγεν Βαβυλώνιος, καὶ
παρά γε τοῖς πολίταις οὐχ Ὅμηρος, ἀλλὰ Τιγράνης καλεῖσθαι·
ὕστερον δὲ ὁμηρεύσας παρὰ τοῖς Ἕλλησιν ἀλλάξαι τὴν προσ-
ηγορίαν.

(b) *Lucian next asked some literary critical questions, concerning
interpolation, the first word of the Iliad, and the sequence of com-
position of the Iliad and Odyssey. He remarks on Homer's alleged
blindness.*

     ἔτι δὲ καὶ περὶ τῶν ἀθετουμένων στίχων ἐπηρώτων, εἰ   10
ὑπ' ἐκείνου εἰσὶ γεγραμμένοι. καὶ ὃς ἔφασκε πάντας αὐτοῦ
εἶναι. κατεγίνωσκον οὖν τῶν ἀμφὶ τὸν Ζηνόδοτον καὶ Ἀρίστ-
αρχον γραμματικῶν πολλὴν τὴν ψυχρολογίαν. ἐπεὶ δὲ ταῦτα
ἱκανῶς ἀπεκέκριτο, πάλιν αὐτὸν ἠρώτων τί δή ποτε ἀπὸ τῆς
μήνιδος τὴν ἀρχὴν ἐποιήσατο· καὶ ὃς εἶπεν οὕτως ἐπελθεῖν   15
αὐτῷ μηδὲν ἐπιτηδεύσαντι. καὶ μὴν κἀκεῖνο ἐπεθύμουν εἰδ-
έναι, εἰ προτέραν ἔγραψεν τὴν Ὀδύσσειαν τῆς Ἰλιάδος, ὡς
οἱ πολλοί φασιν· ὁ δὲ ἠρνεῖτο. ὅτι μὲν γὰρ οὐδὲ τυφλὸς
ἦν, ὃ καὶ αὐτὸ περὶ αὐτοῦ λέγουσιν, αὐτίκα ἠπιστάμην·
ἑώρα γάρ, ὥστε οὐδὲ πυνθάνεσθαι ἐδεόμην.   20

(c) *Lucian mentions Homer's willingness to talk and the result of
a lawsuit brought against him by Thersites, one of his own characters
from the Iliad.*

11. THE HOMERIC QUESTION

διεληλύθεσαν = 3rd pl.
pluperf. of διέρχομαι:
I pass by.
ἄμφω: both (dat. ἀμφοῖν)
τά τε ἄλλα ... καί: es-
pecially (lit. 'other
things too ... and').
τοῦτο: sc. 'the answer to
...'.
εἰσέτι: still.
5 Χῖος, -α, -ον: from Khios
(an island off the
Ionian coast)
Σμυρναῖος, -α, -ον: from
Smyrna (a city on the
mainland of Ionia).
Κολοφώνιος, -α, -ον: from
Kolophon (an Ionian city
in Lydia).
εἶναι (nom. + inf.): he
was ...:
μέντοι γε: nevertheless.
Βαβυλώνιος, -α, -ον: from
Babylon.
Τιγράνης, ὁ: Tigranes.
ὁμηρεύω: I am a hostage.
ἀλλάζω: I change.
προσηγορία, ἡ (1b): nomen-
clature, name.
10 ἔτι: besides.
ἀθετέω: I reject as spurious.
στίχος, ὁ (2a): verse, line.
ἐπερωτάω: I inquire.
εἰσί γεγραμμένοι = 3rd pl.
perf. pass. of γράφω.
καταγιγνώσκω: I charge x (gen.)

with y (acc.).
ἀμφί (+ acc.): around.
Ζηνόδοτος, ὁ (2a): Sdenodotos
(born c.325 B.C., first
librarian at Alexandria,
editor of Homer).
Ἀρίσταρχος, ὁ (2a):
Aristarkhos (c.217-145 B.C.,
head of the library of Alex-
andria, editor of Homer).
γραμματικός, ὁ (2a): critic,
grammarian.
ψυχρολογία, ἡ (1b): nonsense.
ἀπεκέκριτο = 3rd s.plúperf.pass.
of ἀποκρίνω: I answer
(ταῦτα is subject).
15 μῆνις (μηνιδ-), ἡ (3a):
wrath (first word of Homer's
Iliad: μῆνιν ἄειδε, θεά,
Πηληϊάδεω Ἀχιλῆος: 'Sing,
goddess, the anger of
Peleus' son Achilleus ...').
ἐπελθ- = aor. stem of
ἐπέρχομαι (+ dat.): I come
into the mind of.
μηδέν: in no way.
ἐπιτηδεύω: I do something on
purpose.
Ὀδύσσεια, ἡ (1b): Odyssey.
Ἰλιάς (Ἰλιαδ-), ἡ (3a):
Iliad.
ἀρνέομαι: I say no.
οὐδέ: not ... either.
τοφλός, -ή, -όν: blind.
ὃ καὶ αὐτό: tr. 'which is itself
something else ...'
20 *πυνθάνομαι: I enquire, ask
(x (acc.) of y (gen.)).

πολλάκις δὲ καὶ ἄλλοτε τοῦτο ἐποίουν, εἴ ποτε αὐτὸν
σχολὴν ἄγοντα ἑώρων· προσιὼν γὰρ ἄν τι ἐπυνθανόμην αὐτοῦ,
καὶ ὃς προθύμως πάντα ἀπεκρίνετο, καὶ μάλιστα μετὰ τὴν
δίκην, ἐπειδὴ ἐκράτησεν· ἦν γὰρ τις γραφὴ κατ' αὐτοῦ ἀπε-
νηνεγμένη ὕβρεως ὑπὸ Θερσίτου ἐφ' οἷς αὐτὸν ἐν τῇ ποιήσει   25
ἔσκωψεν, καὶ ἐνίκησεν ὁ Ὅμηρος Ὀδυσσέως συναγορεύοντος.

12. 'THE FACE THAT LAUNCHED A THOUSAND SHIPS'

(Ἀληθῶν Διηγημάτων Β - Verae Historiae 2.25-27)

The funeral games, to celebrate the deaths of those on the
island, followed soon after this, but they were interrupted by the
news of an escape from the Place of the Impious. A battle was
fought and the criminals re-imprisoned. Homer, of course, wrote
a version of it which Lucian, of course, lost before reaching home.

(a) As the months went by, Kinyras (whom Lucian had rescued from
the whale; see 10 above) began to show more than a passing interest
in Helen. The lovers planned an escape.

25.   ἤδη δὲ μηνῶν ἐξ διεληλυθότων περὶ μεσοῦντα τὸν ἕβδομον
νεώτερα συνίστατο πράγματα· Κινύρας ὁ τοῦ Σκινθάρου παῖς,
μέγας ὢν καὶ καλός, ἤρα πολὺν ἤδη χρόνον τῆς Ἑλένης, καὶ
αὐτὴ οὐκ ἀφανὴς ἦν ἐπιμανῶς ἀγαπῶσα τὸν νεανίσκον· πολλά-
κις γοῦν καὶ διένευον ἀλλήλοις ἐν τῷ συμποσίῳ καὶ προΰ-   5
πινον καὶ μόνοι ἐξανιστάμενοι ἐπλανῶντο περὶ τὴν ὕλην.
καὶ δή ποτε ὑπ' ἔρωτος καὶ ἀμηχανίας ἐβουλεύσατο ὁ Κινύ-
πας ἁρπάσας τὴν Ἑλένην - ἐδόκει δὲ κἀκείνῃ ταῦτα - οἴχ-
εσθαι ἀπιόντας ἔς τινα τῶν ἐπικειμένων νήσων, ἤτοι ἐς
τὴν Φελλὼ ἢ ἐς τὴν Τυρόεσσαν. συνωμότας δὲ πάλαι προσ-   10
ειλήφεσαν τρεῖς τῶν ἑταίρων τῶν ἐμῶν τοὺς θρασυτάτους.
τῷ μέντοι πατρὶ οὐκ ἐμήνυσε ταῦτα· ἠπίστατο γὰρ ὑπ' αὐτοῦ
κωλυθησόμενος.

(b) Kinyras and Helen sailed off, but Menelaos missed his wife and
raised the alarm. They were intercepted and Kinyras sent to be pun-
ished with the Impious. Lucian and his comrades were given orders to
leave.

63

ἄλλοτε: on other occasions.
κρατέω: I win.
ἀπενηνεγμένη = perf. pass. part.
of ἀποφέρω: I bring a charge
of x (gen.) against y (κατά +
gen.).
25 Θερσίτης, ὁ (1d):
Thersites ('the ugliest man
who came to Troy' according
to Iliad 2.216: he dared to
challenge Agamemnon in
council, and was silenced
and beaten by Odysseus for
his pains).
ἐφ οἷς ...: tr. 'because of
the jokes he made against
...'.
ποίησις, ἡ (3c): poem,
poetry.
σκώπτω: I joke at.
Ὀδυσσεύς, ὁ (3g): Odysseus
(central character of
Homer's Odyssey).
συναγορεύω: I help with the
defence.

12. 'THE FACE THAT LAUNCHED A
THOUSAND SHIPS'

ἕξ: six.
διεληλυθότων = perf. part.
of διέρχομαι: I pass by.
μεσόω: I am in the middle.
ἕβδομος, η, ον: seventh.
νεώτερα ... πράγματα:
innovations.
συνίσταμαι: I arise.
Κινύρας, ὁ (1d): Kinyras.
Σκίνθαρος, ὁ (2a): Skintharos
(also rescued from the
whale by Lucian).
ἐράω (+ gen.): I am in love
with.

Ἑλένη, ἡ (1a): Helen (wife
of Menelaos; cause of the
Trojan War after her elope-
ment with Paris).
ἀφανής, -ές: unnoticed (tr.
'she obviously' - the
same construction is used
with δῆλός εἰμι + part.).
ἐπιμανῶς: madly.
ἀγαπάω (+ gen.): I am in
love with.
5 διανεύω (+ dat.): I nod to.
προπίνω: I drink someone's
health.
ἐξανίσταμαι: I get up and
go out.
πλανάομαι: I wander.
ἔρως (ἐρωτ-), ὁ (3a):
passion.
ἀμηχανία, ἡ (1b): helpless-
ness.
βουλεύομαι: I plan.
ἐπίκειμαι: I lie off the
coast.
ἤτοι ... ἤ: either ... or.
10 Φελλώ, ἡ: Phello ('Cork
Island', where the cork-
foot people lived; see
intro. to piece 10 above).
Τυρόεσσα, ἡ (1c): Tyroessa
('Cheese Island'; Lucian
and his friends had landed
here on the way to the
Island of the Blest).
συνωμότης, ὁ (1d): fellow-
conspirator.
προσειλήφεσαν = 3rd pl. pluperf.
of προσλαμβάνω: I take.
θρασύς, -εῖα, -ύ: bold,
foolhardy.
μηνύω: I inform x (dat.) of
y (acc.).

ὡς δὲ ἐδόκει αὐτοῖς, ἐτέλουν τὴν ἐπιβουλήν. καὶ ἐπειδὴ
νὺξ ἐγένετο - ἐγὼ μὲν οὐ παρήμην· ἐτύγχανον γὰρ ἐν τῷ   15
συμποσίῳ κοιμώμενος - οἱ δὲ λαθόντες τοὺς ἄλλους ἀναλαβ-
26.όντες τὴν Ἑλένην ὑπὸ σπουδῆς ἀνήχθησαν. περὶ δὲ τὸ μεσο-
νύκτιον ἀνεγρόμενος ὁ Μενέλαος ἐπεὶ ἔμαθεν τὴν εὐνὴν
κενὴν τῆς γυναικός, βοήν τε ἠφίει καὶ τὸν ἀδελφὸν παρα-
λαβὼν ἦλθε πρὸς τὸν βασιλέα τὸν Ῥαδάμανθυν. ἡμέρας δὲ   20
ὑποφαινούσης ἔλεγον οἱ σκοποὶ καθορᾶν τὴν ναῦν πολὺ
ἀπέχουσαν· οὕτω δὴ ἐμβιβάσας ὁ Ῥαδάμανθυς πεντήκοντα
τῶν ἡρώων εἰς ναῦν μονόξυλον ἀσφοδελίνην παρήγγειλε
διώκειν· οἱ δὲ ὑπὸ προθυμίας ἐλαύνοντες περὶ μεσημβρίαν
καταλαμβάνουσιν αὐτοὺς ἄρτι ἐς τὸν γαλακτώδη τοῦ ὠκεανοῦ   25
τόπον ἐμβαίνοντας πλησίον τῆς Τυροέσσης· παρὰ τοσοῦτον
ἦλθον διαδρᾶναι· καὶ ἀναδησάμενοι τὴν ναῦν ἀλύσει ῥοδίνῃ
κατέπλεον. ἡ μὲν οὖν Ἑλένη ἐδάκρυέν τε καὶ ᾐσχύνετο καὶ
ἐνεκαλύπτετο, τοὺς δὲ ἀμφὶ τὸν Κινύραν ἀνακρίνας πρότερον
ὁ Ῥαδάμανθυς, εἴ τινες καὶ ἄλλοι αὐτοῖς συνίσασιν, ὡς   30
οὐδένα εἶπον, ἐκ τῶν αἰδοίων δήσας ἀπέπεμψεν ἐς τὸν τῶν
27.ἀσεβῶν χῶρον μαλάχῃ πρότερον μαστιγωθέντας. ἐψηφίσαντο
δὲ καὶ ἡμᾶς ἐμπροθέσμους ἐκπέμπειν ἐκ τῆς νήσου, τὴν
ἐπιοῦσαν ἡμέραν μόνην ἐπιμείναντας.

13. 'THE WAGES OF UNTRUTH'

(Ἀληθῶν Διηγημάτων Β - Verae Historiae 2.31-32)

Lucian was upset at having to leave, until Rhadamanthys promised
him a place on the Island of the Blest after his death. The king
also directed them to go past the Place of the Impious, to Kalypso's
Isle of Ogygia and gave Lucian some sound advice and a mallow to pray
to in times of danger. Homer wrote an inscription for Lucian, Odys-
seus secretly slipped him a letter addressed to Kalypso and the ship
departed. First call was the Place of the Impious, from which roast-
ing human flesh could be smelt and the screams of souls in torment
heard. The place was difficult to approach, but eventually they
arrived at the entrance.

Passing Timon, the misanthropic gatekeeper, Lucian saw many
people including Kinyras, undergoing punishment. The worst tortures
were reserved for liars. Lucian was glad of his own honesty.

τελέω: I carry out.
ἐπιβουλή, ἡ (1a): scheme.
15 πάρημαι: I sit nearby
(παρήμην is pluperf. in
form, imperf. in meaning).
κοιμάομαι: I sleep.
ἀνήχθησαν = aor. of ἀνάγομαι:
I set sail.
μεσονύκτιον, τό (2b): mid-
night.
ἀνεγείρομαι: I wake up (aor.
part. ἀνεγρόμενος).
Μενέλαος, ὁ (2a): Menelaos
(husband of Helen).
εὐνή, ἡ (1a): bed sc. 'was'.
κενός, -ή, -όν (+ gen.): empty
(of).
ἠφίει = 3rd s. imperf. of
ἀφίημι (in Homer Menelaos
is called βοὴν ἀγαθός).
τὸν ἀδελφὸν: i.e. Agamemnon:
his champion, the last time
Helen ran off, as leader of
the punitive expedition
against Troy.
20 'Ραδάμανθυς, ὁ: Rhadamanthys
(one of the 3 judges of
the dead).
ὑποφαίνω: I begin to
break.
σκοπός, ὁ (2a): lookout.
πολύ: far.
ἀπέχω: I am distant/away.
ἐμβιβάζω: I put on board.
ἥρως (ἥρω-), ὁ (3a): hero.
μονόξυλος, -ον: in one
block, made of one
stalk.
ἀσφοδέλινος, -η, -ον: of
asphodel (the heroes were
thought to dwell in fields
of asphodel in Hades).
παραγγέλλω (παραγγειλ-):

I give orders.
προθυμία, ἡ (1b): eager-
ness.
ἐλαύνω: I row.
μεσημβρία, ἡ (1b): mid-
day.
25 γαλακτώδης, -ες: milky.
ὠκεανός, ὁ (2a): sea.
τόπος, ὁ (2a): place,
region.
ἐμβαίνω (ἐς + acc.): I
enter.
παρὰ τοσοῦτον ἔρχομαι (+
inf.): I come so close
to.
διαδρα- = aor. stem of
διαδιδράσκω: I escape.
ἀναδέομαι: I take in tow.
ἅλυσις, ἡ (3e): chain.
ῥόδινος, -η, -ον: of
roses.
καταπλέω: I sail back.
ἐγκαλύπτομαι: I hide my
face.
ἀμφί (+ acc.): around.
ἀνακρίνω: I examine.
30 εἶ: sc. 'to find out ...'
σύνοιδα (+ dat.): I am
implicated with.
δέω: I tie.
χῶρος, ὁ (2a): place.
μαλάχη, ἡ (1a): mallow
(a plant usually noted
for its soothing quali-
ties when used as a
poultice on wounds).
μαστιγόω: I whip.
ἐμπρόθεσμος, -ον: before
the stated time.
ἐπιοῦσαν = pres. part. of
ἐπέρχομαι: I come.
ἐπιμένω (ἐπιμειν-): I stay.

31. εἴσοδος δὲ μία στενὴ διὰ πάντων ἦν, καὶ πυλωρὸς ἐφ-
ειστήκει Τίμων ὁ ᾿Αθηναῖος. παρελθόντες δὲ ὅμως τοῦ
Ναυπλίου καθηγουμένου ἑωρῶμεν κολαζομένους πολλοὺς μὲν
βασιλέας, πολλοὺς δὲ καὶ ἰδιώτας, ὧν ἐνίους καὶ ἐγνω-
ρίζομεν· εἴδομεν δὲ καὶ τὸν Κινύραν καπνῷ ὑποτυφόμενον   5
ἐκ τῶν αἰδοίων ἀπηρτημένον. προσετίθεσαν δὲ οἱ περιηγηταὶ
καὶ τοὺς ἑκάστων βίους καὶ τὰς ἁμαρτίας ἐφ᾿ αἷς κολάζον-
ται· καὶ μεγίστας ἀπασῶν τιμωρίας ὑπέμενον οἱ ψευσάμενοί
τι παρὰ τὸν βίον καὶ οἱ μὴ τὰ ἀληθῆ συγγεγραφότες, ἐν
οἷς καὶ Κτησίας ὁ Κνίδιος ἦν καὶ ῾Ηρόδοτος καὶ ἄλλοι   10
πολλοί. τούτους οὖν ὁρῶν ἐγὼ χρηστὰς εἶχον εἰς τοὐπιὸν
τὰς ἐλπίδας· οὐδὲν γὰρ ἐμαυτῷ ψεῦδος εἰπόντι συνηπιστάμην.
32. ταχέως δ᾿ οὖν ἀναστρέψας ἐπὶ τὴν ναῦν - οὐδὲ γὰρ ἠδυν-
άμην φέρειν τὴν ὄψιν - ἀσπασάμενος τὸν Ναύπλιον ἀπέπλευσα.

14. ODYSSEUS' LETTER

(᾿Αληθῶν Διηγημάτων Β - Verae Historiae 2.35-36)

Leaving the place of the Impious, Lucian and his crew put in
at the Island of Dreams. Here they were entertained by dreams of
kingship and by visits to their homes. From this place they sailed
on to the Island of Ogygia. They had a letter to deliver to Kalypso
from Odysseus.

(a) Once on Ogygia, Lucian opened Odysseus' letter and found that
the hero was planning to return to Kalypso.

35. τριταῖοι δ᾿ ἐκεῖθεν τῇ ᾿Ωγυγίᾳ νήσῳ προσσχόντες ἀπε-
βαίνομεν. πρότερον δ᾿ ἐγὼ λύσας τὴν ἐπιστολὴν ἀνεγίνωσκον
τὰ γεγραμμένα. ἦν δὲ τοιάδε· ᾿Οδυσσεὺς Καλυψοῖ χαίρειν.
῏Ισθι με, ὡς τὰ πρῶτα ἐξέπλευσα παρὰ σοῦ τὴν σχεδίαν
κατασκευασάμενος, ναυαγίᾳ χρησάμενον μόλις ὑπὸ Λευκοθέας   5

13. 'THE WAGES OF UNTRUTH'

εἴσοδος, ἡ (2a): entrance.
στενός, -ή, -όν: narrow.
διά (+ gen.): over.
πάντων: sc. 'the rivers'
(which surrounded the
place).
πυλωρός, ὁ (2a): gatekeeper.
ἐφειστήκει = 3rd s. pluperf.
of ἐφίσταμαι: I am put in
charge.
Τίμων, ὁ (3a): Timon (legen-
dary for his hatred of men;
Lucian wrote a dialogue
in which he used the story
of the loss of his wealth
through generosity, his
regaining of it and subsequent
brutality to all who now
approached him).
παρελθ- = aor. stem of
παρέρχομαι.
Ναύπλιος, ὁ (2a): Nauplios
(one of the Argonauts, lent
by Rhadamanthys as pilot for
this part of Lucian's
journey).
καθηγέομαι: I lead the way.
ἔνιοι, -αι, -α: some.
γνωρίζω: I recognise.
5 ὑποτύφω: I burn (with a smould-
ering fire underneath).
ἀπαρτάομαι: I am suspended.
προστίθημι: I set out.
περιηγητής, ὁ (1d): guide.
ἁμαρτία, ἡ (1b): mistake,
crime.
τιμωρίαι, αἱ (1b): penalties.
ὑπομένω: I submit to.
παρά (+ acc.): during.
συγγεγραφότες = perf. part. of
συγγράφω: I write (esp.
history).
Κτησίας, ὁ (1d): Ktesias (5th
cent. B.C., a doctor at the
Persian court who wrote a
history of Persia and India).
Κνίδιος, ὁ (2a): man from
Knidos (in Ionia).
Ἡρόδοτος, ὁ (2a): Herodotos
(5th cent. B.C., writer of
the history of the Persian

Wars - appearance of the
gods and his concern for a
divine framework will have
motivated the rationalist
Lucian to represent him as
a liar).
τοὔπιὸν = τὸ ἐπιὸν: the
future.
συνεπίσταμαι (ἐμαυτῷ): I am
conscious of (+ dat. part.
agreeing with ἐμαυτῷ).
ἀναστρέφω: I turn back.
ἠδυνάμην = imperf. of
δύναμαι.
ἀσπάζομαι: I say goodbye
to.
ἀποπλέω: I sail away.

14. ODYSSEUS' LETTER

τριταῖος, -α, -ον: on the
third day.
Ὠγυγία, ἡ (1b): Ogygia
(Kalypso' island).
προσσχ- = aor. stem of
προσέχω (+ dat.): I
put in at.
λύω: I undo.
ἐπιστολή, ἡ (1a): letter.
ἀναγινώσκω: I read.
γεγραμμένα = perf. pass. part.
of γράφω.
Καλυψώ, ἡ (dat. Καλυψοῖ):
Kalypso.
χαίρειν sc. 'bids' (tr. 'greet-
ings to K. from O').
ἴσθι = imper. of οἶδα.
ἐκπλέω: I sail away.
σχεδία, ἡ (1b): boat (lit.
'improvised craft').
5 κατασκευάζομαι: I build.
ναυαγία, ἡ (1b): shipwreck.
χράομαι (+ dat.): I experience.
μόλις: with difficulty.
Λευκοθέα, ἡ (1b): Ino (lit.
'the white goddess') (the
sea-goddess who helped Odysseus
to get to the Phaiakians' land:
see Odyssey 5).

διασωθῆναι εἰς τὴν τῶν Φαιάκων χώραν, ὑφ' ὧν ἐς τὴν οἰκ-
είαν ἀποπεμφθεὶς κατέλαβον πολλοὺς τῆς γυναικὸς μνηστῆρας
ἐν τοῖς ἡμετέροις τρυφῶντας· ἀποκτείνας δὲ ἅπαντας ὑπὸ
Τηλεγόνου ὕστερον τοῦ ἐκ Κίρκης μοι γενομένου ἀνῃρέθην,
καὶ νῦν εἰμι ἐν τῇ Μακάρων νήσῳ πάνυ μετανοῶν ἐπὶ τῷ   10
καταλιπεῖν τὴν παρὰ σοὶ δίαιταν καὶ τὴν ὑπὸ σοῦ προτειν-
ομένην ἀθανασίαν. ἢν οὖν καιροῦ λάβωμαι, ἀποδρὰς ἀφίξομαι
πρὸς σέ. ταῦτα μὲν ἐδήλου ἡ ἐπιστολή, καὶ περὶ ἡμῶν, ὅπως
ξενισθῶμεν.

(b) Lucian found Kalypso's cave, delivered the letter and was re-
ceived hospitably. He answered her questions with tact.

36.   ἐγὼ δὲ προελθὼν ὀλίγον ἀπὸ τῆς θαλάττης εὗρον τὸ σπή-   15
λαιον τοιοῦτον οἷον 'Όμηρος εἶπεν, καὶ αὐτὴν ταλασιουρ-
γοῦσαν. ὡς δὲ τὴν ἐπιστολὴν ἔλαβεν καὶ ἐπελέξατο, πρῶτα
μὲν ἐπὶ πολὺ ἐδάκρυεν, ἔπειτα δὲ παρεκάλει ἡμᾶς ἐπὶ ξένια
καὶ εἰστία λαμπρῶς καὶ περὶ τοῦ 'Οδυσσέως ἐπυνθάνετο καὶ
περὶ τῆς Πηνελόπης, ὁποία τε εἴη τὴν ὄψιν καὶ εἰ σωφρονο-   20
οίη, καθάπερ 'Οδυσσεὺς πάλαι περὶ αὐτῆς ἐκόμπαζεν· καὶ
ἡμεῖς τοιαῦτα ἀπεκρινάμεθα, ἐξ ὧν εἰκάζομεν εὐφρανεῖσθαι
αὐτήν.

From here Lucian and his companions sailed towards the continent
on the other side of the world, where they were shipwrecked after
encountering various adventures: pumpkin-pirates; a halcyon's nest;
a Dionysiac portent, in which the ship's mast put out branches and
grew figs and black grapes; a forest in the middle of the sea; Mino-
taurs; phallus-sailors; and some dangerous women called Ass-legs,
whom Lucian escaped by using the mallow given to him by Rhadamanthys.
'What happened there, I shall tell you in another book' says Lucian,
but that too is just another lie!

69

διασῴζω: I bring safely through.
Φαίακες, οἱ (3a): The Phaiakians (inhabitants of the island of Skheria: see Odyssey 6-7 and 13 for their hospitality to O. and provision of transport home).
τὴν οἰκείαν: sc. χώραν.
μνηστήρ (μνηστηρ-), ὁ (3a): suitor (see Odyssey 22 for the battle with the suitors).
ἐν τοῖς ἡμετέροις: sc. 'house'.
τρυφάω: I live in luxury.
Τηλέγονος, ὁ (2a): Telegonos.
ἀναιρέω: I kill.
10 Μάκαρες, οἱ (3a): the Blest.
μετανοέω (ἐπί + dat.): I repent of.
καταλιπ- = aor. stem of καταλείπω.
δίαιτα, ἡ (1c): life, way of life.
προτείνω: I offer.
ἀθανασία, ἡ (1b): immortality.
καιρός, ὁ (2a): opportunity.
ἀποδρα- = aor. stem of ἀποδιδράσκω: I run away.

15

ὅπως (+ subj.): that (the construction is irregular - one would expect opt. in indir. speech, but L. has preferred a purpose construction).
ξενίζω: I entertain.
προελθ- = aor. stem of προέρχομαι: I go forward.
σπήλαιον, τό (2b): cave.
τοιοῦτος, -αύτη, -οῦτο(ν) ... οἷος, -α, -ον: just ... as (Homer's description of the cave may be found in Odyssey 5.55-75).
ταλασιουργέω: I spin wool.
ἐπιλέγομαι: I read.
ἐπὶ πολύ: for a long time.
παρακαλέω: I call in, summon.
20 ξένια, τά (2b): meal.
ἐστιάω: I feast-
ὄψις, ἡ (3e): looks.
σωφρονέω: I behave properly.
κομπάζω: I boast.
εἰκάζω: I guess (for tense of εἰκάζομεν see on εὑρίσκομεν, 7.25 above).
εὐφραίνομαι (fut. εὐφρανέομαι): I am cheered up.

IV   LUCIAN'S AUTOBIOGRAPHY

Lucian was an orator, who for much of his life travelled around the Greek-speaking parts of the Roman world giving performances of his works. He seems to have liked to preface these shows with specially written introductory pieces, in which he would comment on some aspect of his work - he was sometimes, for instance, worried by the originality of his works! Often enough the pieces are pleasantly self-deprecatory, designed to warm up the audience and get them on his side. Sometimes they involve a flattery of those present which may grate upon modern ears.

The Dream (Περὶ τοῦ 'Ενυπνίου), subtitled Lucian's autobiography (Βίος Λουκιανοῦ), is an introductory piece delivered in Lucian's birthplace, Samosata in Syria. It provides an amusing account of his choice of career - an exemplary tale for the impoverished young of an unimportant town from one of its most famous (in his own estimation!) sons, designed (in his own words) 'to encourage the young to choose the better way, the path of culture, especially any who are turning off onto a worse track just because they are poor, ruining talents which are not at all unworthy'.

15. CAREER PROSPECTS FOR LUCIAN

(Περὶ τοῦ 'Ενυπνίου ἤτοι Βίος Λουκιανοῦ - Somnium sive Vita Luciani 1-2)

(a) *Lucian had finished elementary school. A family conference rejected higher education as an option in favour of learning a skill and earning money.*

1.   ἄρτι μὲν ἐπεπαύμην εἰς τὰ διδασκαλεῖα φοιτῶν ἤδη τὴν
ἡλικίαν πρόσηβος ὤν, ὁ δὲ πατὴρ ἐσκοπεῖτο μετὰ τῶν φίλων
ὅ τι καὶ διδάξαιτό με. τοῖς πλείστοις οὖν ἔδοξεν παιδεία
μὲν καὶ πόνου πολλοῦ καὶ χρόνου μακροῦ καὶ δαπάνης οὐ
μικρᾶς καὶ τύχης δεῖσθαι λαμπρᾶς, τὰ δ' ἡμέτερα μικρά τε   5
εἶναι καὶ ταχεῖάν τινα τὴν ἐπικουρίαν ἀπαιτεῖν· εἰ δέ
τινα τέχνην τῶν βαναύσων τούτων ἐκμάθοιμι, τὸ μὲν πρῶτον
εὐθὺς ἂν αὐτὸς ἔχειν τὰ ἀρκοῦντα παρὰ τῆς τέχνης καὶ μη-
κέτ' οἰκόσιτος εἶναι τηλικοῦτος ὤν, οὐκ εἰς μακρὰν δὲ
καὶ τὸν πατέρα εὐφρανεῖν ἀποφέρων ἀεὶ τὸ γιγνόμενον.   10

15. CAREER PROSPECTS FOR LUCIAN

ἐπεπαύμην = 1st s. pluperf. of
  παύομαι.
διδασκαλεῖον, τό (2b):   school.
φοιτάω: I go, resort.
ἡλικία, ἡ (1b): age.
πρόσηβος, -ον: near manhood.
διδάσκομαι: I have x (acc.)
  taught y (acc.).
*παιδεία, ἡ (1b): education,
  culture, learning.
πόνος, ὁ (2a): work, toil.
δαπάνη, ἡ (1a): expenditure.
5 τύχη, ἡ (1a): rank, position
  in life.
τὰ ... ἡμέτερα: tr. 'our
  resources ...'.
ταχύς, -εῖα, -ύ: fast, quick.
ἐπικουρία, ἡ (1b): aid, help.

βάναυσος, ὁ (2a): artisan.
ἅ (+ infin.): would (the
  verb is inf. representing
  what the relatives said
  i.e. 'they said, if ..., I
  would ... etc.').
ἀρκέω: I suffice, am enough.
τὰ ἀρκοῦντα: the neces-
  saries.
οἰκόσιτος, -ον: taking
  one's meals at home.
τηλικοῦτος, -αύτη, -οῦτον:
  so old, of such an age.
οὐκ εἰς μακράν: tr. 'not
  too far in the future'.
10 εὐφραίνω (fut. εὐφρανέω):
  I cheer, make happy.
τὸ γιγνόμενον (2b): produce,
  profit.

Schoolmaster and Pupils.
From a sandstone funerary
relief found at Neumagen in
W. Germany, late 2nd cent.
A.D.; Rheinisches Landes-
museum, Trier.

(b) The family decided that Lucian should learn sculpture from his
maternal uncle. Lucian's father was confident of his son's talent.

2. δευτέρας οὖν σκέψεως ἀρχὴ προύτέθη, τίς ἀρίστη τῶν
τεχνῶν καὶ ῥᾴστη ἐκμαθεῖν καὶ ἀνδρὶ ἐλευθέρῳ πρέπουσα
καὶ πρόχειρον ἔχουσα τὴν χορηγίαν καὶ διαρκῆ τὸν πόρον.
ἄλλου τοίνυν ἄλλην ἐπαινοῦντος, ὡς ἕκαστος γνώμης ἢ
ἐμπειρίας εἶχεν, ὁ πατὴρ εἰς τὸν θεῖον ἀπιδών - παρῆν   15
γὰρ ὁ πρὸς μητρὸς θεῖος, ἄριστος ἑρμογλύφος εἶναι δοκῶν
- Οὐ θέμις, εἶπεν, ἄλλην τέχνην ἐπικρατεῖν σοῦ παρόντος,
ἀλλὰ τοῦτον ἄγε - δεῖξας ἐμέ - δίδασκε παραλαβὼν λίθων
ἐργάτην ἀγαθὸν εἶναι καὶ συναρμοστὴν καὶ ἑρμογλυφέα·
δύναται γὰρ καὶ τοῦτο, φύσεώς γε, ὡς οἶσθα, ἔχων   20
δεξιῶς.

(c) Lucian outlines the grounds for his father's confidence - his
skill as a child at moulding life-like figures out of wax.

ἐτεκμαίρετο δὲ ταῖς ἐκ τοῦ κηροῦ παιδιαῖς· ὁπότε γὰρ
ἀφεθείην ὑπὸ τῶν διδασκάλων, ἀποξέων ἂν τὸν κηρὸν ἢ βόας
ἢ ἵππους ἢ καὶ νὴ Δί' ἀνθρώπους ἀνέπλαττον, εἰκότως, ὡς
ἐδόκουν τῷ πατρί· ἐφ' οἷς παρὰ μὲν τῶν διδασκάλων πληγὰς
ἐλάμβανον, τότε δὲ ἔπαινος εἰς τὴν εὐφυΐαν καὶ ταῦτα ἦν,   25
καὶ χρηστὰς εἶχον ἐπ' ἐμοὶ τὰς ἐλπίδας ὡς ἐν βραχεῖ μαθή-
σομαι τὴν τέχνην, ἀπ' ἐκείνης γε τῆς πλαστικῆς.

16. 'A DREAM DIVINE ...'

(Περὶ τοῦ Ἐνυπνίου ἤτοι Βίος Λουκιανοῦ - Somnium sive Vita Luciani 5-6)

Lucian started straightaway, eager to impress his friends with
the statues of the gods he would carve. But there was no beginner's
luck in this field; his uncle threw him in at the deep end and Lucian
broke a marble slab clean in two. His uncle flew into a temper, and
beat the little Lucian black and blue. He went home and complained to
his mother (uncle's sister) about the beating, putting it down to
jealousy of his talent. He cried himself to sleep.

σκέψις, ἡ (3e): consideration, inquiry.
προτίθημι (augmented πρου-): I propose.
πρέπων, -ουσα, -ον (+ dat.): befitting.
πρόχειρος, -ον: ready to hand.
χορηγία, ἡ (1b): equipment.
διαρκής, -ές: sufficient.
πόρος, ὁ (2a): revenue, income.
ὡς ἕκαστος ... εἶχεν: tr. 'each in accordance with his ... '.
15 ἐμπειρία, ἡ (1b): experience.
*ἀπιδ- = aor. stem of ἀφοράω: I look (away from everything else).
ἑρμογλύφος, ὁ (2a): carver of Hermai, sculptor.
δοκέω: I am reputed.
θέμις: right.
ἐπικρατέω: I prevail.
ἐργάτης, ὁ (1d): worker.
συναρμοστής, ὁ (1d): a fitter-together.
ἑρμογλυφεύς, ὁ (3g): carver of Hermai, sculptor.
20 δύναμαι (+ acc.): I am

capable in.
φύσεως γε ... ἔχων δεξιῶς: tr. 'being clever by ...'.
κηρός, ὁ (2a): wax.
παιδιά, ἡ (1b): childish amusement/creation.
ἀφεθείην = 1st s. aor. opt. pass. of ἀφίημι.
ἀποξέω: I scrape off.
βοῦς, ὁ/ἡ (acc. pl. βόας): bull, cow.
ἀναπλάττω: I model, mould.
εἰκότως: i.e. in a lifelike way.
*πληγή, ἡ (1a): cuff, smack.
25 τότε: i.e. at the time of the discussion.
ἔπαινος, ὁ (2a):(sc. 'the object of') praise.
εἰς (+ acc.): in relation to.
εὐφυΐα, ἡ (1b): natural appearance.
ταῦτα: i.e. his models.
ἐπί (+ dat.): with regard to.
ἐν βραχεῖ: in a short time.
γε: sc. 'to judge'.
πλαστική, ἡ (1a): (sc. 'attempt at') sculpture.

(a) *Lucian warns his audience that his story now requires their avid attention. That night he was visited by a dream which remains clear in his mind to this day.*

5. μέχρι μὲν δὴ τούτων γελάσιμα καὶ μειρακιώδη τὰ εἰρη-
    μένα· τὰ μετὰ ταῦτα δὲ οὐκέτι εὐκαταφρόνητα, ὦ ἄνδρες,
    ἀκούσεσθε, ἀλλὰ καὶ πάνυ φιληκόων ἀκροατῶν δεόμενα· ἵνα
    γὰρ καθ᾽ Ὅμηρον εἴπω,

                θεῖός μοι ἐνύπνιον ἦλθεν ὄνειρος   5
            ἀμβροσίην διὰ νύκτα,

    ἐναργὴς οὕτως ὥστε μηδὲν ἀπολείπεσθαι τῆς ἀληθείας. ἔτι
    γοῦν καὶ μετὰ τοσοῦτον χρόνον τά τε σχήματά μοι τῶν φαν-
    έντων ἐν τοῖς ὀφθαλμοῖς παραμένει καὶ ἡ φωνὴ τῶν ἀκουσ-
    θέντων ἔναυλος· οὕτω σαφῆ πάντα ἦν.   10

(b) *In the dream two women were fighting over him, one in working overalls, the other finely dressed. He was asked to choose between them.*

6. δύο γυναῖκες λαβόμεναι ταῖν χεροῖν εἷλκόν με πρὸς
    ἑαυτὴν ἑκατέρα μάλα βιαίως καὶ καρτερῶς· μικροῦ γοῦν με
    διεσπάσαντο πρὸς ἀλλήλας φιλοτιμούμεναι· καὶ γὰρ ἄρτι μὲν
    ἂν ἡ ἑτέρα ἐπεκράτει καὶ παρὰ μικρὸν ὅλον εἶχέ με, ἄρτι
    δ᾽ ἂν αὖθις ὑπὸ τῆς ἑτέρας εἰχόμην. ἐβόων δὲ πρὸς ἀλλήλας   15
    ἑκατέρα, ἡ μὲν ὡς αὑτῆς ὄντα με κεκτῆσθαι βούλοιτο, ἡ δὲ
    ὡς μάτην τῶν ἀλλοτρίων ἀντιποιοῖτο. ἦν δὲ ἡ μὲν ἐργατικὴ
    καὶ ἀνδρικὴ καὶ αὐχμηρὰ τὴν κόμην, τὼ χεῖρε τύλων ἀνάπλεως,
    διεζωσμένη τὴν ἐσθῆτα, τιτάνου καταγέμουσα, οἷος ἦν ὁ
    θεῖος ὁπότε ξέοι τοὺς λίθους· ἡ ἑτέρα δὲ μάλα εὐπρόσωπος   20
    καὶ τὸ σχῆμα εὐπρεπὴς καὶ κόσμιος τὴν ἀναβολήν.
        τέλος δ᾽ οὖν ἐφιᾶσί μοι δικάζειν ὁποτέρᾳ βουλοίμην συν-
    εῖναι αὐτῶν.

16. 'A DREAM DIVINE ...'

μέχρι (+ gen.): until,
up to.
γελάσιμος, -η, -ον: laugh-
able, ridiculous.
μειρακιώδης, -ες: childish.
είρημένα, τά (perf. pass.
part. of λέγω): what has
been said.
εύκαταφρόνητος, -ον: easy to
look down upon.
ὦ ἄνδρες: Lucian is addres-
sing a gathering (of his
own people, in Samosata).
φιλήκοος, -ον: liking to
listen, attentive.
ἀκροατής, ὁ (1d): listener
(pl. audience).
5 ἐνύπνιον, τό: (sc. as) a
vision in sleep.
ἀμβρόσιος, -η, ον: immor-
tal. (The lines are
Iliad 2.56-7: Agamemnon
has been visited by a false
dream from Zeus.)
ἐναργής, -ές: clear.
μηδέν: in no respect.
ἀπολείπομαι (+ gen.): I
fall short of.
φαν- = aor. stem of φαίνομαι
(Note that Lucian uses the
n. of these parts. (though
what appeared was f. in
form), tr. 'of the things
...'.)
ἐν τοῖς ὀφθαλμοῖς: tr.
'before ...'.
φωνή, ἡ (1b): sound.
10 ἔναυλος, -ον: ringing in
one's ears.
σαφής, -ές: clear.
ταῖν χεροῖν = gen. dual, tr.
'both my hands'.
ἕλκω: I drag.
βιαίως: forcefully.
καρτερῶς: violently.
μικροῦ: almost.
διασπάομαι: I tear in
half/apart.
φιλοτιμέομαι (πρός + acc.):

I compete with.
ἄρτι μὲν ... ἄρτι δὲ: at
one time ... at another.
ἐπικρατέω: I am on top,
prevail.
14 παρὰ μικρόν: almost.
κέκτημαι (inf. κεκτῆσθαι):
I possess.
μάτην: in vain, to no avail.
τῶν ἀλλοτρίων: sc. property'.
ἀντιποιέομαι (+ gen.): I
lay claim to.
ἐργατικός, -ή, -όν: like a
workman.
ἀνδρικός, -ή, -όν: masculine.
αἰχμηρός, -ά, -όν: rough,
unkempt.
κόμη, ἡ (1a): hair.
τὼ χεῖρε = acc. dual, tr.
'on both her hands'.
τύλος, ὁ (2a): callus,
blister.
ἀνάπλεως, -ων (+ gen.): quite
full of.
διεζωσμένη = perf. part. of
διαζώννυμαι: I am girt
up (tr. δ τὴν ἐσθῆτα: 'wear-
ing overalls': it actually
describes the pulling up of
the clothes and the knotting
of them round the waist).
τίτανος, ὁ (2a): marble-
scrapings.
καταγέμω (+ gen.): I am full
of.
οἷος, -α, -ον: such as, as.
20 ξέω: I polish.
εὐπρόσωπος, -ον: beautiful,
with fine features.
κόσμιος, ον: orderly,
attractive.
ἀναβολή, ἡ: (sc. 'way of
wearing her') cloak/
mantle.
ἐφίημι: I allow x (dat.) to
... (inf.).
ὁπότερος, -α, -ον: which
(of two).
βουλοίμην: opt., as if the
introductory verb δικάζειν
were past.

76

17. 'FAME IS THE SPUR ... '

(Περὶ τοῦ Ἐνυπνίου ἤτοι Βίος Λουκιανοῦ - *Somnium sive Vita Luciani 14-16*)

'Sculpture' (in overalls) spoke first, dropping her h's and
hurrying her argument, which consisted chiefly of the claim that
despite her looks she would make him admired by all, just like Phei-
dias and Polykleitos, Myron and Praxiteles before him. 'Culture'
(finely dressed), in polished language countered that, however fam-
ous he became, he would still be a workman, a slave to toil, and
that people might admire his works, but they would not want to change
places with him. Her claim was that she would beautify his soul,
exposing it to all the great works of the past until he became an
object of general admiration, pointed at in the street, a man whose
eloquence would not only amaze everybody now, but would make him im-
mortal. Was he really going to renounce praise, honour and power to
don a workman's overall?

(a) Lucian didn't wait for the end, but rushed towards 'Culture',
leaving 'Sculpture' to turn to stone.

14.   ταῦτα ἔτι λεγούσης αὐτῆς οὐ περιμείνας ἐγὼ τὸ τέλος
τῶν λόγων ἀναστὰς ἀπεφηνάμην, καὶ τὴν ἄμορφον ἐκείνην
καὶ ἐργατικὴν ἀπολιπὼν μετέβαινον πρὸς τὴν Παιδείαν μάλα
γεγηθώς, καὶ μάλιστα ἐπεί μοι καὶ εἰς νοῦν ἦλθεν ἡ σκυτ-
άλη καὶ ὅτι πληγὰς εὐθὺς οὐκ ὀλίγας ἀρχομένῳ μοι χθὲς   5
ἐνετρίψατο. ἡ δὲ ἀπολειφθεῖσα τὸ μὲν πρῶτον ἠγανάκτει καὶ
τὼ χεῖρε συνεκρότει καὶ τοὺς ὀδόντας συνέπριε· τέλος δέ,
ὥσπερ τὴν Νιόβην ἀκούομεν, ἐπεπήγει καὶ εἰς λίθον μετε-
βέβλητο. εἰ δὲ παράδοξα ἔπαθεν, μὴ ἀπιστήσητε· θαυματο-
ποιοὶ γὰρ οἱ ὄνειροι.   10

(b) 'Culture' rewarded Lucian with a trip above the earth in a
winged chariot, accompanied by the praise of the people he flew over.

15.   ἡ ἑτέρα δὲ πρός με ἀπιδοῦσα, Τοιγαροῦν ἀμείψομαί σε,
ἔφη, τῆσδε τῆς δικαιοσύνης, ὅτι καλῶς τὴν δίκην ἐδίκασας,
καὶ ἐλθὲ ἤδη, ἐπίβηθι τούτου τοῦ ὀχήματος - δεῖξασά τι
ὄχημα ὑποπτέρων ἵππων τινῶν τῷ Πηγάσῳ ἐοικότων - ὅπως
εἰδῇς οἷα καὶ ἡλίκα μὴ ἀκολουθήσας ἐμοὶ ἀγνοήσειν ἔμελλες.   15

17. *'FAME IS THE SPUR ...'*

ταῦτα: *i.e. her arguments.*
αὐτῆς: *i.e. Sculpture.*
*περιμένω (περιμειν-): I
    hang around for.*
τέλος, τό: *end.*
ἀναστα- = *aor. stem of*
    ἀνίσταμαι.
ἀπεφηνάμην = *aor. of*
    ἀποφαίνομαι: *I give an
    opinion, show my hand.*
ἄμορφος, -ον: *unlovely,
    ugly.*
ἐργατικός, -ή, -όν: *like a
    workman.*
μεταβαίνω: *I change sides.*
γεγηθώς: *joyful(ly) (perf.
    part. of* γηθέω: *I rejoice).*
σκυτάλη, ἡ (1a): *stick.*
5 ὅτι: *sc.* 'the fact ...'.
ἐντρίβομαι: *I cause x (dat.)
    to be showered with y (acc.)
    ('Sculpture' is the sub-
    ject).*
*ἀγανακτέω: I am angry/
    cut up rough.*
τὼ χεῖρε *(acc. dual):* tr.
    'both her hands'.
συγκροτέω: *I smack to-
    gether.*
ὀδούς (ὀδοντ-), ὁ (3a):
    tooth.
συμπρίω: *I gnash, grind
    together.*
Νιοβή, ἡ (1a): *Niobe (she
    boasted about her large
    family to Leto, mother
    of two - Artemis and
    Apollo - and, after
    seeing them all killed,
    turned to stone in grief
    (Ovid Met. 6.146-312)).*
ἀκούω: *I hear in relation
    to.*
ἐπεπήγει = *3rd s. pluperf. of*
    πύγνυμαι: *I become solid,
    freeze, set.*
μετεβέβλητο = *3rd s. plupf.
    of* μεταβάλλομαι: *I am
    changed.*
ἀπιστέω: *I disbelieve.*

9 θαυματοποιός, -ον: *wonder-
    worker, magician.*
τοιγαροῦν: *well, then.*
ἀμείβομαι: *I pay x (acc.)
    back for y (gen.).*
ἐπίβηθι = *aor. imper. of*
    ἐπιβαίνω (+ gen.): I
    mount.
ὄχημα, τό (3b): *chariot.*
*δειξ- = *aor. stem of*
    δείκνυμι.
ὑπόπτερος, -ον: *winged.*
Πήγασος, ὁ (2a): *Pegasos
    (winged horse who sprang
    from the blood of Medusa's
    head, when Perseus had cut
    it off).*
15 ἡλίκος, -η, -ον: *how great.*
μή (+ part.): *if not.*

ἐπεὶ δὲ ἀνῆλθον, ἡ μὲν ἤλαυνε καὶ ὑφηνιόχει, ἀρθεὶς
δὲ εἰς ὕψος ἐγὼ ἐπεσκόπουν ἀπὸ τῆς ἕω ἀρξάμενος ἄχρι
πρὸς τὰ ἑσπέρια πόλεις καὶ ἔθνη καὶ δήμους, καθάπερ ὁ
Τριπτόλεμος ἀποσπείρων τι εἰς τὴν γῆν. οὐκέτι μέντοι
μέμνημαι ὅ τι τὸ σπειρόμενον ἐκεῖνο ἦν, πλὴν τοῦτο μόνον   20
ὅτι κάτωθεν ἀφορῶντες ἄνθρωποι ἐπήνουν καὶ μετ᾽ εὐφημίας
καθ᾽ οὓς γενοίμην τῇ πτήσει παρέπεμπον.

(c) 'Culture' brought Lucian, dressed now in rich clothes, back to
his father, and reminded him what kind of mistake he had nearly
made. Lucian attributes this dream to fear.

16.   δείξασα δέ μοι τὰ τοσαῦτα κἀμὲ τοῖς ἐπαινοῦσιν ἐκεί-
νοις ἐπανήγαγεν αὖθις, οὐκέτι τὴν αὐτὴν ἐσθῆτα ἐκείνην
ἐνδεδυκότα ἣν εἶχον ἀφιπτάμενος, ἀλλ᾽ ἐμοὶ ἐδόκουν εὐ-   25
πάρυφός τις ἐπανήκειν. καταλαβοῦσα οὖν καὶ τὸν πατέρα
ἑστῶτα καὶ περιμένοντα ἐδείκνυεν αὐτῷ ἐκείνην τὴν ἐσθῆτα
κἀμέ, οἷος ἥκοιμι, καί τι καὶ ὑπέμνησεν οἷα μικροῦ δεῖν
περὶ ἐμοῦ ἐβουλεύσαντο.
        ταῦτα μέμνημαι ἰδὼν ἀντίπαις ἔτι ὤν, ἐμοὶ δοκεῖν ἐκτα-   30
ραχθεὶς πρὸς τὸν τῶν πληγῶν φόβον.

ἀνέρχομαι (ἀνελθ-): I get up.
ἐλαύνω: I drive.
ὑφηνιοχέω: I hold the
  reins (for tense see on
  διηγούμεθα, 7.48 above).
ἀρθείς = aor. pass. part. of
  αἵρω (ἀρ-): I raise.
ὕψος, τό (3c): height.
ἐπισκοπέω: I observe,
  review.
ἕως, ἡ (gen. ἕω): east.
ἄχρι: right.
ἑσπέρια, τά (2b): western
  parts.
ἔθνος, τό (3c): nation,
  tribe.
δῆμος, ὁ (2a): township,
  village.
Τριπτόλεμος, ὁ (2a):
  Triptolemos (given by
  Demeter the task of bring-
  ing her gifts of culti-
  vation to men by riding
  over the earth and scat-
  tering seed, Ovid, Met.
  5.645ff.).
ἀποσπείρω: I scatter like
  seed.
20 σπείρω: I sow.
κάτωθεν: from below.
εὐφημία, ἡ (1b): fair words,
  honour.
κατά (+ acc.): among (lit.
  'over against').
οὕς: tr. 'whomever' (γενοί-
  μην is indefinite in past
  sequence).
πτῆσις, ἡ (3e): flight.
παραπέμπω: I send on his
  way, escort.
ἐπανάγω (ἐπαναγαγ-): I bring
  x (acc.) back to y (dat.).
25 ἐνδεδυκότα: tr. 'wearing'
  (perf. part. of ἐνδύω:
  I put on).
ἀφίπταμαι: I fly away.
ἀλλ': tr. 'but instead ...'
  (construction becomes
  direct).
εὐπάρυφος, ὁ (2a): a V.I.P.
  lit. 'wearing a garment
  with a fine purple border'.
ἐπανήκω: I have returned.

ἑστῶτα = part. of ἕστηκα:
  I stand.
περιμένοντα: sc. 'for my
  return'.
ἐδείκνυε = imperf. of
  δείκνυμι.
καί τι καί: 'and to some
  extent also ...'.
ὑπέμνησεν = aor. of
  ὑπομιμνήσκω: I remind (sc.
  'him').
μικροῦ δεῖν: almost, lit.
  'to lack a little' cf.
  ἐμοὶ δοκεῖν.
βουλεύομαι: I plan.
30 ἀντίπαις, ὁ (3a): a mere lad.
ἐκταραχθείς = aor. part. of
  ἐκταράττομαι (πρός + acc.):
  I am worried (by).

V TARGETS OF SATIRE

As well as dialogues, literary satires and introductory pieces,
Lucian also wrote pamphlets, aimed at debunking various forms of
human endeavour which he considered ridiculous, or, very occasionally,
praising someone whose ideas met with his approval. Three of his
favourite butts are philosophers, the rich, and historians. Philo-
sophers are, in Lucian's opinion, good material for jokes; it is not
always a sign of his ardent antipathy to philosophy when he gets a
laugh out of them. This may be seen from the first piece in this
section, a bon mot which Lucian reports as being the saying of Demo-
nax, a philosopher whom he admired, and whose style of satire was
akin to his own. But the false philosopher, who has the trappings
of philosophy, but betrays his so-called beliefs by his own behaviour,
is a constant theme (see 4 and 6b above).

The rich are also constantly lambasted. What jars most is their
ignorance and lack of taste. Demonax' second saying is also typical
of Lucian's own exposure of the pretensions of the wealthy. The
second excerpt combines the themes of the ignorance of the rich with
the folly of the philosopher putting himself into their hands - the
worst of both worlds.

For Lucian any writer is fair game, but historians are peculiarly
prone, since they are for ever making up impossible incidents and
telling tall tales. They are the primary target of the True Story
(see III above). Lucian devoted a complete work, entitled How to
write History (Πῶς δεῖ ʾΙστορίαν συγγράφειν - see 20 below), to show-
ing up the absurdity of many contemporary historians. The following
passage is from Lucian's Life of Demonax (Δημώνακτος Βίος).

18. TWO EXAMPLES OF DEMONAX' SATIRIC STYLE

(Δημώνακτος Βίος - Demonax 14 and 41)

Lucian much admired Demonax. One of his reasons was that Demonax
did not adhere to one school of thought, but mixed up the best from
each philosophical sect. Another, clearly, was that they shared a
sense of humour.

(a) A sophist claims to have tried every branch of philosophy. He
will heed the call, whichever sect makes it.

Aristotle (384-322 B.C.) was originally a follower of Plato,
but later established his own school in the Lykeion at Athens. His
adherents were known as Peripatetics. Plato (c. 429-347 B.C.)
established his school in the Academy. Zeno of Kition (335-263
B.C.) was the founder of the sect known as the Stoics, because his
school was situated in the Stoa Poikile (the Painted Porch). Pytha-

*goras (sixth century B.C.) established a philosophico-religious
brotherhood at Kroton (on the toe of Italy), one of the rules of which
was that silence should be observed among the members.*

14. τοῦ δὲ Σιδωνίου ποτὲ σοφιστοῦ 'Αθήνησιν εὐδοκιμοῦντος
καὶ λέγοντος ὑπὲρ αὐτοῦ ἔπαινόν τινα τοιοῦτον, ὅτι πάσης
φιλοφοφίας πεπείραται – οὐ χεῖρον δὲ αὐτὰ εἰπεῖν ἃ ἔλεγεν.
'Εὰν 'Αριστοτέλης με καλῇ ἐπὶ τὸ Λύκειον, ἔψομαι· ἂν Πλάτων
ἐπὶ τὴν 'Ακαδημίαν, ἀφίξομαι· ἂν Ζήνων, ἐπὶ τῇ Ποικίλῃ δια-   5
τρίψω· ἂν Πυθαγόρας καλῇ, σιωπήσομαι. ἀναστὰς οὖν ἐκ μέσων
τῶν ἀκροωμένων, Οὗτος, ἔφη προσειπὼν τὸ ὄνομα, καλεῖ σε
Πυθαγόρας.

(b) *A senator is proud of his broad purple stripe. Demonax reminds
him how little difference they made to their original wearer.*

41. ἰδὼν δέ τινα τῶν εὐπαρύφων ἐπὶ τῷ πλάτει τῆς πορφύρας
μέγα φρονοῦντα, κύψας αὐτοῦ πρὸς τὸ οὖς καὶ τῆς ἐσθῆτος   10
λαβόμενος καὶ δείξας, Τοῦτο μέντοι πρὸ σοῦ πρόβατον ἐφόρει
καὶ ἦν πρόβατον.

18. TWO EXAMPLES OF
DEMONAX' SATIRIC STYLE

Σιδώνιος, ὁ (2a): man from
  Sidon.
εὐδοκιμέω: I have a good
  reputation.
ἔπαινος, ὁ (2a): praise.
'Αριστοτέλης, ὁ (3d):
  Aristotle.
Λύκειον, τό (2b): the Lykeion
5 'Ακαδημία, ἡ (1b): Academy.
Ζήνων, ὁ (3a): Zeno.
Ποικίλη, ἡ: the Painted
  Porch.
Πυθαγόρας, ὁ (1d):
  Pythagoras.
ἀναστα- = aor. stem of
  ἀνίσταμαι.

μέσος, -η, -ον: the middle
  of.
ἀκροώμενος, ὁ (2a): listener
  (part. of ἀκροάομαι: I
  listen).
προσειπεῖν: to call/address.
πλάτος, τό (3c): breadth.
πορφύρα, ἡ (1b): purple
  stripe.
10 μέγα φρονέω: I preen my-
  self on (ἐπί + dat.).
κύπτω: I bend.
οὖς (ὠτ-), τό (3b): ear.
φορέω: I wear.
καὶ ἦν: sc. 'still, despite
  that ...'.

19. *THE PHILOSOPHER'S BURDEN*

(Περὶ τῶν ἐπὶ Μισθῷ συνόντων - *De Mercede conductis 33-35)*

In the pamphlet On people who hire themselves out *(Περὶ τῶν ἐπὶ Μισθῷ συνόντων)*, Lucian deals with the misery of the educated man forced to bow to the will of a rich and stupid patron. Such an appointment may begin with good omens (the promise of high financial rewards and an exalted position), but it will of necessity degenerate into menial service. This story, about the Stoic philosopher Thesmopolis, is one of a number of illustrations of Lucian's theme.

(a) Thesmopolis the Stoic was in the employ of a rich woman. On a journey he had to suffer the company of an eccentrically behaved homosexual.

33. οὐκ ὀκνῶ δέ σοι καὶ διηγήσασθαι ὅ μοι Θεσμόπολις οὗτος
ὁ Στωϊκὸς διηγήσατο συμβὰν αὐτῷ πάνυ γελοῖον καὶ νὴ Δί'
οὐκ ἀνέλπιστον ὡς ἂν καὶ ἄλλῳ ταὐτὸν συμβαίη. συνῆν μὲν
γὰρ πλουσίᾳ τινὶ καὶ τρυφώσῃ γυναικὶ τῶν ἐπιφανῶν ἐν τῇ
πόλει. δεῆσαν δὲ καὶ ἀποδημῆσαί ποτε, τὸ μὲν πρῶτον ἐκ-   5
εῖνο παθεῖν ἔφη γελοιότατον, συγκαθέζεσθαι γὰρ αὐτῷ παρα-
δεδόσθαι φιλοσόφῳ ὄντι κίναιδόν τινα τῶν πεπιττωμένων τὰ
σκέλη καὶ τὸν πώγωνα περιεξυρημένων· διὰ τιμῆς δ' αὐτὸν
ἐκείνη, ὡς τὸ εἰκός, ἦγεν. καὶ τοὔνομα δὲ τοῦ κιναίδου
ἀπεμνημόνευεν· Χελιδόνιον γὰρ καλεῖσθαι. τοῦτο τοίνυν   10
πρῶτον ἡλίκον, σκυθρωπῷ καὶ γέροντι ἀνδρὶ καὶ πολιῷ τὸ
γένειον - οἶσθα δὲ ὡς βαθὺν πώγωνα καὶ σεμνὸν ὁ Θεσμόπολις
εἶχεν - παρακαθίζεσθαι φῦκος ἐντετριμμένον καὶ ὑπογεγραμ-
μένον τοὺς ὀφθαλμοὺς καὶ διασεσαλευμένον τὸ βλέμμα καὶ
τὸν τράχηλον ἐπικεκλασμένον, οὐ χελιδόνα μὰ Δί', ἀλλὰ   15
γῦπά τινα περιτετιλμένον τοῦ πώγωνος τὰ πτερά· καὶ εἴ γε

19. THE PHILOSOPHER'S BURDEN

ὀκνέω: I hesitate.

Θεσμόπολις, ὁ (3e): Thesmopolis.

οὗτος: tr. 'Thesm. here'.

Στωϊκός, ὁ (2a): Stoic (a member of the Stoic sect of philosophy: their main doctrines were (a) virtue is based on knowledge (b) the aim of the philosopher is to live in harmony with nature (c) to be virtuous is the only good, not to be the only evil. All else is 'indifferent' - since the Stoic always acts in accordance with reason (nature) he always possesses the only real good and is thus completely independent of the vicissitudes of fortune).

συμβαίνω (συμβα-) (+ dat.): I happen to.

γελοῖος, -α, -ον: funny.

ἀνέλπιστος, -ον: beyond expectation.

τρυφάω: I live in luxury.

ἐπιφανής, -ές: distinguished, famous.

5 δεῆσαν = aor. part. of δεῖ: tr. 'when she needed ...' (acc. abs.).

ἀποδημέω: I make a trip.

ἐκεῖνο: tr. 'the following ...'.

συγκαθέζεσθαι ... παραδεδόσθαι: tr. (sc. 'he said') 'that a homosexual ...' - take παραδεδόσθαι first with συγκαθέζεσθαι depending on it.

συγκαθέζομαι: I sit with.

αὐτῷ: take with φιλοσόφῳ ὄντι.

παραδίδομαι: I am given to x (dat.) to y (inf.) (παραδεδόσθαι = perf. inf.).

κίναιδος, ὁ (2a): homosexual.

πιττόομαι: I remove the hair on (by means of plaster made of pitch!).

περιξυράομαι: I have my x (acc.) shaved all round.

διὰ τιμῆς ἄγω: I hold in honour, I value.

εἰκός, τό: probability, likelihood (sc. 'is').

καὶ ... δέ: and what's more.

10 ἀπομνημονεύω: I call to mind.

χελιδόνιον, τό (2b): Celandine (lit. 'little swallow').

καλεῖσθαι: the inf. depends on sc. 'he said'.

ἡλίκος, -η, -ον: how big.

τοῦτο ...: tr. 'well, what a monstrosity to start with, that a person φῦκος ἐντετριμμένον ... should sit by σκυθρωπῷ ... etc.'.

σκυθρωπός, -ή, -όν: sullen.

πολιός, -ά, -όν: grey.

βαθύν: tr. 'long'.

σεμνός, -ή, -όν: pompous.

παρακαθίζομαι (+ dat.): I sit beside.

φῦκος, τό (3c): rouge, make-up.

ἐντετριμμένον = perf. part. of ἐντρίβομαι: I have rubbed on me.

ὑπογεγραμμένον = perf. part. of ὑπογράφομαι: I have painted.

διασεσαλευμένος: excited, ogling.

βλέμμα, τό (3b): glance, look.

15 τράχηλος, ὁ (3a): neck.

χελιδών (χελιδον-), ἡ (3a): swallow.

γύψ (γυπ-), ὁ (3a): vulture.

περιτετιλμένος: plucked (περιτίλλω: I pluck).

πτέρον, τό (2b): wing.

εἰ γε ...: Lucian treats the εἰ clause as indir. statement. Thus δεηθῆναι is the verb, which would normally be ἐδεήθη, 'he had (not) begged'.

πολλά: tr. 'a great deal'.

84

μὴ πολλὰ δεηθῆναι αὐτοῦ, καὶ τὸν κεκρύφαλον ἔχοντα ἐπὶ
τῇ κεφαλῇ ἂν συγκαθίζεσθαι. τὰ δ' οὖν ἄλλα παρ' ὅλην τὴν
ὁδὸν μυρίας τὰς ἀηδίας ἀνασχέσθαι ὑπάδοντος καὶ τερετί-
ζοντος, εἰ δὲ μὴ ἐπεῖχεν αὐτός, ἴσως ἂν καὶ ὀρχουμένου   20
ἐπὶ τῆς ἀπήνης.

(b) The mistress begged a favour of Thesmopolis, that he look after
her pregnant dog on the journey.

34.   ἕτερον δ' οὖν τι καὶ τοιοῦτον αὐτῷ προσταχθῆναι. καλ-
ἔσασα γὰρ αὐτὸν ἡ γυνή, Θεσμοπόλι, φησίν, οὕτως ὄναιο,
χάριν οὐ μικρὰν αἰτούσῃ δὸς μηδὲν ἀντειπὼν μηδὲ ὅπως ἐπὶ
πλεῖόν σου δεήσομαι περιμείνας.   25
       τοῦ δέ, ὅπερ εἰκὸς ἦν, ὑποσχομένου πάντα πράξειν,
Δέομαί σου τοῦτο, ἔφη, χρηστὸν δρῶσα σε καὶ ἐπιμελῆ καὶ
φιλόστοργον, τὴν κύνα ἣν οἶσθα τὴν Μυρρίνην ἀναλαβὼν εἰς
τὸ ὄχημα φύλαττέ μοι καὶ ἐπιμελοῦ ὅπως μηδενὸς ἐνδεὴς
ἔσται· βαρύνεται γὰρ ἡ ἀθλία τὴν γαστέρα καὶ σχεδὸν ὡς   30
ἐπίτεξ ἐστίν· οἱ δὲ κατάρατοι οὗτοι καὶ ἀπειθεῖς οἰκέται
οὐχ ὅπως ἐκείνης, ἀλλ' οὐδ' ἐμοῦ αὐτῆς πολὺν ποιοῦνται
λόγον ἐν ταῖς ὁδοῖς. μὴ τοίνυν τι σμικρὸν οἰηθῇς εὖ ποι-
ήσειν με τὸ περισπούδαστόν μοι καὶ ἥδιστον κυνίδιον δια-
φυλάξας.   35

(c) Thesmopolis agreed. Lucian pictures the absurd scene, adding
a few details of his own invention. Thesmopolis' homosexual fellow-
traveller joked about his change of philosophical sect.

       ὑπέσχετο ὁ Θεσμόπολις πολλὰ ἱκετευούσης καὶ μονονουχὶ
καὶ δακρυούσης. τὸ δὲ πρᾶγμα παγγέλοιον ἦν, κυνίδιον ἐκ
τοῦ ἱματίου προκῦπτον μικρὸν ὑπὸ τὸν πώγωνα καὶ κατουρῆ-
σαν πολλάκις, εἰ καὶ μὴ ταῦτα ὁ Θεσμόπολις προσετίθει,
καὶ βαῦζον λεπτῇ τῃ φωνῇ - τοιαῦτα γὰρ τὰ Μελιταῖα - καὶ   40

δεηθ- = aor. stem of
δέομαι.
κεκρύφαλος, ὁ (2a): hair-
net.
ἐπί (+ dat.): on.
ᾆν (+ inf.): would (inf. de-
pending on sc. 'he said'.
Lucian appears to be ex-
cited and colloquial -
we would expect an aor.
infin., not present, to
represent 'would have
...').
συγκαθίζομαι: I sit with.
τὰ ... ἄλλα: tr. 'in other
respects'.
μυρίοι, -αι, -α: countless.
ἀηδία, ἡ (1b): nauseous
foible.
ἀνασχ- = aor. stem of
ἀνέχομαι.
ὑπάδοντος: sc. 'Celandine'.
ὑπάδω: I sing in accompani-
ment/along.
τερετίζω: I hum.
20 αὗτός: i.e. Thesmopolis.
ᾆν: sc. ἀνέσχετο, i.e.
would have put up with
(continuing the construc-
tion and extrapolating
from τερετίζοντος, which
Celandine did, to what he
would have done without
T's interference).
ὀρχέομαι: I dance.
ἀπήνη, ἡ (1a): wagon.
ἕτερον ...: sc. 'he said
that ...'. αὐτῷ προστα-
χθῆναι (from προστάττω):
tr. 'was enjoined upon
him'.
οὕτως ὄναιο (from ὀνίνημι):
tr. 'bless you if you do'
(lit. 'thus may you have
profit').
χάρις, ἡ: favour.
αἱτούσῃ: sc. μοι.
ἀντειπ- = aor. stem of
ἀντιλέγω: I speak
against.
ὅπως (+ fut.): (sc. 'forcing
me') to.
24 ἐπὶ πλεῖον: further.

ὅπερ: tr. 'as'.
ὑποσχ- = aor. stem of
ὑπισχνέομαι.
φιλόστοργος, -ον: affection-
ate.
Μυρρίνη, ἡ (1a): Myrrhine.
ἀναλαβ- = aor. stem of
ἀναλαμβάνω.
ὄχημα, τό (3b): vehicle,
chariot.
ἐπιμελέομαι (ὅπως + fut. ind.):
I take care (that).
ἐνδεής -ές (+ gen.): want-
ing for.
30 βαρύνομαι: I am weighed
down.
ἐπίτεξ, ἡ: about to pro-
duce.
κατάρατος, -ον: cursed.
ἀπειθής, -ές: dis-
obedient.
οὐχ ὅπως ... ἀλλ' οὐδέ:
not only not ... but
not even.
ἐκεινῆς: i.e. the dog.
λόγον ποιέομαι (+ gen.): I
have regard for, I pay
attention to.
ὀδός, ἡ (2a): journey.
οἰηθ- = aor. stem of οἶμαι.
περισπούδαστος, -ον: be-
loved.
μοι: tr. 'by my' (dat. of
agent after pass. idea).
*κυνίδιον, τό (2b): little
dog; doggie.
34 διαφυλάττω: I guard care-
fully.
ἱκετευούσης: sc. αὐτῆς.
μονονουχί: almost.
παγγελοῖος, -ον: very
funny, highly ridiculous.
προκύπτω: I peep out.
κατουρέω: I urinate.
προστίθημι: I add.
40 βαὖζω: I bark.
Μελιταῖος, -α, -ον: (sc.
'dogs') from Malta.

τὸ γένειον τοῦ φιλοσόφου περιλιχμώμενον, καὶ μάλιστα εἴ
τι τοῦ χθιζοῦ αὐτῷ ζωμοῦ ἐγκατεμέμικτο. καὶ ὅ γε κίναιδος,
ὁ σύνεδρος, οὐκ ἀμούσως ποτὲ καὶ εἰς τοὺς ἄλλους τοὺς
παρόντας ἐν τῷ συμποσίῳ ἀποσκώπτων, ἐπειδή ποτε καὶ ἐπὶ
τὸν θεσμόπολιν καθῆκε τὸ σκῶμμα, Περὶ δὲ Θεσμοπόλιδος,   45
ἔφη, τοῦτο μόνον εἰπεῖν ἔχω, ὅτι ἀντὶ Στωϊκοῦ ἤδη Κυνικὸς
ἡμῖν γεγένηται.
35.   τὸ δ᾽ οὖν κυνίδιον καὶ τετοκέναι ἐν τῷ τρίβωνι τῷ τοῦ
Θεσμοπόλιδος ἐπυθόμην.

20. THUCYDIDES REDIVIVUS

(Πῶς δεῖ Ἱστορίαν συγγράφειν - Quomodo Historia conscribenda sit 25-26)

In How to write History (Πῶς δεῖ Ἱστορίαν συγγράφειν) Lucian
propounds very little in the way of theory which could not be found
elsewhere; his main message is that history is not poetry and demands
strict adherence to the truth. His main weapon is literary
satire and parody. Each fault is backed up with an exposé of one of
the current rash of histories dealing with Lucian Verus' Parthian
War (A.D. 161-5). In this passage the offender against Lucian's creed
is an imitator of Thucydides, the historian of the Peloponnesian War
(431-404 B.C.).

(a) Lucian has been commenting on the geographical inaccuracy of
one writer, whose narrative had moved his own home town of Samosata
from Syria to Mesopotamia. He goes on here to summarise and satirise
the same writer's account of the strange suicide of Severianus, one
of Lucius Verus' generals.

25.   νὴ Δία κἀκεῖνο κομιδῇ πιθανὸν περὶ τοῦ Σεουηριανοῦ ὁ
αὐτὸς οὗτος εἶπεν ἐπομοσάμενος, ἦ μὴν ἀκοῦσαί τινος τῶν
ἐξ αὐτοῦ τοῦ ἔργου διαφυγόντων· οὔτε γὰρ ξίφει ἐθελῆσαι
αὐτὸν ἀποθανεῖν οὔτε φαρμάκου πιεῖν οὔτε βρόχον ἅψασθαι,
ἀλλά τινα θάνατον ἐπινοῆσαι τραγικὸν καὶ τῇ τόλμῃ ξενί-   5
ζοντα· τυχεῖν μὲν γὰρ αὐτὸν ἔχοντα παμμεγέθη ἐκπώματα
ὑαλᾶ, τῆς καλλίστης ὑάλου, ἐπεὶ δὲ πάντως ἀποθανεῖν ἐγ-

περιλιχμάομαι: I lick.
χθιζός, -ή, -όν: yesterday's.
αὐτῷ: i.e. the beard.
ζωμός, ὁ (2a): soup, sauce.
ἐγκαταμείγνυμαι (+ dat.): I
  am mixed up in.
σύνεδρος, ὁ (2a): companion,
  fellow traveller.
ἀμούσως: untastefully.
ἀποσκώπτω (εἰς + acc.): I
  joke at.
45 καθῆκε = aor. of καθίημι.
σκῶμμα, τό (3b): joke.
Στωϊκός, ὁ (2a): Stoic.
Κυνικός, ὁ (2a): Cynic
  (lit. 'dog-like') (the
  philosophical sect of
  Diogenes and Antisthenes,
  whose main attribute
  was the rejection of
  all possessions
  and conventions and the
  practice of shamelessness).
ἡμῖν: tr. 'for our benefit',
  'as we can see'.
τετοκέναι = perf. inf. of
  τίκτω.
τρίβων (τριβων-), ὁ (3a):
  threadbare cloak.

20. THUCYDIDES REDIVIVUS

κἀκεῖνο: tr. 'the follow-
  ing too...'.
κομιδῇ: altogether, quite.

πιθανός, -ή, -όν: worthy
  of belief.
Σευηριανός, ὁ (2a):
  Severianus.
ὁ αὐτὸς οὗτος: this same
  chap.
ἐπομοσ- = aor. stem of
  ἐπόμνυμι: I swear.
ἦ μην: that in very
  truth.
τινος: tr. 'from one ...'.
ἔργον, τό (2b): action,
  deed.
οὔτε ... οὔτε ... οὔτε:
  sc. 'he said that ...'.
ξίφος, τό (3c): sword.
αὐτὸν: i.e. Severianus.
φάρμακον, τό (2b): poison.
πι- = aor. stem of πίνω
  (+ gen.): I drink some.
βρόχος, ὁ (2a): noose.
5 ἐπινοέω: I contrive.
τραγικός, -ή, -όν: tragic.
ξενίζω: I surprise,
  astonish.
τυχεῖν: sc. 'he said that
  ...', αὐτὸν: i.e.
  Severianus.
παμμεγέθης, -ες: immense.
ἔκπωμα, τό (3b): drinking-
  cup.
ὑαλοῦς, -ῆ, -οῦν: of glass.
ὕαλος, ἡ (2a): glass,
  crystal.
ἔγνωστο (γιγνώσκω): he
  had decided.

νωστο, κατάξαντα τὸν μέγιστον τῶν σκύφων ἑνὶ τῶν θραυ-
μάτων χρήσασθαι εἰς τὴν σφαγὴν ἐντεμόντα τῇ ὑάλῳ τὸν
λαιμόν. οὕτως οὐ ξιφίδιον, οὐ λογχάριον εὗρεν, ὡς ἀν-   10
δρεῖός γε αὐτῷ καὶ ἡρωϊκὸς ὁ θάνατος γένοιτο.

(b) In Thucydides (Book II), Perikles gives a funeral oration for
those who had died for their country in the preceding year; it re-
counts the glories of Athens. Lucian now goes on to show how his
writer, in imitation of Thucydides, has a centurion called Afranius
Silo deliver a funeral oration over Severianus, dwelling mainly on
the past glories of their dinner-parties. Then, in imitation of the
Greek hero of the Trojan War, Ajax, who went mad after failing to
win Achilles' armour in competition with Odysseus, and committed
suicide, Afranius also kills himself over Severianus' grave. Lucian's
final comment is sardonic.

26.   εἶτ' ἐπειδὴ Θουκυδίδης ἐπιτάφιόν τινα εἶπε τοῖς πρώτοις
τοῦ πολέμου ἐκείνου νεκροῖς, καὶ αὐτὸς ἡγήσατο χρῆναι
ἐπειπεῖν τῷ Σεουηριανῷ· ἅπασι γὰρ αὐτοῖς πρὸς τὸν οὐδὲν
αἴτιον τῶν ἐν Ἀρμενίᾳ κακῶν, τὸν Θουκυδίδην, ἡ ἄμιλλα.   15
θάψας οὖν τὸν Σεουηριανὸν μεγαλοπρεπῶς ἀναβιβάζεται ἐπὶ
τὸν τάφον Ἀφράνιόν τινα Σίλωνα ἑκατόνταρχον, ἀνταγωνιστὴν
Περικλέους, ὃς τοιαῦτα καὶ τοσαῦτα ἐπερρητόρευσεν αὐτῷ,
ὥστε με νὴ τὰς Χάριτας πολλὰ πάνυ δακρῦσαι ὑπὸ τοῦ γέλω-
τος, καὶ μάλιστα ὁπότε ῥήτωρ ὁ Ἀφράνιος ἐπὶ τέλει τοῦ   20
λόγου δακρύων ἅμα σὺν οἰμωγῇ περιπαθεῖ ἐμέμνητο τῶν πολυ-
τελῶν ἐκείνων δείπνων καὶ προπόσεων, εἶτα ἐπέθηκεν Αἰάν-
τειόν τινα τὴν κορωνίδα· σπασάμενος γὰρ τὸ ξίφος, εὐγενῶς
πάνυ καὶ ὡς Ἀφρόνιον εἰκὸς ἦν, πάντων ὁρώντων ἀπέσφαξεν ἑαυ-
τὸν ἐπὶ τῷ τάφῳ - οὐκ ἀνάξιος ὢν μὰ τὸν Ἐνυάλιον πρὸ πολλοῦ 25
ἀποθανεῖν, εἰ τοιαῦτα ἐρρητόρευεν. καὶ τοῦτο ἔφη ἰδόντας τοὺς
παρόντας ἅπαντας θαυμάσαι καὶ ὑπερεπαινέσαι τὸν Ἀφράνιον.
ἐγὼ δὲ καὶ τὰ ἄλλα μὲν αὐτοῦ κατεγίγνωσκον, μονονουχὶ
ζωμῶν καὶ λοπάδων μεμνημένου καὶ ἐπιδακρύοντος τῇ τῶν
πλακούντων μνήμῃ, τοῦτο δὲ μάλιστα ᾐτιασάμην, ὅτι μὴ τὸν   30
συγγραφέα καὶ διδάσκαλον τοῦ δράματος προαποσφάξας ἀπέθανεν.

καταξ- = aor. stem of
κατάγνυμι: I break/
shatter.
σκύφος, τό (3c): cup.
θραῦσμα, τό (3b): fragment,
splinter.
εἰς (+ acc.): for.
σφαγή, ἡ (1a): slaughter.
ἐντεμ- = aor. stem of
ἐντέμνω: I cut.
10 λαιμός, ὁ (2a): throat.
Ειφίδιον, τό (2b): dagger,
little sword.
λογχάριον, τό (2b): little
javelin.
ἡρωϊκός, -ή, -όν: heroic.
Θουκυδίδης, ὁ (1d):
Thucydides.
ἐπιτάφιος, ὁ (?a): fun-
eral speech.
τοῖς ...: sc. 'over ...'.
χρῆναι = inf. of χρή.
ἐπειπειν (+ dat.): to
speak over.
ἅπασι ... αὐτοῖς ... ἡ
ἄμιλλα: tr. 'all of
them contest with ...'.
πρός (+ acc.): against.
οὐδέν: in no way.
15 Ἀρμενία, ἡ (1b): Armenia.
κακόν, τό (2b): trouble.
ἄμιλλα, ἡ (1c): contest.
θάπτω: I bury.
μεγαλοπρεπῶς: magnifi-
cently.
ἀναβιβάζομαι: I bring up.
τάφος, ὁ (2a): grave,
tomb.
Ἀφράνιος, ὁ (2a): Afranius.
Σίλων (Σιλων-), ὁ (3a):
Silo.
ἑκατόνταρχος, ὁ (2a):
centurion.
ἀνταγωνιστής, ὁ (1d):
rival.
Περικλῆς, ὁ (3d: uncontr.):
Perikles.
ἐπιρρητορεύω: I declaim
x (acc.) over y (dat.).
Χάρις (Χαριτ-), ἡ (3a):
Grace (goddess of charm,
grace and beauty).
πολλά: at many points.

γέλως (γελως-), ὁ (3a):
laughter.
20 τέλος, τό (3c): end.
οἰμωγή, ἡ (1a): wailing,
lamentation.
περιπαθής, -ές: passionate.
μέμνημαι (+ gen.): I
mention.
πολυτελής, -ές: expensive.
πρόποσις, ἡ (3e): health,
toast.
ἐπέθηκεν = aor. of
ἐπιτίθημι: I finish with.
Αἰάντειος, -ον: befitting
Ajax, Ajax-like.
κορωνίς (κορωνιδ-), ἡ (3a):
flourish.
σπάομαι: I draw.
ξίφος, τό: sword.
εὐγενῶς: nobly.
Ἀφρονίος, ὁ (2a): Afreneticus
(pun on Afranius = 'mindless-
idiot').
εἰκὸς ἦν: tr. 'befitted'.
ἀποσφάζω: I slaughter.
25 ἐπί (+ dat.): on.
τάφος, ὁ (2a): grave, tomb.
ἀνάξιος, -ον: unworthy.
Ἐνυάλιος, ὁ (2a): Ares
(god of war).
πρὸ πολλοῦ: a long time before.
ῥητορεύω: I speak, orate.
τοῦτο obj. of ἰδόντας
ἔφη: sc. 'the author ...'.
ὑπερεπαινέω: I praise to
the skies.
καταγιγνώσκω: I condemn x (gen.)
for y (acc.).
μονονουχί: almost.
ζωμός, ὁ (2a): soup, sauce.
λοπάς (λοπαδ-), ἡ (3a): dish.
ἐπιδακρύω (+ dat.): I weep
at.
30 πλακοῦς (πλακουντ-), ὁ (3a):
cake.
μνήμη, ἡ (1a): mention.
αἰτιάομαι: I hold x (acc.)
against (someone).
συγγραφεύς, ὁ (3g): historian.
διδάσκαλος, ὁ (2a): producer.
προαποσφάζω: I slaughter
first.

VI   LUCIAN   AND   THE   IRRATIONAL

The second century A.D. was a time of rampant superstition. New cults arose with great rapidity and most of them seem to have aimed at some promise of individual salvation in a way which the traditional Olympian religion had not. Educated men as well as simple people involved themselves wholeheartedly with the irrational. Lucian makes great play with the surrender of the educated to paranormal phenomena. The extracts here (21-23) come from the dialogue Pathological Liars *(Φιλοψευδεῖς ἤ ᾿Απιστῶν), and present a character called Tykhiades, a rationalist who is sceptical of all stories of ghosts, reincarnation and magic.*

21.   HOMOEOPATHIC MEDICINE ?

(Φιλοψευδεῖς ἤ ᾿Απιστῶν - Philopseudeis 7-8)

Tykhiades reports to his friend Philokles a conversation in which he participated at the house of Eukrates. Eukrates was ill and seemed to be suffering from gout. At any rate an august body of philosophers was gathered around his bed discussing remedies when Tykhiades arrived.

(a)   Kleodemos (a peripatetic philosopher of Aristotle's school) suggested a cure for gout involving a weasel's tooth and a lion's skin. Deinomakhos the Stoic offered a correction ≈ a deer's skin, not a lion's but Kleodemos explained the correctness of his previous contention.

7.   οἱ μὲν δὴ ἐτύγχανον οἶμαι ὑπὲρ τοῦ νοσήματος τὰ μὲν
ἤδη πολλὰ προειρηκότες, τὰ δὲ καὶ τότε διεξιόντες, ἔτι
δὲ καὶ θεραπείας τινὰς ἕκαστος ὑποβάλλοντες. ὁ γοῦν
Κλεόδημος, Εἰ τοίνυν, φησίν, τῇ ἀριστερᾷ τις ἀνελόμενος
χαμᾶθεν τὸν ὀδόντα τῆς μυγαλῆς οὕτω φονευθείσης, ὡς προ-   5
εῖπον, ἐνδήσειεν εἰς δέρμα λέοντος ἄρτι ἀποδαρέν, εἶτα
περιάψειεν περὶ τὰ σκέλη, αὐτίκα παύεται τὸ ἄλγημα.
    Οὐκ εἰς λέοντος, ἔφη ὁ Δεινόμαχος, ἐγὼ ἤκουσα, ἐλάφου
δὲ θηλείας ἔτι παρθένου καὶ ἀβάτου· καὶ τὸ πρᾶγμα οὕτω
πιθανώτερον· ὠκὺ γὰρ ἡ ἔλαφος καὶ ἔρρωται μάλιστα ἐκ τῶν   10
ποδῶν. ὁ δὲ λέων ἄλκιμον μέν, καὶ τὸ λίπος αὐτοῦ καὶ ἡ
χεὶρ ἡ δεξιὰ καὶ αἱ τρίχες ἐκ τοῦ πώγονος αἱ ὀρθαὶ μεγάλα
δύνανται, εἴ τις ἐπίσταιτο αὐτοῖς χρῆσθαι μετὰ τῆς οἰκείας

21. HOMEOPATHIC MEDICINE?

ὑπέρ (+ gen.): concerning.
*νόσημα, τό (3b): illness,
  disease.
τὰ μὲν ἤδη πολλά ... τὰ δὲ καί
  τότε ...: tr. 'quite a
  few things already ...
  and others right then ...'.
προειρηκότες = perf. part.
  of προλέγω (προειπ-): I
  say beforehand.
διεξιόντες = part. of
  διεξέρχομαι.
ἔτι: besides.
θεραπεία, ἡ (1b): cure,
  treatment.
ὑποβάλλω: I suggest.
Κλεόδημος, ὁ (2a):
  Kleodemos.
ἀριστερά, ἡ (1b): the
  left hand.
ἀνελ- = aor. stem of
  ἀναιρέω.
5 χαμᾶθεν: from the ground.
ὀδούς (ὀδοντ-), ὁ (3a):
  tooth.
μυγαλῆ, ἡ (1a): field-mouse.
φονεύω: I kill.
ἐνδέω: I tie (onto) (εἰς
  + acc.).
*λέων (λεοντ-), ὁ (3a): lion.
ἀποδαρέν = n. aor. pass. part.
  of ἀποδείρω: I skin,
  strip off, flay.
περιάπτω: I tie around.
περιάψειεν ... παύεται: a
  mixed condition 'if x were
  to ... y stops'.
ἄλγημα, τό (3b): pain.
εἰς: sc. δέρμα.
Δεινόμαχος, ὁ (2a):
  Deinomakhos (a Stoic
  philosopher: see on
  Στωϊκός, 19.2 above).
ἔλαφος, ἡ (2a): deer.
θηλύς, -εῖα, -ύ: female.
ἄβατος, -ον: unmounted.
10 πιθανός, -ή, -όν: worthy
  of belief.
ὠκύς, -εῖα, ύ: swift.
ἔρρωμαι (ἐκ + gen.): I have
  strength in.

ἄλκιμος, -ον: stout,
  brave.
λίπος, τό (3c): fat.
χειρ (χειρ-), ἡ (3a): paw.
τριχ-: stem of θρίξ, ἡ (3a):
  hair.
μεγάλα δύναμαι: I have
  great efficacy/power.
οἰκείας: tr. 'requisite'.

ἐπῳδῆς ἑκάστῳ· ποδῶν δὲ ἴασιν ἥκιστα ἐπαγγέλλεται.

Καὶ αὐτός, ἦ δ' ὃς ὁ Κλεόδημος, οὕτω πάλαι ἐγίνωσκον,   15
ἐλάφου χρῆναι τὸ δέρμα εἶναι, διότι ὠκὺ ἔλαφος· ἔναγχος
δὲ Λίβυς ἀνὴρ σοφὸς τὰ τοιαῦτα μετεδίδαξέ με εἰπὼν ὠκυ-
τέρους εἶναι τῶν ἐλάφων τοὺς λέοντας. 'Αμέλει, ἔφη, καὶ
αἱροῦσιν αὐτὰς διώκοντες.

(b) Tykhiades was sceptical: spells and external remedies could not
affect cures. But he was laughed down, though Eukrates' doctor
Antigonos appeared pleased with him.

8.   ἐπήνεσαν οἱ παρόντες ὡς εὖ εἰπόντος τοῦ Λίβυος. ἐγὼ   20
δέ, Οἴεσθε γάρ, ἔφην, ἐπῳδαῖς τισιν τὰ τοιαῦτα παύεσθαι
ἢ τοῖς ἔξωθεν παραρτήμασιν τοῦ κακοῦ ἔνδον διατρίβοντος;
ἐγέλασαν ἐπὶ τῷ λόγῳ καὶ δῆλοι ἦσαν κατεγνωκότες μου
πολλὴν τὴν ἄνοιαν, εἰ μὴ ἐπισταίμην τὰ προδηλότατα καὶ
περὶ ὧν οὐδεὶς ἂν εὖ φρονῶν ἀντείποι μὴ οὐχὶ οὕτως ἔχειν.   25
ὁ μέντοι ἰατρὸς 'Αντίγονος ἐδόκει μοι ἡσθῆναι τῇ ἐρωτήσει
μου· πάλαι γὰρ ἠμελεῖτο, οἶμαι, βοηθεῖν ἀξιῶν τῷ Εὐκράτει
μετὰ τῆς τέχνης οἴνου τε παραγγέλλων ἀπέχεσθαι καὶ λάχανα
σιτεῖσθαι καὶ ὅλως ὑφαιρεῖν τοῦ τόνου.

(c) Kleodemos asked if Tykhiades' criticism was serious. Tykhiades
answered with a reductio ad absurdum of Kleodemos' lion-skin and
weasel cure.

ὁ δ' οὖν Κλεόδημος ὑπομειδιῶν ἅμα, Τί λέγεις, ἔφη, ὦ   30
Τυχιάδη; ἄπιστον εἶναί σοι δοκεῖ τὸ ἐκ τῶν τοιούτων γίγ-
νεσθαί τινας ὠφελείας ἐς τὰ νοσήματα;
"Εμοιγε, ἦν δ' ἐγώ, εἰ μὴ πάνυ κορύζης τὴν ῥῖνα μεστὸς
εἴην, ὡς πιστεύειν τὰ ἔξω καὶ μηδὲν κοινωνοῦντα τοῖς ἔν-
δοθεν ἐπεγείρουσι τὰ νοσήματα μετὰ ῥηματίων, ὥς φατε, καὶ   35
γοητείας τινὸς ἐνεργεῖν καὶ τὴν ἴασιν ἐπιπέμπειν προσαρ-
τώμενα. τὸ δ' οὐκ ἂν γένοιτο, οὐδ' ἢν ἐς τοῦ Νεμείου

*ἐπῳδή, ἡ (1a): spell,
incantation.
ἑκάστῳ: in apposition to
αὐτοῖς.
ἴασις, ἡ (3e): healing,
cure.
14 ἐπαγγέλλομαι: I promise,
offer (take ὁ λεών as
the subject).
χρῆναι = inf. of χρή.
ἔναγχος: recently.
σοφός, -ή, -όν (+ acc.):
wise/versed (in).
μεταδιδάσκω: I convert.
τῶν ἐλάφων: gen. of compari-
son.
ἀμέλει: of course, actually.
20 τοῦ Λίβυος: gen. after
ἐπαινέω.
ἔξωθεν: external, outside.
παράρτημα, τό (3b): amulet.
κακόν, τό (2b): trouble.
καταγιγνώσκω: I charge
x (gen.) with y (acc.).
ἄνοια, ἡ (1b): stupidity.
πρόδηλος, -ον: self-
evident, obvious.
25 εὖ φρονέω: I am in my
senses.
ἀντειπ- = aor. stem of
ἀντιλέγω: I deny.
μὴ οὐχί: tr. 'that it was
...' (double neg. after a
verb with neg. meaning).
Ἀντίγονος, ὁ (2a):
Antigonos.
ἡσθ- = aor. stem of ἥδομαι.
ἐρώτησις, ἡ (3e): answer.
πάλαι: for ages.
ἀμελέομαι: I am disregarded
(with πάλαι tr. imperf.
'he had been being ...').
ἀξιόω: I reckon, expect.
Εὐκράτης, ὁ (3d): Eukrates
(lit. 'Easy Winner').
παραγγέλλω: I order.
λάχανον, τό (2b): vegetable.
σιτέομαι: I eat.
ὑφαιρέω (+ gen.): I grad-
ually take away part of.
τόνος, ὁ (2a): tension.
30 ὑπομειδιάω: I smile gent-
ly/surreptitiously.

Τυχιάδης, ὁ (3d): Tykhiades
(lit. 'Lucky').
ἄπιστος, -ον: unbelievable.
δοκεῖ: its subject is
τὸ ... γίγνεσθαι.
ὠφέλεια, ἡ (1b): help
(ὠφελείας is subject of
τὸ ... γίγνεσθαι).
ἔμοιγε: tr. 'Yes, it does
...'.
κόρυζα, ἡ (1c): snot,
mucus.
ῥίς (ῥιν-), ἡ (3a): nose.
ὡς (+ inf.): (sc. 'so
much') as.
πιστεύω: I believe.
τὰ ἔξω: external applica-
tions.
μηδέν: in no way.
κοινωνέω (+ dat.): I have
to do with.
ἔνδοθεν: internal.
35 ἐπεγείρω: I stir up, cause.
τοῖς ... ἐπεγείρουσι =
n. dat. pl. pres. part.
ῥημάτιον, τό (2b): little
phrase.
γοητεία, ἡ (1b): magic.
ἐνεργέω: I am effective.
ἴασις, ἡ (3e): cure.
ἐπιπέμπω: I send down.
προσαρτάομαι: I am attached,
fastened on.
Νέμειος, -α, -ον: Nemean
(one of Herakles' labours
was to subdue this invulnera-
able lion and bring its skin
back to Eurystheus).

λέοντος τὸ δέρμα ἐνδήσῃ τις ἑκκαίδεκα ὅλας μυγαλᾶς· ἐγὼ
γοῦν αὐτὸν λέοντα εἶδον πολλάκις χωλεύοντα ὑπ' ἀλγηδόνων
ἐν ὁλοκλήρῳ τῷ αὐτοῦ δέρματι.   **40**

22. A JOURNEY FROM THIS WORLD TO THE NEXT

(Φιλοψευδεῖς ἢ Ἀπιστῶν - *Philopseudeis 25*)

Eukrates claimed to have seen Hades through a crack which opened
up in the earth. His account was substantiated by Pyrrhias, one of
his slaves. But Tykhiades was still thoroughly unconvinced. He was
still laughing at this story when Kleodemos broke in with the story
of his own death and resurrection.

Kleodemos was ill with a fever and had been left to get some
sleep. He was conducted down to Hades by a young man. Everything
there was as expected. Pluto discovered that Kleodemos had been
brought down by mistake; so he was sent back and woke from his fever
with the prediction, soon fulfilled, of a neighbour's death.

25. ὁ Κλεόδημος δέ, Οὐ καινά, εἶπεν, οὐδὲ ἄλλοις ἀόρατα
ταῦτα εἶδες, ἐπεὶ καὶ αὐτὸς οὐ πρὸ πολλοῦ νοσήσας τοιόνδε
τι ἐθεασάμην· ἐπεσκόπει δέ με καὶ ἐθεράπευεν Ἀντίγονος
οὗτος. ἑβδόμη μὲν ἦν ἡμέρα, ὁ δὲ πυρετὸς οἷος καῦσος σφοδ-
ρότατος. ἅπαντες δή με ἀπολιπόντες ἐπ' ἐρημίας ἐπικλεισ-   5
άμενοι τὰς θύρας ἔξω περιέμενον· οὕτως γὰρ αὐτὸς ἐκέλευσας,
ὦ Ἀντίγονε, εἴ πως δυνηθείην εἰς ὕπνον τραπέσθαι. τότε
οὖν ἐφίσταταί μοι νεανίας ἐγρηγορότι πάγκαλος λευκὸν ἱμ-
άτιον περιβεβλημένος, εἶτα ἀναστήσας ἄγει διά τινος χάσ-
ματος εἰς τὸν Ἅιδην, ὡς αὐτίκα ἐγνώρισα τὸν Τάνταλον ἰδὼν   10
καὶ τὸν Τιτυὸν καὶ τὸν Σίσυφον. καὶ τὰ μὲν ἄλλα τί ἄν
ὑμῖν λέγοιμι; ἐπεὶ δὲ κατὰ τὸ δικαστήριον ἐγενόμην - παρῆν
δὲ καὶ ὁ Αἰακὸς καὶ ὁ Χάρων καὶ αἱ Μοῖραι καὶ αἱ Ἐρινύες -
ὁ μέν τις ὥσπερ βασιλεύς, ὁ Πλούτων μοῖ δοκεῖ, καθῆστο
ἐπιλεγόμενος τῶν τεθνηξομένων τὰ ὀνόματα, οὓς ἤδη ὑπερ-   15
ημέρους τῆς ζωῆς συνέβαινεν εἶναι. ὁ δὲ νεανίσκος ἐμὲ
φέρων παρέστησεν αὐτῷ· ὁ δὲ Πλούτων ἠγανάκτησέν τε καὶ
πρὸς τὸν ἀγαγόντα με, Οὔπω πεπλήρωται, φησίν, τὸ νῆμα

ἐνδέω: I bind x (acc.)
onto y (ἐς + acc.).
ἐκκαιδέκα: sixteen.
μυγαλῆ, ἡ (1a): field-
mouse.
αὐτὸν λέοντα: tr. 'an
actual lion ...'.
χωλεύω: I limp.
ἀλγηδών (ἀλγηδον-), ὁ (3a):
pain.

40 ὁλόκληρος, -ον: perfect,
complete.

22. A JOURNEY FROM THIS
WORLD TO THE NEXT

καινός, -ή, -όν: novel,
strange.
ἀόρατος, -ον: unseen.
ἄλλοις: tr. 'by ...' (dat.
of agent after a passive
idea).
οὐ πρὸ πολλοῦ: not long ago.
ἐπισκοπέω: I visit.
ἕβδομος, -η, -ον: seventh.
πυρετός, ὁ (2a): fever.
οἷος: tr. like'.
καῦσος, ὁ (2a): bilious
endemic fever.
σφοδρός, -ά, -όν: violent.
5 ἐπί (+ gen.): in.
ἐρημία, ἡ (1b): solitude.
ἐπικλείομαι: I close.
εἶ: sc. 'to see ...'.
δυνηθ- = aor. stem of
δύναμαι.
τραπ- = aor. stem of
τρέπομαι.
ἐγρηγορώς: awake (perf.
part. of ἐγείρομαι).
παγκαλός, -ή, -όν: com-
pletely beautiful.
λευκός, -ή, -όν: white.
περιβεβλημένος = perf. part.
of περιβάλλομαι: I put
round myself.
ἀναστησ- = aor. stem of
ἀνίστημι: I raise.
χάσμα, τό (3b): chasm.
10 Ἅιδης, ὁ (1d): Hades.
γνωρίζω: I recognise.
Τάνταλος, ὁ (2a): Tantalos.

Τιτυός, ὁ (2a): Tityos.
Σίσυφος, ὁ (2a): Sisyphos
(These three were considered
part and parcel of the tradi-
tional Hades scene).
Χάρων, ὁ (3a): Kharon (ferry-
man of the dead).
Μοῖραι, αἱ (1b): the three
goddesses of fate (see intro.
note to piece 5 above).
Ἐρινύς, ἡ (3h): Fury (god-
dess who avenges blood-
guilt).
ὁ μέν τις: tr. 'someone or
other'.
Πλούτων, ὁ (3a): Pluto
(king of the dead).
15 ἐπιλέγομαι: I read.
τῶν τεθνηξομένων: of those
about to die (fut. perf.
part. of θνῄσκω).
ὑπερήμερος, -ον (+ gen.):
past the term of.
ζωή, ἡ (1a): life.
συμβαίνει: x (acc.) happens
to y (inf.) (lit. 'it hap-
pens that ...').
νεανίσκος: presumably Hermes,
as conductor of the dead to
Hades.
παρίστημι (παραστησ-): I set
x (acc.) beside y (dat.).
πληρόω: I fulfil.
νῆμα, τό (3b): (thread of)
destiny (spun by the Fates:
see intro. to 5 above).

αὐτῷ, ὥστε ἀπίτω. σὺ δὲ δὴ τὸν χαλκέα Δημύλον ἄγε· ὑπὲρ
γὰρ τὸν ἄτρακτον βιοῖ. κἀγὼ ἄσμενος ἀναδραμὼν αὐτὸς μὲν   20
ἤδη ἀπύρετος ἦν, ἀπήγγελλον δὲ ἅπασιν ὡς τεθνήξεται Δημ-
ύλος· ἐν γειτόνων δὲ ἡμῖν ᾤκει νοσῶν τι καὶ αὐτός, ὡς
ἀπηγγέλλετο. καὶ μετὰ μικρὸν ἠκούομεν οἰμωγῆς ὀδυρομένων
ἐπ' αὐτῷ.

23. THE SORCERER'S APPRENTICE

(Φιλοψευδεῖς ἢ Ἀπιστῶν - Philopseudeis 33-36)

Kleodemos' story and the ghost story from Eukrates which followed
it met the same response from Tykhiades. But on the arrival of the
Pythagorean philosopher Arignotos, Tykhiades' scorn was held back by
his respect, until he realized that Arignotos was as bad as the others.
This was confirmed by a tale, in which Arignotos described an exorcism
he had performed. Eukrates followed this with a tale of magic.

(a) Eukrates told of a journey he made in his youth to Egypt. There
he met a wise man from Memphis.

33.   ἐγὼ δὲ ὑμῖν καὶ ἄλλο διηγήσομαι αὐτὸς παθών, οὐ παρ'
ἄλλου ἀκούσας· τάχα γὰρ ἂν καὶ σύ, ὦ Τυχιάδη, ἀκούων
προσβιβασθείης πρὸς τὴν ἀλήθειαν τῆς διηγήσεως. Ὁπότε
γὰρ ἐν Αἰγύπτῳ διῆγον ἔτι νέος ὤν, ὑπὸ τοῦ πατρὸς ἐπὶ
παιδείας προφάσει ἀποσταλείς, ἐπεθύμησα εἰς Κοπτὸν ἀνα-   5
πλεύσας ἐκεῖθεν ἐπὶ τὸν Μέμνονα ἐλθὼν ἀκοῦσαι τὸ θαυμασ-
τὸν ἐκεῖνο ἠχοῦντα πρὸς ἀνίσχοντα τὸν ἥλιον ...

34.   κατὰ δὲ τὸν ἀνάπλουν ἔτυχεν ἡμῖν συμπλέως Μεμφίτης
ἀνὴρ τῶν ἱερογραμματέων, θαυμάσιος τὴν σοφίαν καὶ τὴν
παιδείαν πᾶσαν εἰδὼς τὴν Αἰγύπτιον· ἐλέγετο δὲ τρία καὶ   10
εἴκοσιν ἔτη ἐν τοῖς ἀδύτοις ὑπόγειος ᾠκηκέναι μαγεύειν
παιδευόμενος ὑπὸ τῆς Ἴσιδος.

(b) Arignotos recognized this man as his teacher, Pankrates, and
described him. Eukrates related Pankrates' power over crocodiles
and how he himself came to befriend Pankrates.

ἀπίτω = 3rd s. imper. of
ἀπέρχομαι.
χαλκεύς, ὁ (3g): bronze-
smith.
20 Δημύλος, ὁ (2a): Demylos.
βιόω: I live.
ἄσμενος, -η, -ον: joyfully.
ἀναδραμ- = aor. stem of
ἀνατρέχω: I run back.
ἀπύρετος, -ον: without
fever.
τεθνήξεται = fut. perf.
of θνήσκω: I die.
ἐν γειτόνων (+ dat.): next
door to.
μετὰ μικρὸν: sc. χρόνον.
οἰμωγή, ἡ (1a): lamenta-
tion.
ὀδύρομαι (ἐπί + dat.): I
mourn over.

23. THE SORCERER'S
APPRENTICE

τάχα: perhaps.
προβιβάζομαι (πρός + acc.):
I am led on to (sc. 'ac-
cept').
διήγησις, ἡ (3e): narrative.
Αἴγυπτος, ἡ (2a): Egypt.
διάγω: I spend time,
live.
5 πρόφασις, ἡ (3e): purpose.
ἀποσταλ- = aor. pass. stem
of ἀποστέλλω: I send off.
Κοπτός, ὁ (2a): Koptos
(a place on the right
bank of the Nile).
ἀναπλέω (ἀναπλευσ-): I sail
upstream.
Μέμνων (Μεμνον-), ὁ (3a): the
statue of Memnon at Thebes
(between the time of Claudius
and Septimius Severus one of
the two colossal statues re-
presenting Amenophis III came
to be considered as the
statue of Memnon, son of
Aurora and Tithonus, killed
at Troy. Broken in two, the
statue gave out a sound: a
cult arose, but the statue's

noise stopped when
Severus restored it!).
ἠχοῦντα: sc. 'the statue
:...'.
θαυμαστός, -ή, -όν: amazing.
ἐκεῖνο: tr. 'that famous'
ἠχέω: I make x (acc.)
sound.
πρός (+ acc.): about,
at.
ἀνίσχω: I rise.
ἀνάπλους, ὁ (2a contr.):
journey upstream.
συμπλέω (+ dat.): I sail
with.
Μεμφίτης, ὁ (1d): from
Memphis.
ἱερογραμματεύς, ὁ (3g):
sacred scribe.
10 Αἰγύπτιος, -ον: Egyptian.
ἐλέγετο: subject is
'he' (i.e. Μεμφίτης
ἀνήρ).
ἄδυτον, τό (2a): shrine.
ὑπόγειος, -ον: under-
ground.
ᾠκηκέναι = perf. inf. of
οἰκέω.
μαγεύω: I use magic.
παιδεύω: I train.
Ἶσις (Ἰσιδ-), ἡ (3e):
Isis (national diety of
Egypt).

98

Παγκράτην λέγεις, ἔφη ὁ Ἀρίγνωτος, ἐμὸν διδάσκαλον,
ἄνδρα ἱερόν, ἐξυρημένον ἀεί, νοήμονα, οὐ καθαρῶς ἑλλην-
ίζοντα, ἐπιμήκη, σιμόν, προχειλῆ, ὑπόλεπτον τὰ σκέλη.   15
Αὐτόν, ἦ δ' ὅς, ἐκεῖνον τὸν Παγκράτην· καὶ τὰ μὲν
πρῶτα ἠγνόουν ὅστις ἦν, ἐπεὶ δὲ ἑώρων αὐτὸν εἴ ποτε
ὁρμίσαιμεν τὸ πλοῖον ἄλλα τε πολλὰ τεράστια ἐργαζόμενον,
καὶ δὴ καὶ ἐπὶ κροκοδείλων ὀχούμενον καὶ συννέοντα τοῖς
θηρίοις, τὰ δὲ ὑποπτήσσοντα καὶ σαίνοντα ταῖς οὐραῖς,   20
ἔγνων ἱερόν τινα ἄνθρωπον ὄντα, καὶ κατὰ μικρὸν φιλο-
φρονούμενος ἔλαθον ἑταῖρος αὐτῷ καὶ συνήθης γενόμενος,
ὥστε πάντων ἐκοινώνει μοι τῶν ἀπορρήτων.

(c) Pankrates had persuaded Eukrates to go with him alone. Eukrates
described how Pankrates' magical powers made servants out of inanimate
objects.

καὶ τέλος πείθει με τοὺς μὲν οἰκέτας πάντας ἐν τῇ
Μέμφιδι καταλιπεῖν, αὐτὸν δὲ μόνον ἀκολουθεῖν μετ' αὐτοῦ,   25
μὴ γὰρ ἀπορήσειν ἡμᾶς τῶν διακονησομένων· καὶ τὸ μετὰ
35.τοῦτο οὕτω διήγομεν. ἐπειδὴ δὲ ἔλθοιμεν εἴς τι καταγώγιον,
λαβὼν ἂν ἢ τὸν μοχλὸν τῆς θύρας ἢ τὸ κόρηθρον ἢ καὶ τὸ
ὕπερον περιβαλὼν ἱματίοις ἐπειπών τινα ἐπῳδὴν ἐποίει βαδ-
ίζειν, τοῖς ἄλλοις ἅπασιν ἄνθρωπον εἶναι δοκοῦντα. τὸ δὲ   30
ἀπελθὸν ὕδωρ τε ἐπήντλει καὶ ὠψώνει καὶ ἐσκεύαζεν καὶ
πάντα δεξιῶς ὑπηρέτει καὶ διηκονεῖτο ἡμῖν· εἶτα ἐπειδὴ
ἅλις ἔχοι τῆς διακονίας, αὖθις κόρηθρον τὸ κόρηθρον ἢ
ὕπερον τὸ ὕπερον ἄλλην ἐπῳδὴν ἐπειπὼν ἐποίει ἄν.

(d) Eukrates, despite the magician's veto, managed to learn this
trick. He ordered his animated servant to bring water, but could
not stop the process, once started, and flooded the house. Pankrates
returned, undid the damage and then vanished.

τοῦτο ἐγὼ πάνυ ἐσπουδακὼς οὐκ εἶχον ὅπως ἐκμάθοιμι   35
παρ' αὐτοῦ· ἐβάσκαινε γάρ, καίτοι πρὸς τὰ ἄλλα προχειρ-

Παγκράτης, ὁ (1d):
Pankrates (lit. 'All-
powerful').
'Αρίγνωτος, ὁ (2a):
Arignotos (the Pythagor-
ean philosopher: see intro.
to 18a above; his name
means 'Easily known' or
'Infamous').
ἱερός, -ά, -όν: holy.
ἐξυρημένος: shaved (perf.
pass. part. of ξυρέω).
νοήμων, -ον: intelligent.
καθαρῶς: correctly.
ἑλληνίζω: I speak Greek.
15 ἐπιμήκης, -ες: tallish.
σιμός, -ή, -όν: snub-nosed.
προχειλής, -ές: thick-
lipped.
ὑπόλεπτος, -ον: a bit
thin.
αὐτὸν ... παγκράτην: tr.
'P. to the life!'.
εἴ ποτε: i.e. whenever.
ὁρμίζω: I anchor.
τεράστιος, -ον: prodi-
gious, marvellous.
ἄλλα τε ... καὶ δὴ καί:
especially.
κροκόδειλος, ὁ (2a):
crocodile.
ὀχέομαι: I ride.
συννέω (+ dat.): I swim
with.
20 τὰ δέ: i.e. the beasts.
ὑποπτήσσω: I crouch be-
fore (sc. 'him').
σαίνω: I fawn upon.
κατὰ μικρόν: bit by bit.
φιλοφρονέομαι: I treat
kindly.
συνήθης, -ες: intimate.
κοινωνέω: I share x (gen.)
with y (dat.).
ἀπόρρητα, τά (2b): secrets,
mysteries.
25 Μέμφις (Μεμφι-), ἡ (3a):
Memphis.
καταλιπ- = aor. stem of
καταλείπω.
αὐτὸν: tr. 'myself'.
μὴ γὰρ ...: sc. 'he said
that ...'.

ἀπορέω (+ gen.): I lack.
τὸ μετὰ τοῦτο: tr. 'in the
period which followed'.
διάγω: I live.
ἐπειδή (+ opt.): whenever
(past sequence indefinite).
καταγώγιον, τό (2b): inn.
μοχλός, ὁ (2a): bar.
κόρηθρον, τό (2b): broom.
*ὕπερον, τό (2b): pestle.
περιβάλλω (περιβαλ-): I put
x (dat.) on y (acc.).
ἱμάτια, τά (2b): clothes.
ἐπειπ- = aor. stem of
ἐπιλέγω: I pronounce.
τοῖς ἄλλοις ἅπασιν: to all
the others (presumably any-
one apart from Eukrates and
his master).
δοκοῦντα: m. as if agreeing
with μοχλὸν (or attracted
to ἄνθρωπον).
τὸ δέ: i.e. the inanimate
object.
ἐπαντλέω: I pour.
ὀψωνέω: I do the shopping.
σκευάζω: I prepare food.
πάντα: in every way.
δεξιῶς: in the right way.
ὑπηρετέω: I serve.
ἅλις (+ gen.): enough of.
διακονία, ἡ (1b): service.
35 ἐσπουδακώς: sc. 'although'.
οὐκ εἶχον ὅπως (+ opt.):
there was no way for me to
...
βασκαίνω: I am jealous.
καίτοι (+ part.): although.
πρός (+ acc.): with regard
to.
πρόχειρος, -ον: forthcoming.

ὅτατος ὤν. μιᾷ δέ ποτε ἡμέρᾳ λαθὼν ἐπήκουσα τῆς ἐπῳδῆς -
ἦν δὲ τρισύλλαβος - σχεδὸν ἐν σκοτεινῷ ὑποστάς. καὶ ὁ
μὲν ᾤχετο εἰς τὴν ἀγορὰν ἐντειλάμενος τῷ ὑπέρῳ ἃ δεῖ
36. ποιεῖν. ἐγὼ δὲ εἰς τὴν ὑστεραίαν ἐκείνου τι κατὰ τὴν   40
ἀγορὰν πραγματευομένου λαβὼν τὸ ὕπερον σχηματίσας ὁμοίως
ἐπειπὼν τὰς συλλαβάς, ἐκέλευσα ὑδροφορεῖν. ἐπεὶ δὲ ἐμ-
πλησάμενον τὸν ἀμφορέα ἐκόμισεν, Πέπαυσο, ἔφην, καὶ
μηκέτι ὑδροφόρει, ἀλλ᾽ ἴσθι αὖθις ὕπερον· τὸ δὲ οὐκέτι
μοι πείθεσθαι ἤθελεν, ἀλλ᾽ ὑδροφόρει ἀεί, ἄχρι δὴ ἐνέ-   45
πλησεν ἡμῖν ὕδατος τὴν οἰκίαν ἐπαντλοῦν. ἐγὼ δὲ ἀμηχανῶν
τῷ πράγματι - ἐδεδίειν γὰρ μὴ ὁ Παγκράτης ἐπανελθὼν
ἀγανακτήσῃ, ὅπερ καὶ ἐγένετο - ἀξίνην λαβὼν διακόπτω τὸ
ὕπερον εἰς δύο μέρη· τὰ δέ, ἑκάτερον τὸ μέρος, ἀμφορέας
λαβόντα ὑδροφόρει καὶ ἀνθ᾽ ἑνὸς δύο μοι ἐγεγένηντο οἱ   50
διάκονοι. ἐν τούτῳ καὶ ὁ Παγκράτης ἐφίσταται καὶ συνεὶς
τὸ γενόμενον ἐκεῖνα μὲν αὖθις ἐποίησεν ξύλα, ὥσπερ ἦν
πρὸ τῆς ἐπῳδῆς, αὐτὸς δὲ ἀπολιπών με λαθὼν οὐκ οἶδ᾽ ὅποι
ἀφανὴς ᾤχετο ἀπιών.

(e) *Deinomakhos asked if Eukrates still knew the spell. Eukrates'
answer was: 'Yes, but only the first half'* !

      Νῦν οὖν, ἔφη ὁ Δεινόμαχος, οἶσθα κἂν ἐκεῖνο, ἄνθρωπον   55
ποιεῖν ἐκ τοῦ ὑπέρου;
      Νὴ Δί᾽, ἦ δ᾽ ὅς, ἐξ ἡμισείας γε· οὐκέτι γὰρ εἰς τὸ
ἀρχαῖον οἷόν τέ μοι ἀπάγειν αὐτό, ἢν ἅπαξ γένηται ὑδρο-
φόρος, ἀλλὰ δεήσει ἡμῖν ἐπικλυσθῆναι τὴν οἰκίαν ἐπαντλου-
μένην.   60

*Tykhiades could hold himself back no longer, but his outburst
was taken calmly by Eukrates, who began to tell a story about oracles.
Tykhiades explains to his friend how he walked out, leaving Eukrates
in mid-story. But ever since, he's been seeing ghosts everywhere,
so thoroughly infected has he been by these lies. But after all,
the antidote is at hand - truth and common sense.*

λαθών: secretly, unknown
to him.
ἐπακούω (+ gen.): I
overhear.
τρισύλλαβος, -ον: tri-
syllabic.
σκοτεινός, -ή, -όν: dark.
ἐν σκοτεινῷ: sc. 'place'.
ὑποστα- = aor. stem of
ὑφίσταμαι: I conceal
myself.
ἐντέλλομαι (ἐντειλ-) (+ dat.):
I give orders.
40 εἰς τὴν ὑστεραίαν: on the
next day.
πραγματεύομαι: I do busi-
ness (governing τι).
σχηματίζω: I dress.
ὁμοίως: alike, in the
same way.
ἐπειπ- = aor. stem of
ἐπιλέγω: I pronounce.
συλλαβή, ἡ (1a): syllable.
45 ὑδροφορέω: I bring
water (for tense see on
διηγούμεθα 7.28 above).
ἐμπλησ- = aor. stem of
ἐμπίμπλαμαι: I fill (my
own).
κομίζω: I bring.
πέπαυσο: stop! (perf.
imper. of παύομαι).
ἴσθι = imper. of εἰμί.
ἀεί: tr. 'kept on'.
ἄχρι: until.
ἐνέπλησεν = aor. of
ἐμπίμπλημι: I fill x (acc.)
with y (gen.).
ἀμηχανέω (+ dat.): I am at a
loss about.
ἐδεδίειν = past of δείδια:
I am afraid.
ἀξίνη, ἡ (1a): axe.
διακόπτω: I cut.
τὰ δέ: i.e. the pieces.
50 ἐγεγένηντο = 3rd pl. pluperf.
of γίγνομαι.
διάκονος, ὁ (2a): servant.
ἐκεῖνα: i.e. the pestle-
halves.
ξύλον, τό (2b): wood.
ὅποι: to where.

ἀφανής, -ές: mysterious(ly).
55 κἄν: even.
ἐν ἡμισείας γε: tr. 'well,
half of it' (ἡμισύς, -εῖα,
-ύ: half).
ἀρχαῖος, -α, -ον: old. τὸ
ἀρχαῖον: sc. 'form'.
οἷόν τέ μοι: tr. 'I can'.
ἅπαξ: once.
ὑδροφόρος, ὁ (2a): water-
carrier.
ἐπικλύζω: I flood,
deluge.
ἐπαντλέω: I pour over.

102

Exercises

(Note: these exercises should be attempted only after the reading of all the passages has been completed.)

1. Translate these groups of words, all of which have appeared in the text. You will be helped by referring first to *Reading Greek: Grammar etc.*, pp.327-334, 'Language Survey 13: Vocabulary building' for general principles. You may need to use a lexicon for the basic stem.

ἀρτάομαι, ἀναρτάομαι, ἐξαρτάομαι, παράρτημα, προσαρτάομαι

φύομαι, συμφύομαι, ἐκφύομαι, ἀναφύομαι

σπάομαι, ἀνασπάω, κατασπάω, ἀποσπάω, διασπάομαι,

ἀνάσπαστος, -ον

πέτομαι, περιπέτομαι, ὑπερπέτομαι, ἀφίπταμαι, πτέρον, τό,

πτῆσις, ἡ, ὑπότπερος, -ον

ἀνατέμνω, ἀποτέμνω, ἐντέμνω

σκώπτω, ἀποσκώπτω, σκῶμμα, τό

γένειον, τό, ἀγένειος, -ον

καιρός, ὁ, ἄκαιρος, -ον

ἐράω, ἔραμαι, ἔρως, ὁ, ἐρωτικός, -ή, -όν, ἐπέραστος, -ον

μεταβαίνω, μεταδιδάσκω, μετακαθέζομαι, μέτοικος, ὁ

παιδεύω, παῖς, ὁ, παιδεία, ἡ, εὐπαιδία, ἡ

διακονέομαι, διάκονος, ὁ, διακονία, ἡ

χαλκός, ὁ, χαλκοῦς, -ῆ, -οῦν, χαλεύς, ὁ, πολύχαλκος, -ον

σφαγή, ἡ, ἀποσφάζω, προαποσφάζω

ῥέω, ἀπορρέω, ῥεῦμα, τό

κύπτω, κατακύπτω, συμπαρακύπτω, προκύπτω

βιάζομαι, βία, ἡ, βίαιος, -α, -ον

πνέω, ἀποπνέω, ἐπιπνέω, πνεῦμα, τό

γέλως, ὁ, γελοῖος, -α, -ον, γελάσιμος, -η, -ον

ἀποβλέπω, ἀναβλέπω, περιβλεπτός, -ον.

2. Lucian uses the genitive absolute extensively. Translate again the following examples, in each case beginning the gen. abs. clause with a different conjunction in English (e.g. if, when etc.). For a simple explanation of the construction see *Reading Greek: Grammar etc.* §139 p.147.

a) νὴ Δία, τράγου ἴσως τινὸς μοιχεύσαντος αἶγα.   3(a)

b) ἁπάντων δὲ ἤδη σχεδὸν αὐτῷ διῳκημένων ἀπῄειμεν
   ἐς τὸ συμπόσιον.   4(d)

c) ... πῶς ἐγένετο νὺξ ἐν οὐρανῷ τοῦ ἡλίου παρόντος
   ἀεὶ καὶ συνευωχουμένου.   4(e)

d) ... ἐπειδὰν ἐμπεσών ἄνεμος διασείσῃ τὰς ἀμπέλους
   ἐκείνας, τότε πρὸς ἡμᾶς καταπίπτει ἡ χάλαζα
   διαρραγέντων τῶν βοτρύων.   9(d)

e) ... καὶ ἐνείκησεν ὁ Ὅμηρος Ὀδυσσέως
   συναγορεύοντος.   11(c)

f) ἡμέρας δὲ ὑποφαινούσης ἔλεγον οἱ σκοποὶ καθορᾶν
   τὴν ναῦν πολὺ ἀπέχουσαν.   12(b)

3. Translate and compare the underlined phrases.
   You may be helped by *Reading Greek: Grammar etc.*, p.323,
   'Language Survey II: Use of the Cases' s.v. Accusative.

a) ἀλλ' εἰ καὶ <u>τι</u> ἥμαρτον, ὦ Ζεῦ, σύγγωθί μοι.   2(a)

b) εὐδαίμων, ὦ Σώκρατες, ἄνθρωπος εἶ <u>τά γε τοιαῦτα</u>. 6(c)

c) ἦν δὲ καὶ ἰχθῦς ἐν αὐτῷ πολλοὺς ἰδεῖν, οἴνῳ
   μάλιστα καὶ <u>τὴν χρόαν καὶ τὴν γεῦσιν</u> προσ-
   εοικότας.   7(b)

d) <u>τὸ μὲν γὰρ ἀπὸ τῆς γῆς</u>, ὁ στέλεχος αὐτὸς
   εὐερνὴς καὶ παχύς, <u>τὸ δὲ ἄνω</u> γυναῖκες ἦσαν.   7(c)

e) περὶ δὲ τὴν πόλιν ῥεῖ ποταμὸς μύρου τοῦ καλλίσ-
   του, <u>τὸ πλάτος</u> πηχέων ἑκατὸν βασιλικῶν, βάθος
   δὲ πέντε.   10(a)

4. Lucian uses καὶ very frequently simply to emphasise
   what follows it. Translate these examples and compare
   them. (*Reading Greek: Grammar etc.*, p.293 gives a use-

ful conspectus of the uses of καί.)

a) ἦ διότι μὴ πώγωνα μηδὲ πολιὰς ἔφυσας, διὰ ταῦτα
<u>καὶ</u> βρέφος ἀξιοῖς νομίζεσθαι γέρων καὶ πανοῦργος
ὤν;   2(a)

b) τί δαί σε μέγα ἠδίκησα ὁ γέρων ὡς φὴς ἐγώ,
διότι με <u>καὶ</u> πεδῆσαι διανοῇ;   2(a)

c) τίνα <u>καὶ</u> φὴς σου μητέρα;   3(b)

d) τίνες ποτ' εἰσιν ἢ τί δύναται αὐτῶν ἑκατέρα;
πότερον τὰ ἴσα ταῖς Μοίραις ἢ τι <u>καὶ</u> ὑπὲρ
ἐκείνας.   5(c)

5. Translate these sentences and compare the uses made of
the Dative case. For a conspectus of Dative usages
see *Reading Greek: Grammar etc.*, pp.325-6, 'Language
Survey II: Use of the Cases' s.v. Dative.

a) εὖ γε ὁ γενναῖος, ὡς ὅλος <u>ἡμῖν</u> κυοφορεῖ.   1(b)

b) Ὦ παῖ, μήτηρ μέν <u>σοι</u>, ἔφη, ἐγώ εἰμί.   3(b)

c) ἀνεμνήσθην ἐκείνων τῶν Ὁμήρου ἐπῶν, ἐν οἷς
πεποίησαι <u>αὐτῷ</u> ἐν τῇ ἐκκλησίᾳ τῶν θεῶν
δημηγορῶν.   5(d)

d) ἀπὸ δὲ τῶν δακτύλων ἄκρων ἐξεφύοντο αὐταῖς οἱ
κλάδοι καὶ μεστοὶ ἦσαν βοτρύων.   7(c)

e) Περὶ δὲ Θεσμοπόλιδος, ἔφη, τοῦτο μόνον εἰπεῖν
ἔχω, ὅτι ἀντὶ Στωϊκοῦ ἤδη Κυνικὸς ἡμῖν
γεγένηται.   19(c)

APPENDIX: AN INTRODUCTION TO LUCIAN

1 Lucian's life and works

The corpus of Lucian's works consists of 86 items, of which
six are certainly spurious. Of the remaining 80, almost
certainly another four are suppositious works, and debate
continues over a further eight.[1] The 68 undisputedly gen-
uine works cover a wide range, both in form and theme. But
is it difficult to categorise them according to these crit-
eria. A division by form groups works together which have
nothing in common except the fact that they are dialogues.
A division by theme does not take account of either the
diversity of material in any particular work, or the
setting or viewpoint adopted. Nevertheless, a few point-
ers can be given.

There is a group of works which adheres fairly clearly to
the accepted rhetorical genres (see below, p.108 and p.114),
among them the declamations *Tyrannicida* and *Abdicatus*,
and the paradoxical encomium *Muscae Encomium*. In another
group, Lucian introduces a display of his work with short
prefaces, designed to gain the audience's attention and
goodwill: examples are *Bacchus* and *Zeuxis*. A fair pro-
portion of the works is in dialogue form (e.g. *Hesiodus*
and *Timon*) or has a dialogue frame, containing a reported
dialogue (e.g. *Nigrinus* and *Philopseudeis*). But the mat-
erial is very diverse, ranging from vignette (e.g. *Dialogi
Marini*) to philosophical argument (e.g. *Hermotimus*). Much
use is made of moralistic material (e.g. concerning wealth
and poverty in *Gallus*), often presented through fantasy
(it is the cock who speaks to Micyllus of the drawbacks
of wealth in *Gallus*). The delights of storytelling are
indulged in many places (e.g. *Toxaris*, where they are built
around the theme of friendship). Literary satire is another
penchant, whether it is direct (as in *How to Write History*),
or veiled (as in the fictional narrative of *Verae Historiae*).
Several works contain attacks, whether personal (e.g. against
the fraudulent prophet in *Alexander*) or literary (these may
also be personal: e.g. *Rhetorum Praeceptor*), or general
(e.g. against human credulity in *De Sacrificiis*). There
are, equally, many defences, whether of Lucian's works
and ways of writing (e.g. *Bis Accusatus*), or of his grasp
of correct Greek usage (e.g. *Pseudologista*). The range
and flavour of his works is not, even so, exhausted, as a
quick glance at the amusing scenes in *Dialogi Deorum* will
show. The very broad character of his works may be said,
with qualification, to be humorous, with a tendency to-
wards satire.

We have from Lucian's pen one of the rare examples of
ancient autobiography (*Somnium*: see pieces 15-17 in the

selection), but we still know very little about his life.
The biographical notice in the 'Suda' (a Byzantine diction-
ary) is virtually worthless and he is mentioned by only one
contemporary (Galen, see below). What little we do know
has to be gleaned from his own writings, a hazardous pro-
cedure at the best of times with the most straightforward
authors, and with Lucian a veritable minefield. Lucian's
constantly ironical tone makes it difficult to see pre-
cisely where he is to be taken at face value and where
not.[2] Nevertheless the following data can be given with
reasonable certainty.

He was born in Samosata, a city in Commagene, in the Roman
province of Syria (Hist. Conscr. 24, where he objects to an
ignorant historian who has placed his fatherland in
Mesopotamia). The date of his birth may have been c. A.D.
125, but of this there can be no certainty.[3] The people
of his home town are the audience of Somnium, a work in
which we learn that at least his mother's side of the
family was of artisan class (ch.2: his uncle was a sculptor
of herms), but that he pursued the path of fame and fortune,
education in rhetoric (Somn. 18). References to him as an
orator and an advocate (Piscator 9, 25) seem to imply that
he used this skill both for rhetorical displays and for
law-court work. He travelled widely in pursuit of success,
not only in Ionia and Greece, but also to Italy and Gaul
(Bis Accusatus 27). In Gaul he held a public position
in rhetoric and was numbered among the highly paid sophists
(Apologia pro Mercede Conductis 15). But in c.164 he was
back in his home town displaying his wealth (Somn. 18). In
fact, several works can be dated to this period which must
have been composed in Asia Minor. In Imagines and Pro
Imaginibus Lucian praises Panthea, the mistress of Lucius
Verus, co-emperor with Marcus Aurelius, who arrived at
Antioch, probably in 163, ostensibly to conduct the
Parthian campaign. It has been plausibly suggested that
De Saltatione, a work written in praise of pantomine, was
also written here by Lucian about this time to ease his
way into the circle of Verus, who was an avid fan of
dancing.[4] It is unlikely that the attempt succeeded:
Lucian probably travelled from Antioch to Samosata, then
north through Cappadocia, taking his family. On the way,
he made a diversion to visit the new cult of Glykon,
founded by Alexander at Abounoteichos (Alexander 55,56).
Lucian's own attempts to expose the fraudulent oracle
(ibid. 53-4) seem to have been characteristic of the real
man. They are corroborated by Galen's account of a con-
temporary of the same name who exposed the ignorance of a
philosopher by passing on to him a nonsensical treatise
he had composed and ascribed to Heracleitus.[5] Lucian was
back in Greece in 165, attending the Olympic games at
which the Cynic philosopher Peregrinus Proteus immolated
himself (De Morte Peregrini 35). It was in Greece too that

he composed his satire of the historians of the Parthian War (*Quomodo Historia Conscribenda sit* 14 and 17), probably in 166 after the Roman victory, but before the triumph in October.[6] Perhaps he was still trying to get into Lucius Verus' circle. At some stage he travelled to Macedonia (*Zeuxis* 7,8; *Scytha* 9) and to Philippopolis in Thrace (*Fugitivi* 25) in pursuit of patronage, but it is not possible to prove where these journeys fit.

At about the age of forty, Lucian appears to have relinquished the well-worn themes of standard rhetoric ('accusations against tyrants and eulogies of the powerful', *Bis Accusatus* 32) for a new genre, the comic dialogue, invented by himself. At the same period[7] he wrote *Hermotimus*, a refutation of dogmatic philosophy and a recommendation to philosophers to 'live the common life' (*Herm.* 84). These two concerns, coming together at one time in his life, characterise much of Lucian's writing. He often satirised the aridity of sophistic rhetoric (e.g. *J.Tr.* 32) and for him the only good philosopher was one who concerned himself with ethics (*Demonax* - written certainly after 171[8]), while the secret of the universe itself is, in Teiresias' words to Menippus in the Underworld that 'the life of the man in the street is the best and most sensible' (*Nec.* 21).

Late in his life, Lucian gained a position in the administration of Egypt (*Apologia pro Mercede Conductis* 12) probably that of *archistator*, which involved the organisation of recording of lawsuits.[9] That he lived on into the reign of Commodus (i.e. after 180) is clear from the reference to 'divine Marcus' in *Alexander* 48. Whether or not he gave up his sophistic career on his appointment in Egypt, it seems very unlikely that Lucian had not regularly practised as a declaimer for most of his life.[10]

2. Lucian's world and his attitude to it

Lucian was a Syrian (*Piscator* 19, *Bis Accusatus* 27 etc.), living in the Roman world in which he was perfectly at home - witness his flattery of Lucius Verus (*Imagines* 22) and his use of 'us' to describe the Empire (*Quomodo Historia Conscribenda sit* 5: 'If even another war starts (Celts versus Getae or Indians versus Bactrians, for no one would dare to attack us ...).[1] He also knew some Latin (*Pro Lapsu inter Salutandum* 13). Yet he made his fortune in Gaul, practising declamation in Greek. Such paradoxes were commonplace in his age, which is generally known as that of the 'Second Sophistic' - a title lifted from Philostratus, who wrote biographies of many of the sophists of Lucian's day in the 220's (Philostratus, *V.S.* 481).[2] The hermaphrodite sophist Favorinus of Arles, for

instance, 'used to say ... that there were in the story of
his life these three paradoxes: though he was a Gaul he led
the life of a Hellene; a eunuch, he had been tried for
adultery; he had quarrelled with an Emperor and was still
alive.' (Philostratus, *V.S.* 489)

What was a sophist? The term 'appears to be contained with-
in the term *rhetor* and to apply particularly to those tea-
chers of rhetoric (rhetors) whose attainment was of such a
level as to give public *performances*'.[3] It must be noted,
however, that philosophers and others could be classified
as sophists too (Favorinus of Arles is given both titles
by Philostratus, loc.cit.). Lucian qualifies for the title
from two angles. He constantly refers to his audience as
'listeners' (e.g. *Prometheus es in Verbis* 7) and he uses
the term of his public appointment in Gaul (*Apologia pro
Mercede Conductis* 15). But he does not appear in Philostra-
tus' collection of lives. Probably he did not, like most of
those included, have famous teachers. Certainly he was not
from a wealthy and distinguished family (unlike Herodes
Atticus: compare Philostratus, *V.S.*546ff. with *Somnium* 1-2,
piece 15 in the selection). His post in Egypt could not begin
to compare with Herodes Atticus' consulship at Rome (A.D.
143). He could not, despite his show to the citizens of
Samosata (*Somn.* 18), have equalled the munificence of men
like Herodes (who gave the Athenians a stadium and a theatre
(*V.S.* 550 and 551), among many other benefactions). And if
Philostratus could look slightingly upon Hadrian of Tyre for
quipping as he took up the chair of rhetoric at Athens 'once
again letters have come from Phoenicia' (*V.S.* 586-7), the
works of a man 'serious only in raising laughs' (as the
fourth-century writer Eunapius called Lucian, *V.S.* 454) would
certainly not have had the slightest appeal.

The sophists practised the type of rhetoric known as epideic-
tic (show oratory). The vast majority of their themes were
historical, taken from the period of Greek autonomy. Marcus
of Byzantium's oratory, for example, is characterised for
Philostratus by 'his speech of the Spartan advising the Lace-
daemonians not to receive the men who had returned from
Sphacteria without their weapons' (*V.S.* 528). The event in
question had occurred in 425 B.C. In Lucian's works too
there are examples of declamation set in the distant past.
In the speeches in *Phalaris* Lucian argues the case, from two
viewpoints, of accepting as a dedication at Delphi the famous
bronze bull in which the Sicilian tyrant had been said to have
tortured and killed many men. But it is precisely that sort
of thing which Lucian says he gave up (*Bis Acc.* 32), and
often parodies (e.g. *Iuppiter Tragoedus* 32 where Zeus vetoes
the idea of bringing down the Painted Stoa to end an argu-
ment which will prove there is no providence, because the
destruction of its pictures of Marathon, Miltiades and
Kynageirus will deprive the rhetors of their favourite themes).

He could be ruthless in his portrayal of a sophist who had
made his name the easy way (the *Rhetorum Praeceptor* was
probably aimed at Julius Pollux, writer of the *Onomastikon*.
See *Rh. Pr.* 24).[4]

In the treatment of the themes, there was great emphasis on
the technique of variation. Philostratus tells a reveal-
ing story about the visit of Alexander Peloplaton ('Clay-
Plato') to Athens. A theme for extempore oration was pro-
posed to him: 'the speaker endeavours to recall the
Scythians to their earlier nomadic life, since they are
losing their health by dwelling in cities' (the Scythians
were a favourite topic of Lucian's too: see e.g. *Anacharsis*).
During this declamation, Herodes Atticus, who had arranged
to be there, but was late, turned up. Alexander asked
whether he should continue the Scythian speech, and it was
agreed that he should. But in continuing, he gave a remark-
able display of his powers. 'For', says Philostratus, 'the
ideas which he had treated so brilliantly before Herodes'
arrival he recast now that he was here, but with such dif-
ferent words and rhythms that those who were listening to
them for a second time did not think that he was repeating
himself.' The cliché 'when it is stagnant, even water goes
bad', for example, became in Herodes' presence 'even those
waters are sweeter that keep on the move' (*V.S.* 571-3).
No doubt Lucian too practised this sort of skill at some time
during his life. But in his extant works it seems clear
that like any good entertainer, he would often tell the
same jokes, but not in the same way to the same audience
(compare, for instance, the different uses of the theme of
Fate in *Iuppiter Confutatus* 1-4 (piece 5 in this selection)
and *Deorum Concilium* 13, where Momus is the critic of empty
names like Heimarmene and Tykne).[5]

There was archaism in language as well as in theme. The
sophists attempted to write in the Attic Greek of the fifth
and fourth centuries B.C. Compilations like Pollux'
Onomastikon were intended as aids to this end. But moder-
ation in Atticism was recommended ('bad taste in Atticizing
is truly barbarous', says Philostratus, *V.S.* 503; and in
Athenaeus' *Deiphosophistae* 3.97d-98f a Cynic ridicules
Ulpian of Tyre and Pompeianus of Philadelphia for their
hyperatticist absurdities).[6] Lucian was a moderate Atticist,
merciless to sophists who revelled in the use of obsolete
words or common words in an unusual sense. His *Lexiphanes*
was possibly aimed against Ulpian and Pompeianus. In this
work the unlucky victim of Lucian's barbs first treats
us to an unintelligible reworking of Plato's *Symposium*
('I counter-Symposium the son of Ariston' is how Lexiphanes
describes his new work, *Lex.* 1), and then is treated with
an emetic by the doctor Sopolis. But Lucian was not en-
tirely consistent in his criticism. In *Somnium* 16 (piece

17 in this selection) Lucian uses ἀφιπτάμενος though he
condemns ἴπτατο in *Lex.* 25.[7] If anyone had pointed out
the inconsistency, though, it is probable that Lucian would
have gone to great lengths to justify himself, as he did
on several other occasions when he appeared to have been in-
consistent or to have made a mistake. *Apologia pro Mercede
Conductis*, written when he had taken up his post in Egypt,
explains the consistency of his earlier work (*De Mercede
Conductis*: piece 19) with his present action. *Pseudologista*
is a scurrilous attack on someone who laughed at a dubious
usage; *Pro Lapsu inter Salutandum* is an attempt to make up
by a show of ingenious learning for the use of the wrong
greeting to a patron.

Archaism was visible even in historical writing. World
history had become largely history of Rome, while treat-
ment of Greek history tended to be confined to the class-
ical age (including Alexander), neglecting the present.[8]
Contemporary history in Greek mostly meant biographies of
emperors or monographs on particular wars, like Statilius
Crito's *Getica* or Arrian's *Parthica*.[9] Arrian had a part-
icular penchant for modelling his works on those of Xeno-
phon (e.g. *Anabasis*, to recall Xenophon's work of the same
name).[10] The writers satirised by Lucian in *How to Write
History* (piece 20) were all writing monographs on Lucius
Verus' Parthian campaign (A.D. 161-165). Many of them
were indulging in archaism of a ridiculous kind and de-
gree, such as the imitator of Thucydides who began his
account with the first sentence of his model, with only
the names changed (*Hist. Conscr.* 15). The witless his-
torian then imported the plague from Thucydides wholesale,
but for the Pelasgikon and the long walls (ibid.). Lucian
left the recital knowing perfectly well what he would say
even after his departure (ibid.). This is not a critique
of the use of classical models, but of plagiarism. Lucian's
Attic language is not the only archaic thing about his own
works. Some of his dialogues would be hard to date from
their settings (e.g. *Piscator*, where it is classical Athens,
cf. 15-16) and often contemporary institutions, described
in Attic language, nestle side by side with long-obsolete
classical terms (e.g. *Navigium* 24 where distributions of
money are Roman, though the term 'distribution' is class-
ical Attic, but they are made to citizens and metics - the
latter a classification not used since the 3rd century
B.C.).[11]

The relation between history and the sophists is not dif-
ficult to see. Much less clear is the status of the novel,
that popular genre full of parted lovers and exciting ad-
ventures, of which Longus' *Daphnis and Chloe* is a second-
century example.[12] Another tradition, the traveller's
tale, of which Ktesias' *Indica* (Photius, *Bibliotheca* cod.

72) and Iambulus' visit to the Islands of the Sun (Diodorus
Siculus 2.55-60) were examples, certainly earned the con-
tempt of Lucian's contemporary, the Roman writer Aulus
Gellius. He came across some old books for sale in a book-
shop in Brundisium, bought them for a song, and found they
contained tales of marvels such as the Indian tribe with
feathers like birds who live off the smell of flowers
(Noctes Atticae IX. iv. 1-5; 10). Gellius was bored by
them (ibid. 11-12), but he did not reject marvels them-
selves, going on to quote from a more respectable author
(the elder Pliny) some tales of sex-changes and herma-
phrodites (ibid. 14-16).[13] It seems to have been merely
a matter of whose protestations of veracity he was pre-
pared to believe. This seems to indicate that such pro-
ductions differed from the novel proper in claiming to be
based on fact and in receiving the credence of many of
their audience. But already before Lucian's time it seems
that the historical traveller's tale had been assimilated
into the novel. Photius in his account of Antonius Diogenes'
Wonders beyond Thule (Bibliotheca cod. 166) claims that this
work was the 'fount and root' of Lucian's A True History
(pieces 7-14 in this selection; Photius, ibid. 111b), which
is ostensibly a parody of the historical genre (V.H. I,
3 for Ktesias and Iambulus; II. 31 for Herodotus, whom
Lucian spots in the Isles of the Damned being punished for
lying - he thanks his lucky stars he knows he has been hon-
est!), but typically embraces Homer also (V.H. I. 3: the
whole business started with Odysseus' lies to the Phaeacians
in Odyssey IX-XII). Yet Antonius Diogenes' work was not
like Ktesias, Iambulus or Herodotus. Photius reports that
in a letter to Faustinus he admits to writing 'unbelievable
falsehoods' (ibid. 111a). The author himself therefore does
not claim veracity for the tales. Such a claim is made by
a letter from one Balagros (presumably at the start of Book
I), who relates that the twenty-four books which follow are
a transcription of ancient tablets discovered by Alexander
after the capture of Tyre (ibis. 111a). Photius also men-
tions that Antonius Diogenes prefaces each book with a list
of ancient sources for his material 'so that his unbeliev-
able tales should not appear to lack evidence' (ibid. 111a).
So already in Antonius Diogenes (whose date is not known,
though he is earlier than Lucian) pretence has taken the
place of direct historical presentation and substantiation by
reference to 'trustworthy sources' is already part of the
pretence. Thus Lucian's parody is not as destructive as
it seems. He merely presents unmasked fiction (pseudos)
instead of masked, and leaves the spotting of 'trustworthy
sources' (which are only sources of fun) to the audience,
rather than giving them straight (V.H. I. 2). He adds
further fun by deliberately ignoring the distinction bet-
ween fictional and historical writing (hence the references
to Ktesias and Iambulus and the claim that Homer is the

source of the genre to which *V.H.* belongs) and by pretending
that the philosophers claim to be speaking of tangible re-
alities when they speak theoretically or figuratively (*V.H.*
I. 2 for philosophers; in II. 17 Plato was the only absen-
tee from the Isles of the Blest - he was living in a city
he had invented and was using his 'Constitution' (*Republic*)
and 'Laws').[14]

Philostratus (*V.S.* 489) includes among the sophists
Favorinus, whom he styles 'philosopher'. As this example
shows, there was a tendency for the distinctions between
orators and philosophers to become blurred: 'they had many
tasks in common, and both were obliged to use the spoken
and written word.'[15] *Demonax* 14 (piece 18(a) in the sel-
ection) presents a good example of the obverse, a sophist
claiming philosophical interests: his mention of the
famous schools and their founders is purely for effect -
the bubble is effectively burst by the real philosopher,
Demonax.[16] Still, philosophy under its traditional head-
ings was alive in the second century. Marcus Aurelius was
himself a Stoic, and endowed four chairs of philosophy at
Athens in A.D. 176 - for Academics, Peripatetics, Stoics
and Epicureans. Pythagoreanism, Scepticism and particu-
larly Cycicism, though not recognised by such official
appointments, also continued their existence.[17]

Generally Lucian's treatment of the philosophers and the
sects concentrates on the stock attributes of each, which
every schoolboy would know: Socrates' irony (*Dialogi
Mortuorum* 20.4: piece 6(c)), Plato's flattery of Sicilian
tyrants (*D. Mort.* 20.5: piece 6(b)), the Sceptics' in-
ability to come to a firm conclusion (*Icaromenippus* 25:
piece 4(c)), the Epicureans' pursuit of pleasure (*V.H.*
II. 18: they are popular on the Isles of the Blest because
they are 'jolly convivial chaps'), the Stoic's love of
syllogisms (e.g. the 'Horns', *Gallus* 11; Chrysippus' syl-
logisms, *Ic.* 24: piece 4(a)), Pythagoras' aversion to
eating beans (*Gall.* 5), the Cynic's tunic, stick and
pouch and his outspokenness (*Vitarum Auctio* 7-12),
Aristippus' perfume (*D. Mort.* 20.5: piece 6(b)).[18] He
is also keen on exposing the gap between a philosopher's
pretensions and his behaviour (e.g. *Convivium* 22, where
the uninvited Stoic Hetoimokles berates the host
Aristaenetus in a letter for inviting men like Zenothemis
and Diphilus, whom he could refute with one syllogism, and
not himself - not that he cares, of course! Cf. Lucian's
own defence in *Piscator* 31f. before the ancient philo-
sophers whom he put on sale in *Vit. Auct.*). Lucian seems
not to have had any time at all for dogmatic philosophy
(*Hermotimus* is a lengthy refutation of the whole idea,
written at the same period of his life as his defence of
comic dialogue, *Bis Acc.*: see *Herm.* 13 for his age). The
final piece of advice given by Lycinus (i.e. Lucian) to

Hermotimus, the relentless investigator of doctrines, is
'to live the life common to all' (*Herm.* 84) and Menippus,
perplexed by the contradictions of the philosophers (*Menippus sive Necyomantia* 4), is given a similar revelation when
he asks the blind seer Teiresias which is the best life
(*Nec.* 21: 'the life of the man in the street'). Lucian
in fact, when he wasn't joking about them, seems to have
regarded the ancient philosophers as 'lawgivers as to the
best style of life' who had produced standards by which
people could order their own lives properly (*Pisc.* 30).
The contemporaries he admired, Nigrinus the Platonist and
Demonax the Cynic, he valued for their ethical teaching and
their actual conduct (*Nigrinus* and *Demonax* passim).[19] For
Lucian philosophy was a matter of practical ethics; all
else was nonsense.[20]

The second-century followers of Plato, Zeno and Pythagoras
were generally more interested in the religious aspects
of philosophy, presenting their systems as a means of salvation.[21] At this time, too, Christianity was beginning to
spead more widely. Mystery cults, like that of Isis,
gained educated adherents. The healing cult of Asclepius
revived during this period,[22] and the orator Aelius Aristides
regularly treated his respiratory ailments by incubation
(sleeping the night in the temple) and following outlandish prescriptions which he claimed the god gave him in his
dreams. 'When the harbour waves were swollen by the south
wind and ships were in distress, I had to sail across to
the opposite side, eating honey and acorns from an oak
tree, and vomit ...' (*Aelius Aristides* 47.65 Keil).[23]
Lucian's attitude to religion appears to be similar to his
view of philosophy. He is a hater of frauds and a lover of
truth (*Pisc.* 20). Among the frauds he classified the Cynic
Peregrinus (praised by Aulus Gellius, *N.A.* 12.11) and
Alexander of Abunoteichos, against both of whom he claims
to have waged a personal campaign (in *De Morte Peregrini* 39
he tells credulous listeners that he saw a vulture flying
up to heaven from the pyre exclaiming 'I have left the
earth, I am going to Olympus'; in *Alexander* 55, on being
offered Alexander's hand to kiss, he hit it!). As with
philosophy, he is eclectic in his allies. In *Alexander*,
Epicureans get a good press for their opposition to the
prophet (*Alex.* 25) and the work ends with a eulogy of
Epicurus (*Alex.* 61). In general, Lucian mocks those gullible enough to substitute for sound rationality a superstitious credulity. So the Platonists, Stoics and Pythagoreans are, unlike the sensible Epicureans, treated as
friends by Alexander (*Alex.* 25). The butts of Philopseudeis
(selection nos. 21-3) are Kleodemos the Peripatetic, Deinomakhos the Stoic and Ion the Plationist (*Philops.* 6).[24]

But such strictures against irrationality do not betoken
atheism. Tykhiades (i.e. 'Man-in-the-street', the ordinary
person, like Lucian) denies that his rejection of the weasel-
tooth plus lion-skin cure for gout (*Philopseudeis* 7-8:
piece 21) means that he also rejects the gods and their
intervention in effecting cures: 'there's nothing to stop
such things being lies even though the gods exist. But I
both revere the gods and see their cures and the good they
do to the ill, setting them on their feet by means of drugs
and medicine' (*Philops.* 10). There is no reason to think
this could not have been Lucian's view. He certainly seems
to step lightly where Asclepius and Isis are concerned -
their cults may have been supported by many in the audience[25]
who were prepared to laugh heartily at Lucian's mythological
joking (e.g. *Dialogi Deorum*: pieces 1-3, or *Juppiter Confuta-
tus*: piece 5, or *Icaromenippus*: piece 4), which was sanctioned
by the authority of Old Comedy (e.g. Aristophanes, *Birds*
1494f.). His attitude to the Christians, whom he mentions as
victims of Peregrinus' avarice (*Peregr.* 11-13), is in line
with his usual attitudes. He notes, among other things,
their belief in personal immortality which leads them to
treat death lightly, even to the extent of giving themselves
up to it willingly, their rejection of the Greek gods and
worship of Christ, and their shared possessions (*Peregr.* 13).
The main objection seems to be that 'they have no firm
grounds for believing such things' (ibid.), but besides this
there is the fact that for Greeks the gods were most import-
ant for what they could do while you were alive.

3. Lucian's method of composition, and his debts

Lucian was trained as a *rhetor*. This training fell into
two stages, the first with a teacher of *progymnasmata* or
'preliminary exercises' (like those of Hermogenes, Aphthonius
and Theon),[1] the second with a practising sophist (cf.
Scopelian's attendance at the school of Nicetes of Smyrna,
see Philostratus, *V.S.* 516), where the curriculum centred
on *meletai* or 'declamations' ('practice exercises').[2] The
progymnasmata taught the pupil how to dress up and vary a
theme. It might for example be treated by an extended com-
parison (*synkrisis*) or by working proof and disproof of the
same subject (*kataskeue* and *anaskeue*), or enlivened by
simile or description (*ekphrasis*).[3] The *meletai* extended
the use of these techniques to full speeches on themes like
those of Marcus of Byzantium (see above, p.108).

The effect of this training on Lucian is clear.[4] Note the
fondness he shows for presenting the two sides of a case
(often actually in a court, e.g. *Piscator* 24ff. and *Bis
Acc.* 13ff.). His use of *ekphrasis* is particularly notable
(he often describes ancient works of art, like Apelles'
'Calumny' in *De Calumnia* 5). He often uses extended similes

(life of men is like bubbles produced in a fountain, *Charon sive Contemplantes* 19). *Somnium* contains a *synkrisis*, in the comparison between sculpture and education (*Somn.* 6-14: pieces 16(b) and 17(a)). Above all, perhaps, he reworks themes such as 'the false philosopher' in myriad ways. It may be a passing reference (e.g. *D. Mort.* 20.5: piece 6(b)) or be extended to cover a whole dialogue (e.g. *Convivium*, where the 'philosophers' show up the contrast between what they profess and what they practise *in extenso*: see above p.112, or something in between (e.g. Parrhesiades' defence of *Vit. Auct. in Pisc.* 31-37).[5] His purely sophistic works have been mentioned above (p.108), but include also examples of judicial *meletai* (*Tyrannicida* and *Abdicatus*: the first being a claim to the reward for killing a tyrant, by a man who has, he argues, caused the tyrant's suicide by his killing of the tyrant's son; the second a plea by a dis-owned son who studied medicine, saved his father's life and was taken back, then was disowned again when he refused to cure his stepmother of insanity).[6]

Another aspect of Lucian's method of composition is the use of classical models and the reuse of material from the ancient writers either by recasting ('transposition') or quotation or allusion. General use of a classical model may be seen in *Demonax* (piece 18), which is in the form of Xenophon's *Memorabilia* (reminiscences of Socrates).[7] Reuse of material by transposition is most obvious in *V.H.* II, 35 (piece 14(a)), where *Odyssey* V-XXIV (and a bit more) are reduced to a few lines.[8] Quotation contributes to the lit-erary *ambiance*, giving opportunities to the writer to demon-strate his learning. Lucian uses it for this purpose usually when he is defending himself (e.g. *Pro Lapsu* 1) but generally he limits quotation to well known tags (often at or near the beginning of works) because he is aiming at entertaining the audience by placing them in a new and unexpected context (e.g. *Somn.* 5: piece 16(a), where he introduces his own dream by quoting Homer, *Il.* 2. 56-7).[9] Allusion can test the audience's knowledge (and therefore enhance the impression of the writer's superiority), and again Lucian normally uses it to create ironical humour (e.g. *V.H.* II. 20 (piece 11), where scholarly questions about Homer are put to Homer himself or *Icaromenippus* (piece 4(d)), where Menippus con-firms a detail in Homer and remarks that he must have known because he too had seen Heaven!).[10]

Lucian makes no secret of his methods, arguing (as Parrhes-iades) in *Piscator* 6 to the angry philosophers, 'Anyway, where else but from you did I get the material I've gather-ed like a bee, which I use in my public displays?' And (as in *V.H.* I. 3) the recognition of the allusions is an integral part of the audience's enjoyment: 'The audience applaud and recognise each of them the allusion, its source and how I have collected it, in their view envying me for my

flower-picking, but in fact envying you and your meadow'
(ibid.) The writer's art lies in 'understanding how to
select and intertwine and fit together (sc. the various
coloured flowers), so that they aren't out of tune with
one another' (ibid.)

Small wonder with such a doctrine that Lucian was concerned
to make it clear that originality without grace and beauty
was worth nothing (Prometheus es in Verbis 3),[11] nor that
even his most original creation, comic dialogue, was delib-
erately set by its creator within the context of its class-
ical sources.[12] In Bis Accusatus 'the Syrian' is haled
into court by Rhetoric (his wife, for desertion) and
Dialogue (for hybris). Dialogue's complaint (Bis Acc. 33)
is that Lucian 'took away my tragic and sober mask from
me, and put on me a comic, satyr-like and almost ridiculous
one. Then he brought and shut in with me Jest and Iambic
and Cynicism and Eupolis and Aristophanes ... and finally
he even dug up Menippus, one of the old Cynics with a re-
pution for barking and biting and brought him in to me as
well; a really frightened dog he is too, since he hides his
bite inasmuch as he used to laugh as he snapped ...'
Essentially the same point is made by the angry philosophers
in Pisc. 25-6. Lucian sees his novelty as a mixture of
existing elements, in particular, Platonic dialogue, Old
Comedy and the diatribes of the Cynic writer of the third
century B.C., Menippus of Gadara.

How much Lucian took from each is a matter of debate, but
easier to answer for Plato and Old Comedy. As well as the
dialogue form, the language in Lucian's works is redolent
of Plato.[13] Fantasy situations and solutions to problems,
like the journey of Icaromenippus, based in outline on
Aristophanes' Peace, are rife in Old Comedy.[14] Menippus
is more difficult, since only some of the titles of his
works survive, among them a Nekyia (descent to Hades:
Diogenes Laertius VI. 101) and the sale of Diogenes, (ibid.
29-30) which may have given Lucian the idea for Menippus or
The Seeking of Prophecy from the Underworld (Menippus sive
Necyomantia) and the Philosophers for Sale (Vit. Auct.).
Strabo (XVI. 2. 29) notes that he purveys serious messages
through laughter (giving him the epithet σπουδαιογέλοιος).
He wrote in a mixture of prose and verse (Probus on Virgil,
Eclogues VI, 31) and was imitated by M. Terentius Varro
in his Saturae Menippeae (Cicero, Ac. Post. I.2.8; Aulus
Gellius N.A. II. xviii, cf. Quinitilian, Inst. Or. X.1.95)
as well as in the Apocolocyntosis attributed to Seneca.[15]
Lucian may have taken from him the idea of a first person
narrative in which a sceptical observer visits Hades or
Heaven and uses his journey as a vehicle for satirical ob-
servations on human life (mocking its transience: Marcus
Aurelius 6.47).[16] What he did not do, was copy Menippus
(or anyone else) word for word. He condemns plagiarism as

a ludicrous activity (*Hist. Conscr.* 15: see p.110 above) and in speaking of his own originality in mixing comedy and dialogue (*Prom. Es* 7) says 'As for the charge of theft (the god (i.e. Prometheus) has to face that as well, you know), come off it! That's one thing you can't accuse my works of. Who would I have stolen from for a start? Unless, of course, there's some other composer of 'pine-benders' and 'goat-stags' who's slipped my eye.'[17]

4. *Lucian's reputation and influence*

Lucian's reputation in the period following his death was not high among the historians of the sophists. Philostratus omitted him from his work, and Eunapius' comment was des-igned to sting (see p.108 above). Yet his works were pre-served in large numbers,[1] and authors like Aelian, Alciphron, Julian and Aristaenatus, writing soon after his era, seem to have borrowed from them.[2] The Christian writers Lac-tantius (d.325) and Isidore of Pelusium mentioned him for his satire of the pagan gods.[3] One work (*De Calumnia*) was even paraphrased in Syriac in the 6th century.[4]

He emerges from the obscurity of the 'dark-ages' in Byzantium in the scholia of Basilios, archbishop of Adada in Pisidium (fl.870) and Arethas, archbishop of Caesarea (fl. 907). the views of his Byzantine readers could be severe. One wrote, on the passage on Christ and the Christians in *Peregrinus* (see above pp.114) 'What is this drivel, you accursed man, against Christ the saviour?' The entry in the Suda dictionary tells us that Lucian died by being torn apart by wild dogs and comments that 'he was adequately punished in this world, and in the next he will inherit eternal fire with Satan'.[5] The patriarch Photius (d.891) was less inclined to condemn him utterly and so presumably were those who produced imitations.[6] In the twelfth century and beyond, these became more common; Lucian was now a regular school author.[7]

When Greek began to be taught regularly again in Italy, from 1396 onwards, Lucian was one of the first authors to be studied, translated and imitated. The first translations into Latin were done before 1403 (*Timon* by Bertholdus and an anonymous *Charon sive Contemplantes*).[8] From then on-wards, Lucian was a firm part of the western literary tradition. In the 15th century he was regarded as 'a most learned man', 'a philosopher very well known among the Greeks in his own day', 'weighty in speech' and displaying 'propriety in diction', 'wise', 'vehement and biting in criticising vice', a writer who combines 'jollity with severity'.[9] As a consequence of the overstressing of Lucian's moralism, most imitations used only the settings

(*Dialogues of the Gods* or *of the Dead*), but filled them
with humanistic moralising.[10] The best imitator in this
period was Leon Battista Alberti, whose *Intercoenales*
('Supper pieces') contained one dialogue, *Virtus Dea*,
which the author seems to have sent into the world under
Lucian's name: it was still being printed as Lucian's in
the 16th century.[11]

Northern Europeans soon acquired a taste for the Syrian
satirist. The great Dutch humanist Erasmus of Rotterdam
translated many of his works and produced in *Praise of
Folly* one of the finest offshoots of Lucian's influence.[12]
His friend Thomas More also translated Lucian and his
Utopia is in many respects a Lucianic work.[13] But during
the religious upheaval of the Reformation, the use of irony,
characteristic of Lucian and his best students, became
dangerous. Erasmus' use of Lucian was condemned by Luther
and the Catholic church alike.[14] Still, when Sir Thomas
Elyot wrote *The Boke named the Governour* in 1531 he recom-
mended for schoolboys the study of Lucian, if only 'quicke
and mery dialogues ... whiche be without ribaudry or to moche
skorning'.[15] All over Europe, writers of the Renaissance
read Lucian (possibly at school) and learned from him - in
France Rabelais, in Spain Cervantes, in Germany Ulrich von
Hutten, in England not only More, but later Ben Jonson.[16]

In the seventeenth and eighteenth centuries Lucian continued
to exercise a decisive influence. Vernacular translations,
the French version of Perrot D'Ablancourt (published 1654)[17]
and the English *Dryden's Lucian* (1711, 'by various hands')[18]
were important here. In the century between 1680 and 1780
there was an enormous industry producing *Dialogues of the
Dead*. Fontenelle's collection appeared in 1683, Fénelon's
in 1700 and Lord Lyttleton's in 1760.[19] But the chief ex-
ponent in this period of literary techniques learned from
Lucian was Henry Fielding, who owned nine editions of the
Syrian's works, mentioned him often in the *Covent Garden
Journal* and even proposed a translation of his works (alas,
never started).[20] 'A Journey from This World to the Next',
published in 1743 in the second book of the *Miscellanies*,
contains many Lucianic themes, but perhaps takes its start-
ing point from the report of a man who had died and lived
to tell the tale, in *Philopseudeis* 25 (piece 22 in this
selection).[21]

The nineteenth and twentieth century have thrown up a number
of literary and journalistic uses of Lucian's persona. For
instance, Walter Savage Landor's *Imaginary Conversations*
contains a dialogue between Lucian and the fanatical Christian
Timotheus,[22] and W.F.R. Hardie produced in 1922 a 'Lucianic
dialogue between Socrates in Hades and certain men of the
present day'.[23] But the period is chiefly notable for the

study of Lucian. The edition of Hemsterhuys and Reitz had appeared in Amsterdam in 1743, one in a fairly short line of seven since the *editio princeps* of 1496. The nineteenth century saw no fewer than four complete Greek texts published in Germany.[24] Perhaps the oddest line of twentieth-century influence began with a poem called 'Der Zauberlehrling' ('The Sorcerer's Apprentice') written by Goethe in 1797. A century later the French composer Paul Dukas was inspired by this to produce his symphonic poem 'L'apprenti sorcier'. In 1938, Walt Disney had the idea of producing a film with cartoon animations over this piece of music. He mentioned the matter to the well known conductor Leopold Stokowski, who agreed at once to do the music and urged Disney to expand the film to feature length. Hence 'Fantasia'. But Disney's original idea had been to give Mickey Mouse a much needed boost.[25] So it is that in 'Fantasia' Mickey Mouse plays the sorcerer's apprentice, who first saw the light in Lucian's *Philopseudeis* 33-36 (piece 23).

NOTES TO APPENDIX

1. Lucian's life and works

1. Macleod's *O.C.T.* vol.1 v-viii lists 80 genuine works and
   6 *spuria*. Of these 80, *De Saltatoribus* (Macleod no.75)
   is by Libanius and it is almost certain that *Cynicus, Long-
   aevi, Halcyon* and *Ocypus* (Macleod nos.76, 12, 72 and 74)
   are spurious. Debate still continues over *Soloecista,
   Lucius sive Asinus, Amores* and *Demosthenis Encomium* (Mac-
   leod nos.18, 39, 49 and 58) and a few others (*De Syria
   Dea, De Astrologia, Iudicium Vocalium* and *De Parasito*:
   Macleod nos.44, 48, 16 and 33). For recent views and bib-
   liography see G. Anderson, 'Studies in Lucian's Comic Fiction'
   (*Mnemosyne* Supplement 43, Leiden 1976) and J. Hall, *Lucian's
   Satire* (Arno Press, N.Y. 1981) *passim*.

2. I agree basically with B.P. Reardon, *Lucian, Selected Works*
   (Library of Liberal Arts, N.Y. 1965), p.vii: 'For all the
   research that may underlie recent judgements of him, one
   will not go very far wrong in taking him at his face value'.
   Hall devotes Chapter 1 to an examination of the evidence,
   which I have followed. J. Schwartz, *Biographie de Lucien
   de Samosate* (Brussels 1965), relies on an elaborate system
   of cross-references which cannot stand up to the clear-
   minded criticism of Hall (pp.56ff.). See also G. Anderson,
   'Lucian: Theme and Variation in the Second Sophistic'
   (*Mnemosyne* Supplement 41, Appendix I, Leiden 1976). The
   'Suda' article is translated by P. Turner in his introduc-
   tion to the Penguin translation, *Lucian: Satirical Sketches*
   (1961), p.7.

3. See Hall, pp.6-16. References in *Bis Acc.* 2 to events
   around 165 taken together with *Bis Acc.* 32 (Lucian aged 40)
   give 125 as the birthdate. But the references in *Bis Acc.*
   2 may not be to contemporary events. Lucian tends to appear
   in his dialogues under various pseudonyms: Parrhesiades in
   Piscator (ch.19), the Syrian logographos in *Bis Acc.* (ch.25),
   and possibly Tychiades in *Philopseudeis* (see Hall, pp.510-
   11 (n.59); but the others are literary defences and it is
   better to see this character as representative of common
   sense: see p.114). Most regularly he presents himself under
   the Hellenized form of Lucianus, Lykinos (e.g. in *Hermotimus,
   Navigium, Eunuchus, Imagines* etc.). In *V.H.* II.28 he is
   Λουκιανός in an epigram composed for him by Homer!

4. D.S. Robertson, 'The authenticity and date of the *De
   Saltatione*', *Essays and Studies presented to William
   Ridgeway* (Cambridge 1913), pp.180-6, and Hall, pp.21-3.

5. In a part of his commentary on Hippocrates' *Epidemics* which
   has survived only in Arabic. G. Strohmaier, 'Übersehenes
   zur Biographie Lukians', *Philologus* 120 (1976), pp.117-22.
   See Hall's discussion, pp.4-6. On Lucian's debunking activi-

ties, see M.D. Macleod, 'Lucian's activities as a MISALAZON', *Philologus* 1979, pp.326-8.

6. Hall, pp.28-9, citing J.F. Gilliam, 'The plague under Marcus Aurelius', *A.J.P.* 82 (1961), pp.228, 229 and n.16.

7. That is, if we accept that Lykinos = Lucian (see above, n.3), and that the age is not simply arbitrary.

8. Anderson, *Theme*, p.178 accepts Schwartz' date of not later than 177 (Biographie, pp.17-20), but the only positive criterion is the mention of Cethegus as ὑπατικός in *Dem.* 30: 171 was his consulship - Hall, pp.42-3.

9. But C.P. Jones, 'Two enemies of Lucian', *G.R.B.S.* 13 (1972), pp.486-7, thinks it may be ὑπομνηματογράφος and cites Philo, *In Flacc.* 131.

10. Jones (art. cit. n.9, p.485) thinks Lucian gave up his sophistic career, while G.W. Bowersock, *Greek Sophists in the Roman Empire* (Oxford 1969), p.114, denies that he had ever been a rhetorical performer! The evidence is against both assertions: see Hall, pp.17-18.

2. Lucian's world and his attitude to it

1. Hall, pp.250-1. But Lucian's 'anti-Roman tendencies' have been a popular theme with scholars, e.g. A. Peretti, *Luciano, Un Intellettuale Greco contro Roma* (Florence 1946).

2. For a general account of the sophists, see G.W. Bowersock, *Sophists. Approaches to the Second Sophistic*, edited by G.W. Bowersock (Pennsylvania 1974), contains discussions of Philostratus' reliability (C.P. Jones, pp.11-16) and the sophists as declaimers (G. Kennedy, pp.17-22), and two useful appendices: (I) is a selective bibliography of the second sophistic (G. Kennedy and M. Barnard), (II) is a guide to the sophists in Philostratus' *V.S.* (Bowersock and Jones). For a useful account of late Greek literature see K.J. Dover (and others) *Ancient Greek Literature* (Oxford 1980), a chapter entitled 'Greek literature after 50 B.C.' (E.L. Bowie).

3. E.L. Bowie, 'Greeks and their past in the Second Sophistic', *Past and Present* 46 (1970), p.5. Cf. Bowersock, *Sophists*, pp.12-14.

4. Hall, pp.273ff. for a discussion. She suggests (pp.277-8) that Lucian has added traits from other sophists, e.g. Scopelian and Hadrian, much as Aristophanes did with Socrates and the sophists in *Clouds*.

5. Anderson, *Theme*, sees Lucian's technique differently, as constant self-imitation with a very narrow set of themes. Hall, in her review of this and his *Studies* in *J.H.S.* 1980,

pp.229-32 regards most of Anderson's parallels as totally unrelated to one another. In my view, Anderson has not succeeded in showing that Lucian is a typical sophistic performer (not therefore 'a sophist's sophist' as he is dubbed by Anderson in *Y.C.S.* XXVII, 1982, pp.61-92), nor that Lucian's classical reading was severely limited ('Lucian's Classics: some short cuts to culture', *B.I.C.S.* 1976, pp.59-68). Limitation in quotation is not proof of limited reading, just a necessity in an entertainer: besides, it seems to me exceedingly unlikely that Lucian would lay himself as wide open as Anderson thinks to the charge of inconsistency - see his attack on the short-cut-taking rhetor in *Rh. Pr.* 9-26, and my remarks, p.109 above). But he has penetrated deeper than anyone else into Lucian's 'turn of mind' and investigated in a new and interesting way the manner in which one idea may spark off another, which ends up looking quite different.

6. Hall, pp.287ff. Cf. B. Baldwin, *Studies in Lucian* (Toronto 1973), pp.50-3.

7. Hall, p.358.

8. Bowie, pp.10-13.

9. Bowie, p.15.

10. Bowie, p.26.

11. J. Delz, *Lukians Kenntnis der Athenischen Antiquitäten* (Freiburg in der Schweiz 1950), p.156. διανομή in e.g. Plato, *Rep.* 535a: see *L.S.J.* s.v.

12. B.P. Reardon, 'The Second Sophistic and the novel' in Bowersock, *Approaches*, pp.23-9.

13. See also Hall, p.339.

14. See Hall, pp.342ff. for how little of *V.H.* can be traced back to Antonius Diogenes. Cf. Anderson, *Studies*, pp.1-7, who also urges against K. Reyhl's attempt to reconstruct Antonius' lost work from Lucian (*Antonios Diogenes, Untersuchungen zu den Roman-Fragmentender 'Wunder jenseits von Thule' und zu den 'Wahre Geschichten' des Lukian*, diss. Tübingen 1969). The question of whether Lucian himself wrote a standard novel depends on the vexed and complex question of *Lucius sive Asinus*, its authenticity, and its relation to the lost *Metamorphoses* of Lucius of Patrae. See B.E. Perry, *The Ancient Romances* (Berkeley, California, 1967), pp.211-82; Anderson *Studies*, pp.34-67; Hall, pp. 354ff.

15. Bowersock, *Sophists*, p.11.

16. J. Bompaire, *Lucien Écrivain* (Paris 1958), p.132, n.1, reports Fritzsche's view (edition of Lucian II.1, p.198) that this Sidonian sophist was Maximus of Tyre. But he was a Platonist philosopher (M. Caster, *Lucien et La*

Pensée Réligieuse de son Temps (Paris 1937), p.30) not a rhetorician. Possibly it was Hadrian of Tyre (Philostratus, *V.S.* 585).

17. Caster, p.11; Reardon, pp.xivff. On Lucian and Scepticism see Caster, pp.59ff.; Pythagoreanism, ibid. pp. 40ff.; Cynicism ibid. pp.65ff.

18. Hall, pp.165ff.

19. Hall, pp.173ff. Bowie, p.17, calls Demonax a Stoic, but J.L. Moles is correct in calling him a Cynic (*J.H.S.* 1983, p.113). He was, however, like many others, highly eclectic (see *Dem.* 62): Hall, pp.173-4.

20. There was a strong ethical bias in contemporary philosophy. Cf. e.g. Marcus Aurelius' list of ethical characteristics inherited from or taught him by others (A, α-ιζ', *O.C.T.*). It has been at times irrestistible for scholars to try to set Lucian in some sort of philosophical 'development': e.g. C. Gallavotti, *Luciano nella sua Evoluzione Artistica e Spirituale* (Lanciano 1932) and most disastrously J.J. Chapman, *Lucian, Plato and Greek Morals* (Boston and NY 1933). See Hall, pp.35-8 and 155ff. The 'conversion' to philosophy is based on misinterpretation of *Bis Acc.* 32.

21. Caster, p.11.

22. Bowersock, *Sophists*, p.69. See Apuleius, *Apol.* 55, for another educated adherent of Asclepius.

23. Bowersock, *Sophists*, p.70.

24. Hall, p.176.

25. Hall, p.212. See Caster, p.306 for Lucian's lack of antagonism to any mysteries but those of Glykon established by Alexander at Abunoteichos.

3. *Lucian's method of composition, and his debts*

1. *Hermogenes*, ed. H. Rabe (Leipzig 1913). Apthonius and Theon in Spengel, *Rhetorés Graeci*, vol.II.

2. Kennedy, 'The Sophists as Declaimers' in Bowersock, *Approaches*, pp.18-20. For a fuller treatment of rhetoric in this period see G. Kennedy, *The Art of Rhetoric in the Roman World* (Princeton 1972), especially ch.8, pp.553-613, 'The age of the sophists'.

3. Anderson, *Theme*, p.3.

4. Bompaire has exhaustively investigated the rhetorical basis of Lucian's works and is indispensable.

5. Thus far in general only with Anderson, *Theme*, pp.11-12, See n.5 of section 2 above for views of his work,

6. *Abdicatus* is a theme of Latin rhetoric also (Seneca the Elder, *Controversiae* 4. 5). Kennedy, 'The sophists as declaimers', Bowersock, *Approaches*, p.20.

7. Bompaire, pp.463-4.

8. See Bompaire, pp.670-1.

9. See n.5 of section 2 above for my view of Anderson's attempt to reduce the scope of Lucian's reading by a study of his quotations. The basic material is collected in F.W. Householder, *Literary Quotation and Allusion in Lucian* (NY 1941). See also G. Anderson, 'Patterns in Lucian's quotations', *B.I.C.S.* 25 (1978), pp.97-100.

10. On *Ic.* 27 *contra* Bompaire, p.591, who says 'On ne peut donner plus nettement que Homère a menti'. Lucian's irony does not involve εἰρωνεία (reversal of surface meaning), but is designed to raise a smile by using the shared Greek culture as a resonator.

11. In *Zeuxis* 1-2 also Lucian expresses dismay at being praised simply for novelty. Bompaire, p.139, says 'Lucien n'aurait déprécié l'originalité que pour mieux souligner la sienne', but it still seems to me that Lucian is keener to set him-self within the boundaries of the accepted literary conventions.

12. I cannot accept Anderson's view that Lucian did not invent the comic dialogue - Anderson calls it 'satiric dialogue' (Anderson, *Sophist* p.85). If so, his defences in *Pisc.* and *Bis Acc.* would have been wide open to critical derision and he could not have reported his audience's views in *Zeuxis* 1-2.

13. W.H. Shewring, 'Platonic influence in Lucian's clausulae', *Ph. Woch.* 1934, pp.814-6 for stylistic elements; W. Schmid, *Der Atticismus* (Stuttgart 1887-96; repr. Olms, Hildesheim 1964) vol.I for vocabulary and style. *Parasitus* is paro-died from Plato (but may not be genuine: see Hall pp.331ff.). See also Anderson, *Theme*, pp.6-7; Bompaire, *passim*.

14. E.g. Eupolis' *Demes* where dead politicians come back to life (as in *Piscator*). See Bompaire, *passim*; Anderson, *Theme*, p.6.

15. See Hall, pp.104-8.

16. Hall, pp.128-31.

17. Yet R. Helm, *Lukian und Menipp* (Leipzig and Berlin 1906), tried to reconstruct Menippus' works from Lucian by assuming that this was Lucian's approach. His arguments were met by Barbara M. McCarthy, 'Lucian and Menippus', *Y.C.S.* 4 (1934), pp.3-58. See Hall, pp.64-150 for the fullest recent dis-cussion.

4. Lucian's reputation and influence

1. See above, p.105 and n.1 of section 1 and the list of works.

2. For Aelian (2nd/3rd cent. A.D.), Alciphron (4th cent. A.D.) and Julian (d.363) (*Misopogon* and *Caesares*) see my unpublished Cambridge Ph.D. dissertation (1975) 'Lucian of Samosata in the Italian Quattrocento', p.64. Aristaenetus (date unknown) wrote letters from Lucian to Alciphron and vice-versa (I.22 and 5).

3. Lactantius, *Inst. Div.* I.9; Isidore, *Epistolae* IV, 55, p.1105c (*Migne, Patrologia Graeca*, vol. LXXVIII).

4. Macleod, no.15 and preface, p.ix.

5. For references see Sidwell, *Lucian*, p.65. Most recently C. Robinson, *Lucian*, London 1979, pp.68-81 and E. Mattioli, *Luciano e L'Umanesimo*, Naples 1980, pp.9-38. Scholion on *Peregrinus* 11 in Jacobitz' edition IV, p.247. For the *Suda* entry, see n.2 to section 1, above.

6. *Bibliotheca*, cod. 128. Philopatris has been thought to belong to the tenth cent.; but see now B. Baldwin in *Y.C.S.* XXVII, pp.321-44, who casts doubt on the confidence with which this dating has been made.

7. E.g. *Timarion*, which has come down with Lucian's works in one MS (Macleod, p.x), is based on *Necyomantia*; Theodorus Prodromus' *Sale of Poetic and Political Lives* is based on *Vitarum Auctio*. See Sidwell, *Lucian*, p.66; Robinson, pp. 76-8 for *Timarion* and pp.69-72 for *Prodromus*. Mattioli, pp.26-30 for *Timarion*, 23-6 for *Prodromus*.

8. Sidwell, *Lucian*, pp.13-16. Mattioli, pp.39-44. Generally, Robinson, pp.81ff.

9. References in Sidwell, *Lucian*, pp.75-84.

10. E.g. Maffeo Vegio's *Palinurus*, a dialogue of the dead, and Giorgio Valagussa's *Deorum Diologus*; Sidwell, *Lucian*, pp.222ff. and 243ff. Robinson, pp.84-6 for *Palinurus*; Mattioli, pp.148-52 for *Palinurus* and pp.157-9 for Valagussa.

11. Sidwell, *Lucian*, pp.173-81; Mattioli, pp.79ff; Robinson, pp.86-7.

12. For Erasmus' translations see C.F. Robinson 'Erasmus. Luciani dialogi' in *Opera omnia Desiderii Erasmi Roterodami recognita et adnotatione critica instructa notisque illustrata*, I.i, Amsterdam 1969, pp.362-627. *Praise of Folly* is available in the Penguin translation of Betty Radice (1971). For Lucian's influence on Erasmus in general see Robinson, pp.165-97.

13. For More's translations see C.R. Thompson, *The Translations of Lucian by Erasmus and St. Thomas More* (Ithaka, NY 1940), pp.23-8. For *Utopia* see Robinson, pp.131-3.

14. E.g. Luther said of Erasmus, 'Totus Lucianum spiras' (*De Servo Arbitrio* 127). Robinson, p.168, cites Luther's views of the *Colloquia Familiaria* of Erasmus: 'On my deathbed I shall forbid my son to read Erasmus' *Colloquies* ... He is much worse than Lucian, mocking all things under the guise of holiness'. On the other side, Alberto Pio da Carpi condemned his use of Lucian in the *Praise of Folly* and *Colloquia*. See N. Caccia, *Note su la Fortuna di Luciano nel Rinascimento* (Florence 1907), pp.37-8.

15. Book I, ch.x (ed. H.H.S. Croft (London 1880), pp.57-8).

16. For Rabelais see Robinson, pp.133-5. For Cervantes see A. Vives Coll, *Luciano de Samosata en Espana (1500-1700)* (Canary Islands 1959), pp.120-33. For Ulrich von Hutten see Robinson, pp.110-15 and Caccia, op. cit., n.14 above, pp.99ff. For Ben Jonson see Robinson, pp.103-9.

17. Robinson, pp.66-7.

18. Robinson, pp.67-8. Dryden wrote his *Life of Lucian* in 1696, which became the preface to the final work, published eleven years after his death. See Hardin Craig, 'Dryden's Lucian', *Classical Philology* 1921, pp.141-63.

19. Robinson, pp.144-63 for the genre and these writers.

20. See H. Knight Miller, *Essays on Fielding's Miscellanies: a commentary on vol.i* (Princeton 1961), ch.vi, and Robinson, pp.198-235.

21. See Robinson, pp.211-18 for discussion of Lucianic themes. This motif is not mentioned.

22. Volume II, pp.1-50, ed. T. Earle Welby (NY and London 1927-36; repr. 1969). It appeared first in 1846.

23. *Gaisford Greek Prose* (Oxford 1922). See the *Spectator* for Oct. 28th 1922.

24. Lehmann (Leipzig 1822-31); Jacobitz (Leipzig 1836-41 and 1851): the text still cited by most scholars; Bekker (Leipzig 1853); Dindorf (Leipzig 1858). In addition Fritzche published thirty works (Rostock 1860-82) and Sommerbrodt several (Berlin 1886-99). The twentieth century is poorer, with Nilen's truncated edition of nineteen works (Leipzig 1906-23), the Harmon-Kilburn-Macleod Loeb (1913 - 67), and Macleod's O.C.T. vols.I-III (1972, 1974, 1980), vol. IV forthcoming.

25. R. Schickel, *The Disney Version; the Life, Times, Art and Commerce of Walt Disney* (NY 1969), pp.238ff.

EDITIONS AND TRANSLATIONS: LIST OF WORKS: ABBREVIATIONS

Editions and translations for further study

The most convenient available text (with translation facing) is the Kilburn-Harmon-Macleod Loeb edition (8 vols., 1913-67). The best text is M.D. Macleod's Oxford Classical Text (vols. I-III, 1972, 1974 and 1980, vol. IV forthcoming). The only near-complete modern English translation (apart from Loeb) is that of H.W. and F.G. Fowler (Oxford 1905, four vols.). Useful also are Paul Turner's racy *Lucian: Satirical Sketches*, Penguin 1961 (now out of print) and B.P. Reardon's *Lucian: Selected Works*, Library of Liberal Arts (Bobbs-Merrill) (NY 1965). Bolchazy-Carducci have recently reissued C.S. Jerram's edition of *Vera Historia* (1879), the notes of which are useful.

List of Lucian's works, with short titles used in appendix

The numbering, the Greek titles and most of the Latin titles are from Macleod's O.C.T. Works 81-86 are omitted as certainly spurious, as are 12, 72 and 74-6. Other dubious works are marked *. See n.1 to section 1 above. A list of the usual English titles may be found in Robinson, pp.239-41. The English title is not given where it is the same as the Latin. An abbreviation occurs in brackets after the Latin title where it is used in the appendix.

1. Φάλαρις A   *Phalaris 1*
2. Φαλαρις B   *Phalaris 2*
3. ῾Ιππίας ἤ Βαλανεῖον   *Hippias*
4. Διόνυσος   *Bacchus*
5. ῾Ηρακλῆς   *Hercules*
6. Περὶ τοῦ ῾Ηλέκτρου ἤ τῶν Κύκνων   *Electrum*   Amber
7. Μυίας ῾Εγκώμιον   *Muscae Encomium*   The Fly
8. Νιγρίνου Φιλοσοφία   *Nigrinus (Nigr.)*
9. Δημώνακτος Βίος   *Demonax (Dem.)*   Life of Demonax
10. Περὶ τοῦ Οἴκου   *De Domo*   The Hall
11. Πατρίδος ῾Εγκώμιον   *Patriae Encomium*   In Praise of my Country
13. ῾Αληθῶν Διηγημάτων A   *Verae Historiae 1 (V.H.I)*   A True Story 1
14. ῾Αληθῶν Διηγημάτων B   *Verae Historiae 1 (V.H.II)*   A True Story 2
15. Περὶ τοῦ μὴ ῥᾳδίως πιστεύειν Διαβολῆ   *De Calumnia (Cal.)*   Slander
*16. Δίκη Συμφώνων   *Iudicium Vocalium*   The Consonants at Law
17. Συμπόσιον ἤ Λαπίθαι   *Convivium*   The Banquet
*18. Ψευδοσοφιστής ἤ Σολοικιστής   *Soloecista*   The Sham Sophist
19. Κατάπλους ἤ Τύραννος   *Cataplus*   The Downward Journey
20. Ζεὺς ἐλεγχόμενος   *Iuppiter Confutatus (J.Conf.)*   Zeus proved wrong

128

21. Ζεὐς Τραγῳδός *Iuppiter Tragoedus (J.Tr.)* Zeus Rants
22. "Ονειρος ἢ 'Αλεκτρυών *Gallus (Gall.)* The Cock
23. Προμηθεύς *Prometheus*
24. 'Ικαρομένιππος ἢ 'Υπερνέφελος *Icaromenippus (Ic.)* Menippos at Ikaros
25. Τίμων *Timon*
26. Χάρων ἢ 'Επισκοποῦντες *Charon sive Contemplantes (Charon)* Charon
27. Βίων Πρᾶσις *Vitarum Auctio (Vit.Auct.)* Philosophers for Sale
28. 'Αναβιοῦντες ἢ 'Αλιεύς *Piscator (Pisc.)* The Dead come to Life
29. Δίς κατηγορούμενος *Bis Accusatus (Bis Acc.)* The Double Indictment
30. Περὶ Θυσιῶν *De Sacrificiis* On Sacrifices
31. Πρὸς τὸν ἀπαίδευτον καὶ πολλὰ Βιβλία ὠνούμενον *Adversus Indoctum* The Ignorant Book Collector
32. Περὶ τοῦ 'Ενυπνίου ἤτοι Βίος Λουκιανοῦ *Somnium sive Vita Luciani (Somn.)* The Dream or Lucian's Autobiography.
*33. Περὶ Παρασίτου ὅτι Τέχνη ἢ Παρασιτική *De Parasito* The Parasite
34. Φιλοψευδεῖς ἢ 'Απιστῶν *Philopseudeis (Philops.)* Pathological Liars
35. Θεῶν Κρίσις *Dearum Iudicium* The Judgement of the Goddesses
36. Περὶ τῶν ἐπὶ Μισθῷ συνόντων *De Mercede conductis* On People Who Hire Themselves Out
37. 'Ανάχαρσις ἢ Περὶ Γυμνασίων *Anacharsis*
38. Μένιππος ἢ Νεκυομαντεία *Menippus sive Necyomantia (Nec.)* Menippus
*39. Λούκιος ἢ "Ονος *Lucius sive Asinus* The Ass
40. Περὶ Πένθους *De Luctu* On Funerals
41. 'Ρητόρων Διδάσκαλος *Rhetorum Praeceptor (Rh.Pr.)* A Professor of Public Speaking
42. 'Αλέξανδρος ἢ Ψευδόμαντις *Alexander (Alex.)*
43. Εἰκόνες *Imagines (Im.)* Essays in Portraiture
*44. Περὶ τῆς Συρίης Θεοῦ *De Syria Dea* The Syrian Goddess
45. Περὶ 'Ορχήσεως *De Saltatione* On the Dance
46. Λεξιφάνης *Lexiphanes (Lex.)*
47. Εὐνοῦχος *Eunuchus* The Eunuch
48. Περὶ τῆς 'Αστρολογίης *De Astrologia* Astrology
*49. "Ερωτες *Amores* Affairs of the Heart
50. 'Υπὲρ τῶν Εἰκόνων *Pro Imaginibus* 'Essays in Portraiture' Defended
51. Ψευδολογιστής ἢ Περὶ τῆς 'Αποφράδος *Pseudologista* The Mistaken Critic
52. Θεῶν 'Εκκλησία *Deorum Concilium* The Parliament of the Gods
53. Τυραννοκτόνος *Tyrannicida* The Tyrannicide
54. 'Αποκηρυττόμενος *Abdicatus* Disowned
55. Περὶ τῆς Περεγρίνου Τελευτῆς *De Morte Peregrini (Peregr.)* The Death of Peregrinus

56. Δραπέται   Fugitivi (Fug.)   The Runaways
57. Τόξαρις ἤ Φιλία   Toxaris
*58. Δημοσθένους Ἐγκώμιον   Demosthenis Encomium   In Praise
    of Demosthenes
59. Πῶς δεῖ Ἱστορίαν συγγράφειν   Quomcdo Historia Conscrib-
    enda sit (Hist.Conscr.)   How to Write History
60. Περὶ τῶν Διψάδων   Dipsades   The Dipsads
61. Τὰ πρὸς Κρόνον κτλ.   Saturnalia
62. Ἡρόδοτος ἤ Ἀετίων   Herodotus (Herod.)
63. Ζεῦξις ἤ Ἀντίοχος   Zeuxis
64. Ὑπὲρ τοῦ ἐν τῇ Ποοσαγορεύσει Πταίσματος   Pro Lapsu
    inter Salutandum (Pro Lapsu.)   A Slip of the Tongue
    In Greeting
65. Ἀπολογία   Apologia Pro Mercede Conductis (Apol.)
    'On Salaried Posts' Defended
66. Ἁρμονίδης   Harmonides
67. Διάλογος πρὸς Ἡσίοδον   Hesiodus   A Conversation with
    Hesiod
68. Σκύθης ἤ Πρόξενος   Scytha (Scyth.)   The Scythian
69. Ποδάγρα   Podagra   Gout
70. Ἑρμότιμος ἤ Περὶ Αἱρέσεων   Hermotimus (Herm.)
71. Πρὸς τὸν εἰπόντα Προμηθεὺς εἶ ἐν τοῖς Λόγοις   Prom-
    etheus es in Verbis (Prom.Es)   A Literary Prometheus
73. Πλοῖον ἤ Εὐχαί   Navigium (Nav.)   The Ship
77. Νεκρικοὶ Διάλογοι   Dialogi Mortuorum (D.Mort.)   Dialogues
    of the Dead
78. Ἐνάλιοι Διάλογοι   Dialogi Marini   Dialogues of the Sea
    Gods
79. Θεῶν Διάλογοι   Dialogi Deorum (D.Deor.)   Dialogues of
    the Gods
80. Ἑταιρικοὶ Διάλογοι   Dialogi Meretricii   Dialogues of
    the Courtesans

Works of other ancient authors abbreviated in appendix

Apuleius, Apol.   Apologia
Aulus Gellius, N.A.   Noctes Atticae
Cicero, Ac. Post.   Academica Posteriora
Eunapius, V.S.   Vitae Sophistarum
Homer, Il.   Iliad
Lactantius, Inst.Div.   Institutiones Divinae
Philo, In Flacc.   In Flaccum
Philostratus, V.S.   Vitae Sophistarum
Plato, Rep.   Republic
Quintilian, Inst. Or.   Institutiones Oratoriae

130

Abbreviations and short titles of modern works referred to
more than once in the notes to the appendix

A.J.P.	American Journal of Philology
Anderson, *Sophist*	G. Anderson, 'Lucian: a sophist's sophist', *Yale Classical Studies*, XXVII, pp.61-92
Anderson, *Studies*	G. Anderson, 'Studies in Lucian's comic fiction', *Mnemosyne* Supplement 43 (Leiden, 1976)
Anderson, *Theme*	G. Anderson, 'Lucian: theme and variation in the Second Sophistic', *Mnemosyne* Supplement 41 (Leiden, 1976)
B.I.C.S.	Bulletin of the Institute of Classical Studies, London
Bompaire	J. Bompaire, *Lucien Écrivain* (Paris, 1958)
Bowersock, *Approaches*	G.W. Bowersock (ed.), *Approaches to the Second Sophistic* (Pennsylvania, 1974).
Bowersock, *Sophists*	G.W. Bowersock, *Greek Sophists in the Roman Empire* (Oxford, 1969)
Bowie	E.L. Bowie, 'Greeks and their past in the Second Sophistic', *Past and Present*, 46 (1970), pp.3-41
Caster	M. Caster, *Lucien et la Pensée Réligieuse de son Temps* (Paris, 1937)
Hall	J. Hall, *Lucian's Satire* (Arno Press, N.Y., 1981)
J.H.S.	Journal of Hellenic Studies
L.S.J.	Liddell-Scott-Jones, *Greek-English Lexicon*
Macleod	M.D. Macleod, Oxford Classical Text of Lucian, vols. I-III, Oxford, 1972, 1974, 1980
Mattioli	E. Mattioli, *Luciano e L'Umanesimo* (Naples, 1980)
O.C.T.	Oxford Classical Text
Ph.Woch.	Philologische Wochenschrift
Reardon	B.P. Reardon, *Lucian, Selected Works* (Library of Liberal Arts (Bobbs-Merrill), N.Y., 1965)
Robinson	C. Robinson, *Lucian* (London, 1979)
Sidwell, *Lucian*	K.C. Sidwell, *Lucian of Samosata in the Italian Quattrocento*, unpublished Cambridge University Ph.D 1975
Y.C.S.	Yale Classical Studies

VOCABULARY

This vocabulary contains:

(i) words which occur in this selection and in the Total Vocabulary of *Reading Greek* (C.U.P., 1978). Such words appear *only* in this vocabulary and will not be found glossed where they occur in the text.

(ii) words which occur in three separate places in this selection with similar meanings. These are glossed on first appearance. The asterisk beside them denotes that you should learn them, but that you will find them in this vocabulary should you forget them.

Stems and difficult parts of verbs are given either in the text or here. For concise instructions on finding verbs see 'Finding the lexicon form of a verb' in *Reading Greek: Grammar, Vocabulary and Exercises*, pp. 335-6.

Conventions

1. Nouns are grouped 1, 2 or 3 as in *Reading Greek*, p. 270 i.e.:

1a βοή	2a ἄνθρωπος	3a λιμήν
1b ἀπορία	2b ἔργον	3b πρᾶγμα
1c τόλμα		3c πλῆθος
1d ναύτης, νεανίας		3d τριήρης
		3e πόλις, πρέσβυς
		3f ἄστυ
		3g βασιλεύς
		3h ὀφρῦς

2. Adjectives are quoted as follows: καλός, -ή, -όν, βραχύς, -εῖα, -ύ, ἀληθής, -ές, κακοδαίμων (κακοδαιμον-).

3. The most common alternative stem(s) of verbs are quoted unaugmented in brackets after the lexicon form, e.g. μανθάνω (μαθ-).

A

ἀγαγ-: *aor. stem of* ἄγω.
ἀγαθός, -ή, -όν: good.
ἀγανακτέω: I am angry, annoyed.
ἀγνοέω: I do not understand/ perceive/know.
ἀγορά, ἡ (*1b*): gathering (-place); market-place; agora.

ἄγω (ἀγαγ-): I lead, I live in, am at.
ἀδελφός, ὁ (*2a*): brother.
ἀδικέω: I wrong.
ἄδω: I sing.
ἀεί: always.
ἀήρ (ἀερ-), ὁ (*3a*): air.
Ἀθῆναι, αἱ (*1a*): Athens.
Ἀθηναῖος, ὁ (*2a*): Athenian.
Ἀθήνησι: at Athens.

ἄθλιος, -α, -ον: pathetic,
miserable, wretched.
αἰδοῖα, τά (2b): genitals.
αἰεί = ἀεί.
αἴξ (αἰγ-), ἡ (3a): nanny-
goat.
αἱρέομαι (ἑλ-): I choose
(aor. pass. ἡρέθην).
αἱρέω (ἑλ-): I take/
capture.
αἰσχύνομαι: I am ashamed,
I feel shame (before).
αἰτέω: I ask (for), I ask
x (παρά + gen.) to y (inf.).
αἴτιος, -α, -ον (+ gen.):
responsible (for), guilty
of.
ἀκολουθέω (+ dat.): I
follow, accompany.
ἀκούω (+ gen. of person,
gen. or acc. of thing):
I hear, listen (to)
(fut.: ἀκούσομαι).
ἀκριβῶς: accurately.
ἀκρόπολις, ἡ (3e):
Acropolis, citadel.
ἀλήθεια, ἡ (1b): truth.
ἀληθής, -ές: true.
ἀλλά: but.
ἀλλήλους (2a): each other,
one another.
ἄλλος, -η, -ον: other, the
rest of.
ἄλλος ... ἄλλον: one ...
another.
ἀλλότριος, -α, -ον: someone
else's.
ἅμα: at the same time.
ἁμαρτάνω (ἁμαρτ-): I do
wrong.
ἄμπελος, ἡ (2a): (grape-)
vine.
ἀμφορεύς, ὁ (3g): amphora,
storage-jar.
ἄν (+ imperf. indic.): would
be ...ing (conditional);(+
opt.): would, will, may,
could (potential); (+ subj.)
-ever (indefinite).
ἄν (+ subj.) = ἐάν: if.
ἀνάγκη ἐστί: it is obliga-
tory (for x (acc. or dat.)
to (inf.)).

ἀναιρέω (ἀνέλ-): I pick up.
ἀναίτιος, -ον: innocent.
ἀναλαμβάνω (ἀναλαβ-): I take
up.
ἀνατέμνω (ἀνατεμ-): I cut
open.
ἀνδρεῖος, -α, -ον: brave,
manly.
ἄνεμος, ὁ (2a): wind.
ἄνευ: without (+ gen.).
ἀνέχομαι (+ gen.): I put up
with.
ἀνήρ (ἀνδρ-), ὁ (3a): man.
ἄνθρωπος, ὁ (2a): man.
ἀνίσταμαι (ἀναστα-): I get
up, I stand up.
ἀντί (+ gen.): instead of.
ἄνω: above.
ἀπαγγέλλω (ἀπαγγειλ-): I
announce, report.
ἀπάγω (ἀπαγαγ-): I lead,
take.
ἀπαιτέω: I demand back.
ἅπας, -ασα, -αν (ἁπαντ-):
all, the whole of.
ἀπέβην aor. of ἀποβαίνω.
ἀπέθανον aor. of ἀποθνήσκω.
ἀπελθ- aor. stem of ἀπέρχομαι.
ἀπέρχομαι (ἀπελθ-): I go away,
depart (fut. ἄπειμι).
ἀπέχομαι (ἀποσχ-) (+ gen.): I
refrain, keep away from.
ἀπιών, -οῦσα, -όν part. of
ἀπέρχομαι/ἄπειμι.
ἀπό (+ gen.): from, away from.
ἀποβαίνω (ἀποβα-): I disembark.
ἀποθαν- aor. stem of
ἀποθνήσκω.
ἀποθνήσκω (ἀποθαν-): I die.
ἀποκρίνομαι (ἀποκριν-): I
answer.
ἀποκτείνω (ἀποκτειν-): I kill.
ἀπολείπω (ἀπολιπ-): I leave
behind, desert.
ἀπολύω: I release.
ἀποπέμπω: I send away.
ἀπορέω: I am at a loss.
ἀποφαίνω: I reveal / show
(x·(acc.) as y (acc.)).
ἀποφέρω (ἀπενεγκ-): I carry
back.
ἅπτομαι (+ gen.): I touch.
ἅπτω: I fasten, fix.

ἄρα: then, consequently
(*marking an inference*).
ἆρα: ? (*used to introduce
a direct question*).
ἄριστος, -η, -ον: best,
very good.
ἁρπάζω: I seize, snatch.
ἄρτι: just now, recently.
ἀρχή, ἡ (1a): beginning.
ἄρχομαι (*mid.*): I begin
(x-ing (*gen. part.*)).
ἄρχω (+ gen.): I rule.
ἀσεβής, -ές: impious,
unholy.
ἀσπάζομαι: I greet,
welcome.
ἄτρακτος, ὁ (2a): spindle
(of the Fates).
αὖθις: again.
αὔτη: f. of οὗτος.
αὐτίκα: at once.
αὐτόν = ἑαυτόν
αὐτόν, -ήν, -ό: him, her,
it, them.
αὐτός, -ή, -ό: self.
ὁ αὐτός: the same.
ἀφ' = ἀπό.
ἀφαιρέω (ἀφελ-): I remove.
ἀφελ- aor. stem of ἀφαιρέω.
ἀφίημι (ἀφε-): I release,
let go.
ἀφικνέομαι (ἀφικ-): I ar-
rive, come (fut. ἀφίξομαι).
ἀφικόμην aor. of ἀφικνέομαι.
ἀφοράω (ἀπιδ-): I look
(away from everything else).

B

βαδίζω: I walk.
βαθύς, -εῖα, -ύ: deep.
βαίνω (βα-): I go, come,
walk.
βασιλεύς, ὁ (3g): king.
βασιλεύω: I am king
(over x (gen.)).
βιάζομαι: I use force.
βίος, ὁ (2a): life.
βοάω: I shout.
βοή, ἡ (1a): shout.
βοηθέω (+ dat.): I help.

βότρυς, ὁ (3h): bunch of
grapes.
βούλομαι: I wish, want.
βραχύς, -εῖα, -ύ: short,
brief.
βρέφος, τό (3c uncontr.):
foetus, new-born baby.
βωμός, ὁ: altar.

Γ

γαῖα (1c) = γῆ, ἡ (1a).
γαμέω (γημ-): I marry.
γάμος, ὁ (2a): marriage.
γάρ: for (second word).
γαστήρ (γαστερ-), ἡ (3a):
stomach.
γε (enclitic): at least
(denotes some sort of
reservation).
γεγένημαι perf. of γίγνομαι.
γείτων (γειτον-), ὁ (3a):
neighbour.
γελάω (γελασ-): I laugh.
γεν- aor. stem of γίγνομαι.
γένειον, τό (2b): beard.
γενναῖος, -α, -ον: noble,
fine, excellent.
γένος, τό (3c): race.
γέρων (γεροντ-), ὁ (3a): old
man.
γεωργός, ὁ (2a): farmer.
γῆ, ἡ (1a): land, earth.
γίγνομαι (γεν-): I become,
am born, happen, arise, am.
γιγνώσκω (γνο-): I know,
think.
γίνομαι = γίγνομαι.
γινώσκω = γιγνώσκω.
γνώμη, ἡ (1a): judgement,
mind.
γοῦν: at any rate.
γραφή, ἡ (1a): indictment,
charge.
γράφω: I write.
γυνή (γυναικ-), ἡ (3a): wife,
woman.

Δ

δακ- aor. stem of δάκνω.
δάκνω (δακ-): I bite.
δακρύω: I weep.
δάκτυλος, ὁ (2a): finger.
δέ: and, but.
δεήσει fut. of δεῖ.
δεήσομαι fut. of δέομαι.
δεῖ: it is necessary (for
  x (acc.) to y (inf.)).
δείκνυμι (δειξ-): I show.
δεινός, -ή, -όν: terrible,
  dire, astonishing.
δειξ- aor. stem of δείκνυμι.
δεῖπνον, τό (2b): dinner.
δένδρον, τό (2b): tree.
δεξιός, -ά, -όν: right,
  clever.
δέομαι (+ gen.): I need,
  ask, beg.
δέρμα, τό (3b): skin.
δεσπότης, ὁ (1d): master.
δεύτερος, -α, -ον: second.
δή: then, indeed.
δῆλος, -η, -ον: clear,
  obvious.
δηλόω: I show, reveal.
Δι- stem of Ζεύς.
διά (+ acc.): because
  of;(+ gen.) through.
διακονέομαι: I act as a
  servant (to x (dat.)).
διανοέομαι: I intend.
διατρίβω: I pass time.
διαφεύγω (διαφυγ-): I get
  away, flee.
διαφθείρω (διαφθειρ-): I
  kill.
διδάσκαλος, ὁ (2a): teacher.
διδάσκω: I teach.
δίδωμι (δο-): I give,
  grant.
διεξέρχομαι (διεξελθ-): I go
  through, relate.
διηγέομαι: I relate, go
  through.
δικάζω: I make a judgement.
δίκαιος, -α, -ον: just.
δικαιοσύνη, ἡ (1a): justice.
δικαστήριον, τό (2b): law-
  court.
δίκη, ἡ (1a): lawsuit.

διοικέω: I administer.
διότι: because.
διώκω: I pursue.
δο- aor. stem of δίδωμι.
δοκεῖ: it seems a good idea
  (to x (dat.) to do y (inf.);
  x (dat.) decides to y (inf.)).
δοκέω: I seem, consider
  (myself) to be.
ἐμοὶ δοκεῖν: in my opinion,
  as it seems to me.
δ'οὖν: however that may be,
  all the same.
δρᾶμα (δραματ-), τό (3b):
  play, drama.
δρόσος, ὁ (2a): dew.
δύναμαι: I am able.
δυνατός, -ή, -όν: able,
  possible.
δύο: two.

E

ἐάν (+ subj.): if (ever).
ἑαυτόν, -ήν, -ό: himself,
  herself, itself, themselves.
ἐγενόμη- aor. of γίγνομαι.
ἔγνων aor. of γιγνώσκω.
ἐγώ: I.
ἔγωγε: I at least, for my
  part.
ἔδωκα aor. of δίδωμι.
ἐθέλω (ἐθελησ-): I wish,
  want.
εἰ: if; whether (indirect
  question); if (x were to y
  (opt.)); if ever (indef.).
  εἰ καί: even if.
εἶ 2nd sing. of εἰμί (I am).
εἰδέναι inf. of οἶδα.
εἶδον aor. of ὁράω.
εἰδώς, -υῖα, -ός (εἰδοτ-):
  knowing (part. of οἶδα).
εἴην opt. of εἰμί (I am).
εἴθε (+ opt.): I wish that!
  would that! if only!
εἰκός: probably, reasonable,
  fair.
εἴκοσι(ν): twenty.
εἰκότως: reasonably, rightly.

εἰμί: I am.
εἶναι *inf. of* εἰμί (I am).
εἰπ- *aor. stem of* λέγω.
εἶπον *aor. of* λέγω.
εἰς (+ *acc.*): to, into,
  onto.
εἷς μία ἕν (ἑν-): one.
εἴσομαι *fut. of* οἶδα.
εἶτα: then, next.
ἐκ (+ *gen.*): out of,
  from.
ἕκαστος, -η, -ον: each.
ἑκάτερος, -α, -ον: each
  (*of two*).
ἐκεῖ: there.
ἐκεῖθεν: from there.
ἐκεῖνος, -η, -ο: that,
  (s)he, it, they.
ἐκκλησία, ἡ (1b): assembly.
ἐκμανθάνω (ἐκμαθ-): I learn
  well, thoroughly (*how to:
  inf.*).
ἐκπέμπω: I send out.
ἔλαθον *aor. of* λανθάνω.
ἐλάττων, -τον (ἐλαττον-):
  smaller.
ἐλεύθερος, -α, -ον: free.
ἐλθ- *aor. stem of* ἔρχομαι.
Ἕλλην (Ἑλλην-), ὁ (3a):
  Greek.
ἐλπίς (ἐλπιδ-), ἡ (3a): hope,
  expectation.
ἐμαυτόν, -ήν: myself.
ἔμβρυον, τό (2b): embryo,
  baby.
ἐμός, -ή, -όν: my.
ἐμπεσ- *aor. stem of* ἐμπίπτω.
ἐμπίπτω (ἐμπεσ-) (+ *dat.*): I
  fall into, on, upon.
ἐν (+ *dat.*): in, on, among.
  ἐν τούτῳ: meanwhile.
ἕν *n. of* εἷς.
ἐνάντιος, -α, -ον: opposite.
ἔνδον: inside.
ἕνεκα (+ *gen.*): because, for
  the sake of (*usually follows
  its noun*).
ἔνθα: where.
ἐνθάδε: here.
ἐνταῦθα: here, there.
ἐντεῦθεν: from then, from
  there.
ἐντίθημι (ἐνθε-): I place in,

put in.
ἐξ = ἐκ.
ἐξάγω (ἐξαγαγ-): I bring
  out.
ἐξελέγχω: I refute,
  expose.
ἐξετάζω: I question closely.
ἔξω (+ *gen.*): outside.
ἔοικα: I seem; (+ *dat.*):
  I resemble.
ἔοικε: it seems, is
  reasonable.
ἔπαθον *aor. of* πάσχω.
ἐπαινέω (ἐπαινεσ-): I
  praise.
ἐπανελθ- *aor. stem of*
  ἐπανέρχομαι.
ἐπανέρχομαι (ἐπανελθ-): I
  return.
ἐπεί: since, when.
ἐπειδάν (+ *subj.*): when
  (ever).
ἐπειδή: when, since.
ἔπειτα: then, next.
ἐπέχω (ἐπισχ-): I restrain,
  check.
ἐπί (+ *acc.*): against, at,
  to; (+ *gen.*): on; (+ *dat.*):
  at; for the purpose of; for,
  because of.
ἐπιδημέω: I come to town,
  am in town.
ἐπιθυμέω: I desire.
ἐπιμελέομαι (+ *gen.*): I
  care for.
ἐπιμελής, -ές: careful.
ἐπίσταμαι: I know how to
  (+ *inf.*): I understand.
ἕπομαι (σπ-) (+ *dat.*): I
  follow.
ἔπος, τό (3c: *uncontr. pl.*
  ἔπεα): word.
ἑπτά: seven.
ἐπῳδή, ἡ (1a): spell,
  incantation.
ἐργάζομαι: I work, perform.
ἔργον, τό (2b): task, job.
ἐρέω *fut. of* λέγω.
ἔρχομαι (ἐλθ-): I go,
  come.
ἐρωτάω (ἐρ-): I ask.
ἐς = εἰς.
ἐσθής (ἐσθητ-), ἡ (3a):

clothing.

ἔσται 3rd s. fut. of εἰμί
(I am).

ἑταῖρος, ὁ (2a): (male)
companion, comrade.

ἔτεκον aor. of τίκτω.

ἕτερος, -α, -ον: one (or
the other, of two).

ἕτερος ... ἕτερον: one
... another.

ἔτι: still, yet.

ἑτοῖμος, -η, -ον: ready.

ἔτος, τό (3c): year.

ἔτυχον aor. of τυγχάνω.

εὖ: well.

εὖ ποιέω: I treat
well, do good to.

εὐδαίμων, -ον (εὐδαιμον-):
happy.

εὐθύς: at once, straight-
away.

εὐπρεπής, ές: seemly.

εὑρ- aor. stem of εὑρίσκω.

εὑρίσκω (εὑρ-): I find,
come upon.

εὐχή, ἡ (1a): prayer.

εὔχομαι: I pray.

ἔφην imperf. of φημί.

ἐφίσταμαι (ἐπιστα-) (+ dat.):
I stand over, near.

ἔχω (σχ-): I have, hold;
(+ adv.): am (in x (adv.)
condition); I wear.

ἔχων: with.

ἑώρων imperf. of ὁράω.

ἕως, ἡ (acc. ἕω): dawn.

Z

Ζεύς (Δι-), ὁ: Zeus
(3a: voc. Ζεῦ).

ζητέω: I look for, seek.

H

ἤ: or; than.

ἤ ... ἤ: either ... or.

ἤ δ'ὅς: he said.

ἡγέομαι: I lead, (+ dat.)
I think, consider.

ἤδη: by now, now, already.

ἥδομαι (+ dat.): I enjoy.

ἡδύς, -εῖα, -ύ (sup. ἥδιστος):
sweet, pleasant.

ἥκιστα: least of all.

ἥκω: I come, have come.

ἦλθον aor. of ἔρχομαι / εἶμι.

ἥλιος, ὁ (2a): sun.

ἡμεῖς: we.

ἡμέρα, ἡ (1b): day.

ἡμέτερος, -α, -ον: our.

ἦν 1st or 3rd s. imperf.
of εἰμί (I am).

ἦν δ'ἐγώ: I said.

ἤν (+ subj.) = ἐάν: if.

ἠπιστάμην imperf. of
ἐπίσταμαι.

Ἡρακλῆς, ὁ (3d uncontr.):
Herakles.

ἡρέθην aor. pass. of
αἱρέομαι.

ἦσαν 3rd pl. imperf. of
εἰμί (I am).

ἡσυχία, ἡ (1b): quiet,
peace.

Θ

θάλαττα, ἡ (1c): sea.

θάνατος, ὁ (2a): death.

θαυμάζω: I wonder at.

θαυμάσιος, -α, -ον: wonder-
ful, amazing.

θεά, ἡ (1b): goddess.

θεάομαι: I watch, gaze at.

θεῖος, ὁ (2a): uncle.

θεῖος, -α, -ον: divine.

θεός, -ό, -ή (2a): god.

θεραπεύω: I look after,
tend.

θέω: I run.

θηρίον, τό (2b): beast.

θνήσκω (θαν-): I die.

θνητός, -ή, -όν: mortal.

θρόνος, ὁ (2a): throne,
seat.

θυγάτηρ (θυγατ(ε)ρ-), ἡ (3a):
daughter.

θύρα, ἡ (1b): door.

θυρίς (θυριδ-), ἡ (3a): open-
ing.

θυσία, ἡ (1b): sacrifice.

θύω: I sacrifice.

I

ἰατρός, ὁ (2a): doctor.
ἰδ- aor. stem of ὁράω.
ἰδιώτης, ὁ (1d): private
citizen.
ἰδού: look!
ἱκανός, -ή, -όν: sufficient.
ἱκανῶς: sufficiently.
ἱκετεύω: I beg.
ἱμάτιον, τό (2b): cloak.
ἵνα (+ subj./opt.): in order
to/that.
ἵππος, ὁ (2a): horse.
ἴσασι(ν) 3rd pl. of οἶδα.
ἴσος, -η, -ον: equal (to:
dat.).
ἴσως: perhaps.

K

καθ᾽ = κατά
καθάπερ: like, as.
καθεύδω: I sleep.
κάθημαι: I am seated.
καθίημι (καθε-): I let
fall, I let/put down.
καθοράω (κατιδ-): I see,
look down at.
καί: and, also, even;
actually.
καί ... καί: both ... and.
τε ... καί: both ... and.
καί γάρ: in fact.
καί δή: and really; as a
matter of fact.
καί δή καί: moreover.
καί μάλα: yes, indeed.
καί μήν: what's more;
yes, and; and anyway.
καίτοι: and yet.
καλέω (καλεσ-): I call
(x (acc.) y (acc.)).
κάλλιστος, -η, -ον: most
(very) fine, good, beauti-
ful.
καπνός, ὁ (2a): smoke.
καρπός, ὁ (2a): fruit,
κατά (+ acc.): in, on, by,
according to; (+ gen.):
against.
καταλαμβάνω (καταλαβ-): I

overtake, come across.
καταλείπω (καταλιπ-): I leave
behind.
κατατίθημι (καταθε-): I put
down.
κάτω: below.
κεῖμαι: I lie, am placed.
κελεύω: I order.
κεφαλή, ἡ (1a): head.
κίνδυνος, ὁ (2a): danger.
κλάδος, ὁ (2a): branch.
κολάζω: I punish.
κομήτης, ὁ (1d): wearing
long hair; long-haired
person.
κυνίδιον, τό (2b): little
dog, doggie.
κύων (κυν-), ὁ/ἡ (3a): dog,
bitch.
κωλύω: I prevent, stop.

Λ

λαβ- aor. stem of λαμβάνω.
λαθ- aor. stem of λανθάνω.
λαμβάνομαι (λαβ-) (+ gen.): I
take hold of.
λαμβάνω (λαβ-): I take,
capture.
λαμπρός, -ά, -όν: illustrious,
famous; splendid; bright,
shining.
λανθάνω (λαθ-) (perf. λέληθα):
I escape the notice of (x
(acc.) y-ing (nom. part.)).
λέγω (εἰπ-): I speak, say,
tell, mean (fut. ἐρέω).
λέληθα perf. of λανθάνω.
λεπτός, -ή, -όν: thin, weak.
λεών (λεοντ-), ὁ (3a): lion.
Λίβυς, ὁ (3h): Libyan.
λίθος, ὁ (2a): stone.
λόγος, ὁ (2a): speech, tale,
argument.

M

μά (+ acc.): (in oaths) no,
by ...!

138

μαϑ- aor. stem of μανθάνω.
μαθήσομαι fut. of μανθάνω.
μακρός, -ά, -όν: long.
μάλα: very, quite, virtu-
ally.
καί μάλα: yes, indeed.
μάλιστα (μάλα): especially,
particularly.
μᾶλλον (μάλα): rather.
μανθάνω (μαϑ-): I learn.
μέγας, -άλη, -α (μεγαλ-):
great, big.
μέγεθος, τό (3c): size.
μέγιστος, -η, -ον (sup.
of μέγας): greatest.
μείζων μεῖζον (μειζον-)
(comp. of μέγας): greater.
μείς (μην-), ὁ (3a): month.
μέλας, -αινα, -αν (μελαν-):
black.
μέλλω: I am about to (+
fut. inf.).
μέμνημαι: I remember (perf.
of μιμνήσκομαι).
μέν ... δέ: on one hand ...
on the other.
μέντοι: however, but.
μέρος, τό (3c): part.
μεστός, -ή, -όν: full of
(+ gen.).
μετά (+ acc.): after; (+
gen.): with.
μέτριος, -α, -ον: moderate,
reasonable, fair.
μή: not; (+ imper.): don't!;
(+ aor. subj.): don't!; (+
subj.): lest, in case.
μηδέ: and not; not even.
μηδείς, -εμία, -έν (μηδεν-):
no, no one.
μηκέτι: no longer.
μην- stem of μείς
μήτηρ (μητ(ε)ρ-), ἡ (3a):
mother.
μία f. of εἷς.
μικρός, -ά, -όν: small,
short, little.
μιμνήσκομαι (μνησϑ-): I
remember.
μοιχεύω: I commit adultery
with.
μόνος, -η, ον: alone.
μόνον: only.

μύρον, τό (2b): myrrh,
Chanel No.5 (?).
μῶν: surely not?

N

ναῦς, ἡ (3 irreg.): ship.
νεανίας, ὁ (1d): young
man.
νεανίσκος, ὁ (2a): young
man.
νεκρός, ὁ (2a): corpse.
νέος, -α, -ον: young.
νεώς gen. s. of ναῦς.
νή (+ acc.): (in oaths)
yes, by ...!
νῆσος, ἡ (2a): island.
νικάω: I win.
νομίζεται: it is customary.
νομίζω: I think (x (acc.) to
be y (acc. or acc. + inf.)).
νόμος, ὁ (2a): law.
νοσέω: I am sick.
νόσημα, τό (3b): illness,
disease.
νοῦς, ὁ (νόος) (2a): mind.
νῦν: now.
νύξ (νυκτ-), ἡ (3a): night.

Ξ

ξένος, ὁ (2a): foreigner.

Ο

ὁ αὐτός: the same.
ὁ δέ ...: and/but he ...
ὁ μέν ... ὁ δέ: one ...
another.
ὅδε ἥδε τόδε: this.
ὁδός, ἡ (2a): road, way.
ὅθεν: from where.
οἶδα: I know (fut. εἴσομαι).
οἰκεῖος, -α, -ον: related,
domestic, family.
οἰκέτης, ὁ (1d): house-slave.
οἰκέω: I dwell (in), live.
οἰκία, ἡ (1b): house.
οἶμαι (οἰηϑ-): I think.
οἶνος, ὁ (2a): wine.

οἷος, -α, -ον: what a
...! what sort of a
...!
οἴχομαι: I am off,
depart.
ὀλίγος, -η, -ον: small,
few.
ὅλος, -η, -ον: whole of,
complete.
ὅλως: completely,
altogether.
ὅμοιος, -α, -ον (+ dat.):
like, similar to.
ὅμως: nevertheless, however.
ὄνειρος, ὁ (2a): dream.
ὄνομα (ὀνοματ-), τό (3b):
name.
ὀντ- m./n. stem of ὤν.
ὁποῖος, -α, -ον: of what
kind.
ὁπόσος, -η, -ον: how many,
how great; as much as.
ὁπόταν (+ subj.): whenever.
ὁπότε: when; (+ opt.):
whenever.
ὅπως (+ fut. indic.): see to
it that; (+ subj. or opt.)
= ἵνα: in order to/that.
ὁράω (ἰδ-): I see; I see to
(+ acc.); I see that (μη
+ subj.) x doesn't happen.
ὀρθός, -ή, -όν: straight.
ὅρκος, ὁ (2a): oath.
ὄρος, τό (3c): mountain.
ὅς, ἥ, ὅ: who, what, which.
ὅς: he.
ὅσον: as far as, about.
ὅσος, -η, -ον: how great!;
as much/many as.
ὅσπερ, ἥπερ, ὅπερ: who/which
indeed; the very ...
who/which.
ὅστις, ἥτις, ὅτι: who (ever),
which (ever).
ὅτε: when.
ὅτι: that, because.
οὐ (οὐκ, οὐχ): no, not.
οὐδαμῶς: in no way, not at
all, by no means.
οὐδέ: and not, not even.
οὐδείς, -εμία, -έν (οὐδεν-):
no, no one, nothing.
οὐδέπω: not yet.
οὐκ = οὐ: no, not.

οὐκέτι: no longer.
οὐκοῦν: therefore, so.
οὖν: therefore (second word).
οὔπω: not yet.
οὐρά, ἡ (1b): tail.
οὐρανός, ὁ (2a): sky,
heavens.
οὔτε ... οὔτε: neither ...
nor.
οὗτος, αὕτη, τοῦτο: this;
(s)he.
οὗτος: hey there! you
there!
οὕτως/οὕτω: thus, so, in
this way.
οὐχ = οὐ.
ὀφθαλμός, ὁ (2a): eye.
ὄψις, ἡ (3e): sight.

Π

παθ- aor. stem of πάσχω.
παιδεία, ἡ (1b): education,
culture, learning.
παιδίον, τό (2b): child.
παίζω: I joke.
παῖς (παιδ-), ὁ/ἡ (voc. παῖ):
child.
πάλαι: long ago.
πάλιν: again.
παντ- stem of πᾶς.
πάνυ: very (much).
πάνυ μὲν οὖν: certainly,
of course.
παρά (+ acc.): along, beside;
to; (+ gen.): from; (+ dat.):
with, beside, in the presence
of, among.
παραδίδωμι (παραδο-): I hand
over.
παράδοξος, -ον: incredible,
paradoxical, unexpected.
παραλαβ- aor. stem of
παραλαμβάνω.
παραλαμβάνω (παραλαβ-): I
take.
παραμένω (παραμειν-): I stay
near/behind/put.
παρασχ- aor. stem of παρέχω.
πάρειμι (+ dat.): I am at
hand, am present.
παρελθ- aor. stem of
παρέρχομαι.

παρέρχομαι (παρελθ-): I
pass, go by, come forward.
παρέχω (παρασχ-): I give
to, provide.
παρθένος, ἡ (2a): maiden.
πᾶς πᾶσα πᾶν (παντ-): all.
πασχω (παθ-: perf. πέπονθα):
I suffer, experience.
πατήρ (πατ(ε)ρ-), ὁ (3a):
father.
παύομαι (+ part.): I stop.
πείθομαι (πιθ-) (+ dat.):
I obey.
πείθω: I persuade.
πειράομαι (πειρασ-) (+ gen.):
I test, try.
πένης (πενητ-), ὁ (3a): poor
man.
πέντε: five.
πεντήκοντα: fifty.
περί (+ acc.): about; around;
(+ gen.): about.
περιμένω (περιμειν-): I hang
around (for x (acc.)).
πηγή, ἡ (1a): spring,
source.
πίνω (πι-): I drink.
πιστεύω (+ dat.): I trust.
πλεῖστος, -η, -ον (sup. of
πολύς): very much, most.
πλέω (πλευσ-): I sail.
πληγή, ἡ (1a): cuff, smack.
πλήν (+ gen.): except.
πλησίον (adv.): near;
(prep. + gen.): near.
πλοῖον, τό (2b): vessel,
ship.
πλούσιος, -α, -ον: rich,
wealthy.
πόθεν: from where?
ποιέομαι: I make.
ποιέω: I make, do; I
make x (acc.) y (acc.);
I make x (acc.) do y (inf.).
ποιητής, ὁ (1d): poet.
πόλεμος, ὁ (2a): war.
πόλις, ἡ (3e): city.
πολίτης, ὁ (1d): citizen.
πολλάκις: many times,
often.
πολύς, πολλή, πολύ (πολλ-):
much, many.

πολύ (adv.): much.
Ποσειδῶν (Ποσειδων-), ὁ (3a:
voc. Πόσειδον; acc.
Ποσειδῶ): Poseidon.
ποταμός, ὁ (2a): river.
ποτε (enclitic): once,
ever.
πότερον ... ἤ: whether
... or.
που (enclitic): somewhere,
anywhere: at all.
ποῦ: where?
πούς (ποδ-), ὁ (3a): foot.
πρᾶγμα (πραγματ-), τό (3b):
thing, matter, affair.
πράττω: I do.
πρό (+ gen.): before.
πρόβατον, τό (2b): sheep.
πρόθυμος, -ον: ready,
eager, willing.
πρός (+ acc.): to, towards.
προσελθ- aor. stem of
προσέρχομαι.
προσέρχομαι (προσελθ-) (+
dat.): I go/come towards.
προσέχω (τὸν νοῦν) (+ dat.):
I pay attention to.
προσιών, -οῦσα, -όν (προσιοντ-)
part. of προσέρχομαι /
πρόσειμι.
προσλέγω (προσειπ-): I
address.
προστάττω (προσταξ-) (+ dat.):
I order.
πρότερον: formerly,
previously; first.
πρότερος, -α, -ον: first (of
two), previous.
πρῶτα or τὰ πρῶτα
πρῶτον or τὸ πρῶτον}: first,
at first, for the first
time.
πρῶτος, -η, -ον: first.
πυθ- aor. stem of
πυνθάνομαι.
πύλη, ἡ (1a): gate.
πυνθάνομαι (πυθ-): I learn,
hear, get to know; I ask,
enquire x (acc.) of y
(gen.).
πῦρ (πυρ-), τό (3b): fire.
πώγων (πωγων-), ὁ (3a): beard.

πως (enclitic): somehow.

πῶς: how?

Ρ

ῥᾴδιος, -α, -ον: easy.
ῥᾳδίως: easily.
ῥᾷστος, -η, -ον: very easy.
ῥήτωρ (ῥητορ-), ὁ (3a): orator.

Σ

σεαυτόν: yourself(-lves).
σελήνη, ἡ (1a): moon.
σημεῖον, τό (2b): sign.
σῖτος, ὁ (2a): food.
σιωπάω: I am quiet (fut. σιωπήσομαι).
σκέλος, τό (3c): leg.
σκοπέομαι: I look at, consider.
σκοπέω: I consider.
σμικρός, -ά, -όν: small.
σός, σή, σόν: your(s).
σοφία, ἡ (1b): wisdom.
σοφιστής, ὁ (1d): sophist.
στόμα (στοματ-), τό (3b): mouth.
στρωμνή, ἡ (1a): bed.
σύ: you (s.).
συγγνώμη, ἡ (1a): pardon, forgiveness.
συμπόσιον, τό (2b): dinnerparty, symposium.
σύν (+ dat.): together with.
σύνειμι (+ dat.): I am with, have intercourse with.
συνίημι (συνε-): I understand, am aware of.
σφόδρα: very much, exceedingly.
σχεδόν: near, nearly, almost.
σκῆμα, τό (3b): dress, appearance; form, figure.
σχολή, ἡ (1a): leisure.

Σωκράτης, ὁ (3d): Socrates.
σῶμα, τό (3b): body.

Τ

ταυτ- f./n. stem of οὗτος.
ταχέως: quickly.
τε ... καί: both ... and.
τεῖχος, τό (3c): wall (of a city).
τεκμαίρομαι: I conclude, infer.
τέκνον, τό (2b): child.
τέλος: in the end, finally.
τέχνη, ἡ (1a): skill, art, expertise.
τήμερον: today.
τί: what? why?
τίθημι (θε-): I put, place.
τίκτω (τεκ-): I bear, give birth to (perf. τέτοκα).
τιμάω: I honour.
τιμωρία, ἡ (1b): revenge, vengeance.
τις, τι (τιν-) (enclitic): a certain, someone.
τίς, τί (τίν-): who? what? which?
τοίνυν: well, then (resuming argument).
τοιόσδε, -άδε, -όνδε: of this kind, like this.
τοιοῦτος, -αύτη, -οῦτο: of this kind, of such a kind, like this.
τόλμα, ἡ (1c): daring.
τοσοῦτος, -αύτη, -οῦτο: so great, so much.
τότε: then.
τουτ- m./n. stem of οὗτος.
ἐν τούτῳ: meanwhile, during this.
τραγός, ὁ (2a): billy-goat.
τρεῖς, τρία: three.
τρέπομαι (τραπ-): I turn (myself).
τρέφω (θρεψ-): I feed, nourish.
τρόπος, ὁ (2a): way, manner.
τροφή, ἡ (1a): food, nourishment.
τυγχάνω (τυχ-): I chance, I

happen (to be *x-ing* (*nom.*
part.)); I am actually
x-ing (*nom. part.*).
τύχη, ἡ (1a): chance,
good/bad fortune.

Y

ὑάλινος, -η, -ον: of crystal,
of glass.
ὕβρις, ἡ (3e): aggression,
violence, insult,
humiliation.
ὕδωρ (ὑδατ-), τό (3b):
water.
υἱός, ὁ (2a): son.
ὕλη, ἡ (1a): wood, forest.
ὑμεῖς: you (*pl.*).
ὑπέρ (+ *acc.*): over, beyond,
above; (+ *gen.*): for, on
behalf of; over.
ὕπερον, τό (2b): pestle.
ὑπισχνέομαι (ὑποσχ-): I
promise.
ὕπνος, ὁ (2a): sleep.
ὑπό (+ *acc.*): under; (+
gen.) by; through,
because of; (+ *dat.*)
under, beneath.
ὕστερον: later.

Φ

φαίνομαι (φαν-): I appear.
φαλακρός, -ά, -όν: bald.
φάσκω: I allege, claim,
assert.
φέρω (ἐνεγκ-, *fut.* οἴσω):
I bear, endure; I lead;
I carry.
φεύγω (φυγ-): I run off,
flee.
φημί (*imperf.* ἔφην; *fut.*
φήσω): I say.
φής: you say.
φήσω *fut. of* φημί.
φιλέῶ: I love, kiss.
φίλος, ὁ (2a): friend.
φιλοσοφία, ἡ (1b):
philosophy.
φιλόσοφος, ὁ (2a):

philosopher.
φόβος, ὁ (2a): fear.
φρονέω: I think, consider.
φύλαξ (φυλακ-), ὁ (3a):
guard.
φυλάττω: I guard.
φύλλον, τό (2b): leaf.
φύσις, ἡ (3e): nature.
φύω (*trans.*): I grow.
φωνή, ἡ (1a): voice,
language.
φῶς (φωτ-), τό (3b): light.

X

χαῖρε: greetings! hello!
χαίρω (χαρ-): rejoice.
χαλεπός, -ή, -όν: difficult,
hard.
χαλκοῦς, -ῆ, -οῦν: of
bronze.
χαρίζομαι: I oblige, please;
(+ *dat.*): I am dear to.
χάρις (χαριτ-), ἡ (3a):
grace.
χείρ (χειρ-), ἡ (3a): hand.
χείρων, χεῖρον (χειρον-)
(*comp. of* κακός): worse.
χθές: yesterday.
χίλιοι, -αι, -α: thousand.
χορός, ὁ (2a): dance.
χράομαι (+ *dat.*): I use,
employ.
χρή: it is necessary for
x (*acc.*) to *y* (*inf.*).
χρῆμα, τό (3b): thing.
χρηματίζω: I do business.
χρηστός, -ή, -όν: good.
χρόνος, ὁ (2a): time.
χρυσοῦς, -ά, -οῦν: golden.
χώρα, ἡ (1b): land.
χωρίον, τό (2b): place;
region.

Ψ

ψεύδομαι: I lie, tell lies.
ψηφίζομαι: I vote.
ψυχή, ἡ (1a): soul.

Ω

ὤ (+ *voc./nom.*): O
  (*addressing someone*).
ὧδε: thus, as follows.
ὤν οὖσα ὄν (ὀντ-) *part.*
  of εἰμί.
ὡς: how!; as; that;
  since; when; (+ *acc.*):
  to, towards; (+ *sup.*):
  as ... as possible; (+
  subj./opt.) = ἵνα: in
  order to/that.
ὥσπερ: like, as, just as.
ὥστε (+ *inf./indic.*): so
  that, with the result
  that, consequently.

144

LIST OF PROPER NAMES

Names which occur more than once (in different sections)
are listed here, with relevant details.

Αἰακός, ὁ (2a): Aiakos (one
of the three judges of the
dead; he receives them as
they enter Hades).

Ἀντίγονος, ὁ (2a):
Antigonos (doctor of
Eukrates, centre of
attention in the debate
on cures for gout and
other superstitious
stories satirised by
Tykhiades).

Ἀπόλλων ('Ἀπολλων-), ὁ
(3a): Apollo (god of
prophecy and music whose
chief shrine was at Delphi).

Ἀρκαδία, ἡ (1b): Arkadia
(mountainous district of
the Peloponnese, home of
the god Pan).

Γανυμήδης, ὁ (3d): Ganymede
(Phrygian boy, abducted by
Zeus to be his wine stew-
ard).

Δάφνη, ἡ (1a): Daphne (daugh-
ter of a river-god; loved
unsuccessfully by Apollo -
she became the laurel tree
rather than submit to him).

Δεινόμαχος, ὁ (2a):
Deinomakhos (a Stoic philos-
opher satirised by Tykhiades
for believing in miraculous
cures).

Διόνυσος, ὁ (2a): Dionysos
(son of Semele and Zeus;
god of wine).

Ἑλένη, ἡ (1a): Helen (of

Troy) (wife of Menelaos;
went with Paris to Troy and
thus caused the Trojan War).

Ἑρμῆς, ὁ (1d): Hermes (son
of Zeus and Maia and messen-
ger of Zeus; father of Pan).

Ζεύς (Δι-), ὁ (3a): Zeus (fath-
er of gods and men; often
alters his appearance to visit
mortal women).

Ἡρακλῆς, ὁ (3c uncontr.):
Herakles (son of Zeus and
Alkmena, in classical Greek
literature often a glutton;
famed for his twelve labours
at the behest of Eurystheus).

Ἡσίοδος, ὁ (2a): Hesiod
(Boeotian poet of c. 7th
cent. B.C.; a farmer whose
works include the didactic
poems Works and Days and
Theogony - a genealogy of
the gods).

Θεσμόπολις, ὁ (3d): Thesmopolis
(a Stoic philosopher who took
paid employment with a rich
lady).

Κινύρας, ὁ (1d): Kinyras (son
of Skintharos, an old man dis-
covered by Lucian living on an
island in the stomach of the
whale by which he and his
ship were swallowed; had an
affair with Helen of Troy).

Κλεόδημος, ὁ (2a): Kleodemos
(a peripatetic philosopher
satirised by Tykhiades for
believing in miraculous
cures).

Κύνισκος, ὁ (2a): Kyniskos (interviewer of Zeus; his name has associations with the words 'dog' and 'Cynic philosopher').

Μοῦσα, ἡ (1c): Muse (one of nine goddesses of the arts and music who lived on Mt. Parnassus).

Ναύπλιος, ὁ (2a): Nauplios (one of the Argonauts; lent by Rhadamanthys to Lucian as a pilot to the Place of the Impious).

Ὀδυσσεύς, ὁ (3g): Odysseus (central character of Homer's *Odyssey*; rejected immortality offered him by the nymph Kalypso to return to Ithaka and his wife Penelope).

Ὅμηρος, ὁ (2a): Homer (composer of the epic poems *Iliad* and *Odyssey*; reputedly blind and claimed as a citizen of Chios, Smyrna and Colophon, among others).

Πάν (Παν-), ὁ (3a): Pan (son of Hermes and Penelope; half-goat, half-man, a pastoral god also worshipped at Athens).

Παγκράτης, ὁ (1d): Pankrates (Egyptian sage, teacher of Arignotos and Eukrates: his name means 'all-powerful').

Πηνελόπη, ἡ (1a): Penelope (daughter of Ikarios and wife of Odysseus; also, by another tradition, mother of Pan).

Πλάτων (Πλατων-), ὁ (3a): Plato (c.429-347 B.C.: philosopher, founder of Academy. His works are largely centred on the character of Sokrates. He meddled in practical poli-

tics in Sicily, but without success).

Ποσειδῶν (Ποσειδων-), ὁ (3a): Poseidon (god of the sea, brother of Zeus).

Ῥαδάμανθυς, ὁ (3h): Rhadamanthys (one of the three judges of the dead).

Σευηριανός, ὁ (2a): Severianus (one of the generals of Lucius Verus, involved in the Parthian War A.D.161-165; committed suicide in a singular fashion).

Σωκράτης, ὁ (3c): Sokrates (5th cent.B.C. Greek Philosopher famous for his irony - the claim that he knew that he was nothing. Wrote nothing, but was immortalised by Plato and Xenophon. Put to death in 399 B.C., on a charge of corrupting the youth and introducing new gods).

Τυρόεσσα, ἡ (1c): Tyroessa ('Cheese-Island': Lucian and his crew had landed here on the way to the Island of the Blest).

Τυχιάδης, ὁ (3d): Tykhiades (a rationalist, who pours scorn on the superstition of Eukrates and his philosopical friends: his name means 'Lucky').